FIRST
PERSON
RURAL

BOOKS BY HODDING CARTER

Lower Mississippi (Rivers of America Series)
The Winds of Fear
Flood Crest
Southern Legacy
John Law Wasn't So Wrong
Where Main Street Meets the River
Robert E. Lee and the Road of Honor
The Marquis de Lafayette: Bright Sword for Freedom
The Angry Scar: The Story of Reconstruction
First Person Rural

In Collaboration

Civilian Defense of the United States
  (with Colonel R. Ernest Dupuy)
The Aspirin Age (contributor)
Gulf Coast Country (with Anthony Ragusin)
So Great a Good (with Betty W. Carter)
This Is the South (contributor)

FIRST
PERSON
RURAL

Hodding Carter

GREENWOOD PRESS, PUBLISHERS
WESTPORT, CONNECTICUT

We are grateful for permission to use the following articles by Hodding Carter:

"An Unforgettable Character," from *Reader's Digest*. Copyright 1954 by The Reader's Digest Association.

"Quartee Beans, Quartee Rice," by permission of *American Heritage*.

"A Bugle Call and Coffee and a Sapling Pine" from *What's New*, Special Christmas Edition. Copyright © 1956 by Abbott Laboratories.

"Little Miss Rachel and D. O. Volenty," from *Reader's Digest*. Copyright © 1963 by The Reader's Digest Association.

"In the Buckboard Summertime," from *Down East*, The Magazine of Maine, issue of September 1954.

"The Time God Didn't Strike Us Dead," from *Reader's Digest*. Copyright 1954 by The Reader's Digest Association.

"The Liberal Arts and the Bill of Rights," from the *Randolph-Macon College Bulletin*, issue of September 1955.

"Faulkner and His Folk," from *The Princeton University Li-*

Library of Congress Cataloging in Publication Data

Carter, Hodding, 1907-1972.
  First person rural.

    Autobiographical.
    Reprint of the ed. published by Doubleday,
Garden City, N.Y.
    1. Carter, Hodding, 1907-1972. 2. Journalists
--United States--Biography. I. Title.
[PN4874.C27A32 1977]   070'.92'4 [B]   77-10014
ISBN 0-8371-9727-9

To my brother
John

Originally published in 1963 by Doubleday & Company, Inc.,
Garden City, New York

Reprinted with the permission of Doubleday and Company, Inc.

Reprinted in 1977 by Greenwood Press, Inc.

Library of Congress catalog card number   77-10014

ISBN 0-8371-9727-9

Printed in the United States of America

Contents

FIRST
PERSON
RURAL

PART I

Looking Backward, with Love

AN UNFORGETTABLE CHARACTER

1954

Back in 1913, when I was six, and for a good many years before and afterward, so many citizens of my South Louisiana home parish had such a fine disregard for constituted law that the parish was known far and wide as Bloody Tangipahoa. The reason I have singled out 1913 is that on an autumn Saturday in that year I put my young, sun-browned father in a special category from which I have never removed him.

He was a city-bred collegian, turned farmer and Tangipahoan because of—I am sure—an inner compulsion of which I want to tell later. Tangipahoa parish lay some fifty miles above New Orleans, which had been my father's home, and between them intruded two lakes and a maze of swamps and bayous. It was another world from low, sub-tropical New Orleans, a lovely rolling land of pine forests and small farms, cleft by dark, swift rivers and creeks. Along the river bottoms dwelt those farmer-hunters whose feuding zeal and low boiling point in matters of personal honor gave accuracy to our parish's nickname.

These independent frontiersmen, many of them descendants of the Tennessee and Mississippi riflemen who had fought under Jackson at New Orleans nearly a hundred years before, were not the only kind of folk who populated Tangipahoa. It was, in a small way, a melting pot which set it apart in the then largely homogeneous South. The Southern Scots-Irish and Anglo-Saxon base had been broadened by farmers, including Scandinavians, from the Midwest who had been induced by railroad land agents to come South; by dark little Sicilian immigrants and chunky Hungarians who had also been brought to Louisiana by steamship companies and land development groups; by French-speaking Cajun trappers and fishermen who lived along the bayous at the parish's southern tip; and, of course, by Negroes, though not in the numbers found elsewhere, for this was not cotton plantation country, but a region of truck and strawberry and dairy farms.

Our farm home was four dirt road miles from Hammond, the parish's principal community, which then had all of 1200 population. The farm consisted of 300 acres, not large by plantation standards but of considerable size in this land of compact, intensively cultivated farms. Our tenants were mostly Sicilian, parents and children alike bewilderingly alien to my brother and sister and me. We liked to play around their garlic-and-wine smelling cabins with the ever-present clay baking ovens and goats in the back yards. But more than such nearby adventures, we liked to go to Hammond in one of the family's horse-drawn vehicles, a fast, two-seater buggy, too small to accommodate all of us at once, or a larger surrey, which actually had a fringed top.

The surrey was usually drawn by Sue, a Kentucky thoroughbred, who was my father's pride. He also entered and drove her in trotting races. Sue was in the shafts on that memorable day in 1913.

He and my pretty, blue-eyed mother had taken me to Hammond that day, leaving my younger brother and sister back home with the nurse. Of Hammond's Main Street conglomerate of one-story brick and frame buildings, the most attractive to me was the ramshackle B-B Lunchroom. I could spell out its sign—"B-B Lunchroom, Two Hamburgers for a Nickel"—because my mother, with time on her hands and ambition for her first-born in her heart, had taught me to read by the time I was five. Once I had asked if I could have the hamburger bargain. My mother had told me that such meat at such a price was found to be poisonous. But I still hankered after the B-B's specialty.

It is probable that my hopes rose that day when my father reined in Sue just across from the B-B, in front of which a number of men were milling around. Maybe my parents would relent and give me a nickel for two hamburgers. And then someone was telling my father that trouble was brewing. Inside the B-B a local bad man, ugly drunk, had run everyone out at gun point and had promised to shoot anyone who came in after him. Meanwhile he was practicing marksmanship on the B-B's fixtures. The town marshal, a pleasant, aging man, stood outside the lunchroom, not wanting to go in.

My father looked at my mother. She said, "No, Will," and he said, "Somebody has to do it," and handed her the reins. I remember that I began to cry as my father walked across the dusty little street and into the B-B Lunchroom unarmed; and my mother began crying, too. Before we knew it, my father came out of the B-B Lunchroom with a pistol, not his, in his hand and a sheepish, drunken man trailing behind him. Somebody let out a happy yelp, and some others joined in. My father turned the pistol over to the marshal and then climbed back into the surrey. As we drove home, my father explained to my mother that he had just told the man, whom he knew, that he ought to come on out with him. And once again he said to my mother, who was sitting close to him on the front seat, "Somebody has to do it."

That was more than forty years ago. My father is very much alive, and, since then, I have heard him explain his sometimes otherwise inexplicable behavior in exactly those words, times beyond all counting. He used them after he had plunged at the harness of a runaway horse and had been dragged half a block before the horse gave up, and Dad rose to his feet, his clothes streaked and torn; and again I heard them when I was eight. We were living in a newly acquired house in town so that we could attend public school, and Dad came near being burned to death when he entered a burning two-story house after some spectator had screamed, in error, that an aged occupant was still inside. A year or so later, because somebody had to do it, he was going out night after night for nearly a month, booted and heavily armed, to search swamp and forest and remote cabin for a backwoods feudist who had shot and killed a member of a rival clan. I was old enough then to understand and approve my father's more extended explanation. Feeling was so high, and loyalties to the two warring groups so divided, that authorities feared that some members of an ordinary citizens' posse would almost inevitably let their allegiances or enmities get the better of them if they found the killer.

And so, again because somebody had to do it, my father, together with two businessmen and a doctor who could and would shoot, and a minister who had once been a Texas ranger, scoured the river bottoms and farming settlements until they surprised and arrested the culprit without bloodshed.

Then there was the September of the terrible 1916 hurricane which almost blew away New Orleans and the rest of South Louisiana. Our family had been in Maine for the summer. But Dad had come home earlier than the rest of us and was to meet us in New Orleans when we arrived. The hurricane struck several days before we left Maine. Dad telegraphed that everything was all right, but that was all we heard from him. When three or four days later our train pulled into New Orleans, after a long detour, it was nighttime. The street lights were still out because of the hurricane's damage. In the lamp-and-candle-lit station, Dad met us with a flashlight and began herding us to a city uncle's automobile.

Most of the other pedestrians also had flashlights, which they played on the sidewalks in front of them. I can never forget my childish embarrassment when one such flashlight betrayed my father's feet. They were shoeless, and he was carrying his shoes. In the glare of the flashlights his white socks stood out like beacons. For a block or more, seemingly every passer-by saw Dad's feet and snickered. Then we noticed that Dad was limping.

The story gradually came out. When the hurricane had struck Pass Manchac, a fishing and trapping region between Lake Pontchartrain and Lake Maurepas, some twenty miles below Hammond, a call had gone out for volunteers to succor the living and search for the dead in the battered lake and swampland. Dressed in everyday business clothes, Dad joined the first contingent that piled onto flatcars of the Illinois Central Railroad, whose main line crossed the stricken Pass. For two days he and his companions braved storm and snakes and alligators in that infested area, carrying out marooned men and women and children, giving first aid to the injured and seeking out the dead. The rescuers were working knee-deep and more in water. Dad had on low-quarter shoes—not having waited to change them—and consequently his feet became chafed and blistered and finally infected. The infection had not reached its worst stage when he met us that night, but even then it was torture to wear shoes; and for days afterwards he was in agony while the doctors wondered whether one foot might have to be amputated.

I could go on, on, on. There was the afternoon when I was in high school and two of our high school club teams were playing baseball in the then unused county fairgrounds, with only students and a handful of teachers as spectators. A drunken deputy sheriff, who was also the fairgrounds caretaker, lurched out on the diamond, waving a pistol, cursing loudly, and demanding that we leave. An older student, who had driven his family's car to the game, and I made it to the automobile and started in it for the entrance gate. The deputy beat us there, and, as we drove past, he hit me on the shoulder with his gun barrel and cursed us. Get Dad, I said, all thought of police assistance gone. We got Dad, and luckily my companion also picked up a town policeman on the way out; but it was Dad who whaled into the deputy's cocked pistol, knocked it out of his hand and, while policeman and students watched approvingly, taught the child-bullier not to terrorize high school students.

Now these stories of my father's unending determination to do whatever somebody had to do primarily illustrate only physical courage. He was not simply a fighter. A strongly built and unusually handsome man, just under six feet, he preferred using his hands to crumble lovingly the soil of his farm or to play his violin. I marvel even now at how his hard, strong fingers touched bow and strings so lightly, his nostrils flaring slightly to the violin's keening and his wide, sensitive mouth tautening as he played. My mother was only an indifferent pianist, but Dad's youngest sister, who with her family was a frequent visitor from New Orleans, was a gaily accomplished one. I can see the two of them playing for us the olden hymns and sentimental melodies we loved.

He worked hard on the farm and at anything else he did, but he always had time for fun; fun for us and for himself. He and my mother used to hunt quail from horseback; and later on he would take my brother and me fishing or hunting for dove and snipe and quail behind Don and Sport. In those days we never had to leave our farm and the adjoining ones to hunt, which makes this a long time ago. And once a week for as long as I can remember he played poker with the same cronies, almost all of whom are gone now. Ritualistically, when he won, he gave my mother half the winnings, or at least he told her he did. The game was not a big one. But one Friday night Dad won several hundred dollars, a real windfall, and quickly concluded that half that sum was much too much to share with Mother. So he hid most of the money under the living-room rug and waked Mother up to divide with her the thirty dollars he said were his full winnings. The next morning he found no chance to rescue the winnings before leaving—by then we were living in town—for work at the farmers' association; and before he came home for midday dinner, our long-time maid, giving the living room a thorough cleaning, found the poker roll under the rug. She turned it over to my mother, who guessed immediately what had happened. She loved to tease, so when Dad came home she absented herself from the living room long enough for him to look for the money. Dad waited long and painful minutes before he told Mother that the money had been hidden from her and was now missing. Then Mother returned to him exactly half of what the maid had found.

He and my mother indulged us more than they could afford. We moved to a house in town when I, the eldest, was seven, because it was almost impossible to get me to school in town every day, and the rural school near by was a poor one. My mother had been teaching me since I was four and when I entered grammar school at seven I was ready for the fourth grade, but she felt this home teaching a makeshift.

The house in town which my father eventually bought occupied almost an entire block. On its shaded grounds he provided everything that small boys could ever hope for: a tennis court and ponies, a complete track and field layout, a fully equipped gymnasium over the carriage house, and, for warm-weather use, a lighted outdoor boxing ring where every week after Boy Scout meeting the town's small fry would gather to box while Dad served as referee. He put much emphasis on our knowing how to take care of ourselves; and in return for all he did he exacted from my brother and me only the promise to stand up to anyone, man or boy, who threatened either of us.

But I must repeat that physical courage—in himself and others—was not his primary concern. Certainly he has shown such courage in full measure all his life; and this would be enough for him to be remembered pridefully in a region still frontier enough to put an especial value on personal bravery. But there were other and, in terms of community building, more meaningful expressions, about which I want to tell.

My boyhood years passed and our town grew. Now that we were living in Hammond proper—though keeping the farm—Dad was in the forefront of everything that helped change the little community from rural village to thriving small city. Was there a new bank to be organized, a bond issue to be approved, a farmers' association to be formed, a multi-parish fair to be set up? Dad was in everything—everything, my mother would say though not disapprovingly, that took time and money and brought only satisfaction as dividend. He was anything but wealthy, and nothing he did has made him so; but his sense of community obligation in time enriched many. In a day when our often ignorant small farmers looked scornfully upon purebred cattle, avenged themselves upon any man who fenced in his range land, and held that the debilitating cattle tick was an act of God not to be interfered with, Dad brought together a small blooded herd, fenced some of his land, and began dipping his cattle to show what good stock and proper care could do. They cut his fences and blew up the dipping vat, and his herd got tick fever and was mostly wiped out; but in his wake came believers as well as skeptics.

Remember, this was an undeveloped and rough country. Some could take it, and some couldn't; and a few found wealth in it, though not many. Dad did not, but he found something else again, and there is no better word for it than satisfaction. It came, for a personal reason, in helping to make Tangipahoa parish a good place.

For many years he served on the parish's governing body, called in Louisiana the Police Jury. His ward's roads were the best and most cheaply graveled in the parish; and he saw to it that our Police Jury kept its records straight in a state and at a time not especially known for strict public accounting. During his service as a police juror, I heard two men whom I didn't know discuss in a barber shop the merits of a third. "He's as honest," one of the men said as a clincher, "as Will Carter." I think this is why in 1940 Dad got the biggest percentage of votes in the state when he ran for the state legislature as an anti-Long candidate—his only real venture in politics—in the fateful election when the Louisiana voters unshackled themselves, for a time, from Longism and corrupt tyranny.

His most enjoyable few minutes as a legislator came, I am sure, when during a free-for-all on the floor of the House of Representatives in the first frenzied session after the anti-Long victory he came to the rescue of a fellow anti-Long lawmaker and, at sixty-one, knocked down the assailant.

His civic devotion brought to him its most satisfying result and to our whole area the most lasting benefit in the creation some thirty years ago of what is now the accredited, four-year Southeastern Louisiana College in Hammond. Dad was on the school board in the mid-twenties, and so was the doctor who had been one of his fellow posse men years before. The high school superintendent was a stern, visionary North Louisianian, who worried over the lack of higher educational opportunity for so many of the high school students. Their families simply could not afford to send them away to college. Why not start a junior college right here, Superintendent Sims asked my father and the other board members? Dad and his doctor friend were especially taken with the seemingly preposterous idea.

By the following fall, Hammond Junior College was offering two college years to seventeen students in the high school building. The trustees were the superintendent, the doctor, and Dad. They were also the principal and unofficial benefactors. Dad got the Police Jury to make about $20,000 available. By next year the college had been moved to a spacious home on the edge of town, bought together with fifty or so acres from a New Orleans owner, and the parish had approved a modest millage to support the junior college.

Dad was a trustee for eleven years. During that time he helped put more than twenty boys and girls through the school—a few dollars whenever he could to each—as it grew from a two- to a four-year institution. Then Huey Long had him removed, as all of Long's opponents were removed, from any position which the Kingfish could control. I don't think anything ever made Dad as angry or heartsick as did being kicked off the board of the college he helped start. And I was as proud as he was, four years ago, when I gave the Commencement talk at the twenty-seventh anniversary of Southeastern's founding, while Dad, the only survivor of the original trustees, sat with me on the platform.

Thirty years before, I had ridden my pony and camped in the woods which were now Southeastern's campus, so close to the house in town which Dad had quitted for the farm as soon as my sister, the youngest, entered college. Almost twenty years before, I had started, in my home town, my first newspaper, a small daily. And, sitting there that Commencement day in cap and gown, I knew that I wouldn't have been there as speaker had not that first newspaper stayed alive during Longism and the Depression; and I knew too that I could not have weathered either had it not been for my father. My wife and I like to boast that as newlyweds we had founded the little *Daily Courier* with less than $400 in cash. That is true enough. But we could not have kept going had Dad not been near in those fantastically difficult times to endorse the notes for the small loans that seemed so big and were so all-important. Nor would a brash twenty-five-year-old editor have been as secure in his generally intemperate comments on state and local politicians and on the parish's continuing high rate of unpunished homicides, had not friend and foe alike known that Dad stood behind everything we wrote. And while we were able to maintain a little home of our own after the first few months, we did find ample room and fare on the farm both at the beginning of that first newspaper venture and again three years later when my mother died and my bereaved father asked us to make the house less lonely for him.

I doubt that my father, not being of a particularly meditative nature, has ever pondered the reasons he has lived and acted as he has. I have said it is because of very special reasons. I think I know what they are. I hope I am not selling my own and my sons' generations short when I say that words—concepts—like duty, honor, citizenship, loyalty, patriotism had a more active meaning a half century ago, when my father was helping build a town in what was essentially the backwoods, than they do now when we have fewer towns to build and more tools with which to build them. Too, they had more personal meaning to the men of his own father's prime, and these were the men to whom he listened in his own childhood, the broken survivors of the Confederacy who had come home to rebuild from ashes.

And there was, I think, another reason, even more personal and perhaps a subconscious one. My father, I have said, was city-raised; but Tangipahoa parish was in his blood. One of his great-grandfathers, a young Kentuckian with a Yale law degree, had moved to New Orleans in 1807, soon after the Louisiana Purchase. He became famed as a jurist and wealthy; and in time he bought tens of thousands of acres in the highlands of Tangipahoa and St. Tammany parishes, across Lake Pontchartrain from New Orleans. There he built a splendid estate, for recreation and as a refuge from the yellow fever, and created a great game preserve.

These holdings had remained in the family, though not in my father's immediate, long after he had reached manhood. The estate, named first Mt. Hennen after the lawyer forebear, and then Morris Retreat, for the son-in-law who took over the property after the Civil War, was a lodestar for my father no less than for his mother and grandmother in their own times. His Virginia father had met and married my grandmother soon after the Civil War. Bitter in defeat, he had taken her to Europe, where they remained for several years; but eventually they wound up in Louisiana, dividing their time between New Orleans and the home in Tangipahoa parish where my father was born, and Dad's own life had been spent between city and country.

I know that Mt. Hennen and Tangipahoa parish were always an emotional part of him, even after the old home had passed at last into other hands. He saw the Tangipahoa and St. Tammany parish countryside as his unowned inheritance and responsibility. Through it in his boyhood he had hunted and fished and camped and ridden. His roots went deep. They still do. And it was only natural that as soon as he could after his college days were over he returned to Tangipahoa as a farmer. He had been nourished by that soil. Now he would nourish it in turn.

But Dad, who is now pushing seventy-five, wouldn't think

of putting it that way. Nor does he consider that it's time for him to slow down. A few months ago he asked me if I would like a pair of old millstones for the terrace of our home in Mississippi. We said, gladly, that we would and thought no more about it until he phoned a few weeks later to say that he was bringing the millstones up to us. Late the next afternoon he stopped his car in our driveway, after a 260-mile drive. With him was my stepmother, and hitched to the car was a cumbersome old trailer. In it were the upper and nether millstones, weighing together more than 600 pounds. We called for Lawyer Phillips, our husky yardman, who, after dubiously surveying the load, got a crowbar, climbed into the trailer, and began gingerly nudging the bar at the nearer millstone. It didn't budge. Dad watched impatiently for a few seconds. Then he clambered into the trailer and took the crowbar from Lawyer.

"Move out the way," he ordered, and before we knew what was happening he had pried the millstone several inches.

"Will!" called out my stepmother. "Stop that, stop it." Dad looked up and started to speak.

But we beat him to the inevitable answer.

"Somebody has to do it," we chorused. And Dad handed the crowbar to Lawyer Phillips.

2

QUARTEE BEANS, QUARTEE RICE

1956

The singsong chant went something like this, and in my Louisiana boyhood it had an amusing meaning:

"A quartee of beans, a quartee of rice,
An' a lil' salt meat to make it nice."

Not many people outside of Louisiana and not a great multitude within it can tell you what that bit of doggerel means; for the custom of *lagniappe*—which is roughly pronounced *lanyap*—and the whimsical folklore that rose from it were alike dying out soon after the century's turn. And that was and is too bad.

Quartee beans, quartee rice. . . . Children would chant it to storekeepers in the hope of getting something for nothing, like candy or a bit of fruit or maybe even a soda on certain auspicious occasions. But unless you know that a quartee was two and a half cents and unless you know also that the cheapest and one of the most nourishing and flavorsome of Creole dishes was and is red beans and rice, you'll be lost at the first line. You will still be confused unless you are further aware that red beans and rice, Creole style, are as nothing unless the beans are enriched in the iron pot with a sizable hunk of salt meat or ham hock, the whole to be pungently seasoned with bay leaf and green peppers, red pepper and tomato paste, an onion or two, some celery tops if available, a few pods of garlic and almost anything else at hand; the mixture whole to be dished out, after hours of simmering, on a heaping mound of boiled rice, each white kernel distinct and individual.

I can't recall the quartee as a unit of value, though I can remember when an individual heaping bowl of red beans and rice, so prepared, commanded only fifteen cents in certain aromatic if not too spotless lunchrooms in New Orleans' French Quarter. But even in the days of the two and a half cents quartee, a miracle was needed to make five cents' worth of beans and rice either sufficient for a family or tasty. A lil' salt meat was needed. And this is where lagniappe came in, a pleasant and gracefully friendly little custom of giving something for nothing, that served chiefly to make customer and vendor warmly aware, now and then, that there were other considerations in life beside the precise measure, the dollar's worth for a dollar, good bookkeeping, and prompt payment of bills. Of course, the purchaser of only a nickel's worth of beans and rice had his nerve to ask for salt meat lagniappe unless he were poor indeed—and this is where the humor of the song came in; for it makes fun of the parsimonious who wanted too much for nothing, not the hungry and needy. But I myself can remember sometimes surprisingly generous largess handed out to children of families which were neither poor nor deserving nor even far behind on their bills.

I was long grown before some idle browsing in South American history brought discovery of how lagniappe got its name. I had always thought it to be an archaic French word. But reading one night of bloody Pizarro and his butchery of a civilized Indian people in Peru 400 years ago, I discovered that the plundering Spaniards had discovered the custom of lagniappe among the trustful Indians. For lagniappe is a French corruption of the Spanish *la napa,* and *napa,* I learned, was originally *yapa,* which in Quechuan, the most cultured of the linguistic stocks of South America, means a present given to a customer.

And so, from the Incas the Spaniards took not only lives and gold but a happy custom of giving; and they brought the custom to Louisiana, where in time the French, as is their uncanny habit, took over the ritual and the word; and in time it came down as a Creole custom to us who were neither Indian nor French nor Spanish but only heterogeneous small boys who canted "lagniappe, lagniappe," as had our parents before us, and begged to be allowed to bear the monthly or longer-due check to the grocery or the drug or the dry goods' store because it meant almost always a sweet if trifling present, thrown in for good measure even when the storekeeper didn't know just why he did it.

I am sure this hindsight bit of scholarly knowledge would not have interested the four merchants whom I recall most vividly from my lagniappe days: Mr. Morgan who ran the corner grocery, Mr. Graziano in his meat market, Rol Fellows of the Central Drug Store, and the dour and terrifying German, Mr. Seib, who ran a crammed notions store called Noah's Ark. We who were young were influenced not so much by the quality of their goods as by their varied responses to our appeal for lagniappe when, check or cash in hand, we entered to pay a parental account or make a purchase of a size that we thought deserved something in turn.

Looking back, I liked best the way Mr. Morgan, the grocer, behaved. He always came through. Sometimes Mr. Graziano, an Italian émigré not long among us, would pretend sulkily that he didn't understand what we were saying. And when he gave, he confined his generosity mostly to a piece of pickled pigs' foot, submerged in disintegrated loneliness in a vinegar jar, or a mouth-puckering pickle, or, occasionally, a sliver of hard Italian cheese. But at least he usually gave and we enjoyed going to his market, which was like traveling to a foreign country, for most of the new Sicilian farmers traded there, and their speech and the foods they bought were both strange.

Mr. Seib was the unapproachable. A grim-visaged, suspicious man, he watched us like a surly bear from the moment we entered his den. He gave us value for our money, but no more. The word *lagniappe* was repulsive to him, and the practice even more so, and it was only as a joke that we asked him for anything for nothing. But his prices were fair enough and his stock large, and, as a result, I am sure Mr. Seib alone helped sound the death knell of lagniappe by his strict but nickel-worthy dealings.

Rol Fellows, the druggist, was a trader of another breed.

Sometimes he was jovially generous, sometimes he was tight-fisted. We never knew when he would be either way or why, except that he was generally friendlier during quail season. He liked to hunt. But he was responsible for the only time to this day that I have ever felt that I had out-smarted a businessman. I had brought in the check for the family drug account, no small amount, and, knowing the size of the bill, I asked boldly for plenty of lagniappe. Rol Fellows asked me, unaccountably, what I wanted and I said mixed fruit tablets. Fruit tablets were the forerunners of Charms and Lifesavers and other such hard candies, and they were kept in stock in enormous glass containers that today are collectors' items. Only one of the Fellows' jars held assorted fruit tablets, and these were for the most part stuck to the bottom and sides of the container, a multitude of strawberry and pineapple and raspberry and cherry fla-vored morsels, all seemingly solidly annealed. Rol Fellows tried to dislodge them with a pencil, but with little success; and finally he said, "Take the darn jar for lagniappe." And so I did. Back home our cook, Effie, steamed the fruit tab-lets loose by putting the jar in a big pot of boiling water, and I had candy enough for weeks ahead.

And now for Mr. Morgan, the best lagniappe-giver, whom I've saved for last and whose store still stands, right where it stood so long ago. Only, Mr. Morgan is gone and that is a pity, for something pleasant went with him.

I am not even sure he owned the outskirts grocery when we first traded there or was just working there. Later he did become owner. It stood on the western edge of town, closer than any other by half a mile to our farm home, and, later, even closer to our house in town. It was not nearness, how-ever, that endeared Mr. Morgan's store to us. There were other and closer if less practical ties. His wife-to-be was my first and favorite teacher and the best I had in grammar school. Her sister worked as secretary in my father's farm-association office. Mr. Morgan's store telephone number was the first my mother called each morning, for this was before the days of supermarkets, cash purchases, and carefully calculated prices per pound or dozen.

My mother would say, "Good morning, Mr. Morgan," and then inquire as to the freshness and tenderness of his fruits and vegetables and steaks or chops or chickens.

At the other end of a primitive telephone system, Mr. Morgan would assure her of the blue-ribbon quality of all she sought; then, with no more ado, she would place her order, with no regard to weight or count or cost: a tender roast, Mr. Morgan, and an assortment of fruit, and do you have any good fresh asparagus, and when do you expect some seafood from New Orleans, and. . . .

She wouldn't ask him the price of any single item or the daily total, and he probably would have felt bad if she had. We never knew where we stood until the bill arrived each month, although in each order of groceries, picked up at the store in our country years or delivered by wagon after we moved to town, there was an order-slip carbon, completely undecipherable, it seemed to me, except for the cumulative amount, to which Mother paid no attention. And then, at month's end would come Mr. Morgan's bill, the end result of many days of unconcerned orders by telephone.

That day always produced domestic drama. My father would be the spit and image of outraged astonishment that any one family could buy as much from any one store. My mother would sometimes promise to be more economical; more often she challenged Dad to be less demanding gastronomically. Once she silenced him for many weeks, by putting us on what Dad decided after a few days was a Spartan diet, though it would have satiated most families. When he protested, Mother produced her slips, showing how much she had saved. That ended the grocery-bill rebellion.

Sometimes Mr. Morgan waited a long time for his money, for our family finances weren't always on an even keel. My brother and I enjoyed those delays for they meant more lagniappe when the eventual settlement was made, just as did the payments of accounts after such spendiferous peri-

ods as Christmas, or the prolonged visits of relatives, when
Mr. Morgan's bill would become gastronomically astronom-
ical. It was at such times especially that we clamored to bear
the magic checks.

"Lagniappe, Mr. Morgan," we'd say as soon as we pushed
open the screen door. "We want a lot of lagniappe." Then
we'd hand Mr. Morgan the check. The protocol in those
long-ago days never varied.

"Think it's good?" he would ask, inspecting the check.

"Sure," we would chorus. "Good as gold." And again,
"Lagniappe," moving meanwhile to the candy counter.

Those were the days when jawbreakers were three to five
for a penny, a half-pound peppermint stick a dime, and a
big candy bar, two for a nickel. Cookies were seemingly
free, so many came out of the barrel for a nickel, and dill
pickles were three for a dime. I wish I could remember the
name of an especially famous molasses-and-coconut candy
bar, which must have been cheaper wholesale than any
other candy, because we always got at least one. We'd make
our selection. Then Mr. Morgan would decide how much of
what we wanted for free we would get for free. The quantity varied, of course, with the size of the check and the
length of time he'd had to wait for it. But we were never
disappointed. Lagniappe was unfailing at Mr. Morgan's.

Or at least it was always forthcoming until World War I
came along and the air filled with slogans about saving food
and money; and the woods filled with profiteers, and small
folk everywhere were jolted or prodded or shocked out of
the old days. Lagniappe didn't survive the war, though Mr.
Morgan did.

He lasted for a good many years after, when so many like
him failed, victims of the inevitable. Most of them couldn't
stand up against the new techniques: the cheaper for cash,
the big volume and small profit per item basis, the come-
and-get-it system, the orderly, clean, emotionally sterile,
and impersonal stores that in time became the like-as-like
supermarkets, each bringing us more variety for less, but
never something for nothing. Like lagniappe.

3

A BUGLE CALL AND COFFEE AND A SAPLING PINE
1956

It is simple to explain why even today a telephone makes me uneasy about Heaven, and why the unexpected blare of an automobile horn puts me in mind of horses. But it will take more time to tell why a boxed green fern can bring back all the wonder of the earliest Christmases I remember. Which is what I want to do.

As for the telephone, the first such instrument in our Louisiana farm home was installed at about the time I had heard and learned a song that began:

"Hello, central, give me Heaven, for my mother's there.
You will find her with the angels on the golden stair."

This song convinced me that even though my mother was often at the earthly end of the telephone herself, an angelic operator lurked at the other extremity of the mysterious wires that ran down the road to infinity.

And as for the automobile, I saw my first horseless carriage from the seat of a surrey driven by my mother and drawn by a fine Kentucky mare named Sue. We had just rounded the last curve on the dirt road to Hammond, the town nearest to our farm, when the auto driver, coming our way, saw us and let loose a blast on his horn, and Sue bolted; and even though a gallant, linen duster-clad passenger in the automobile leaped manfully from his seat—the speed must have been all of fifteen miles an hour—and grabbed Sue's bridle before any harm was done, I was frightened out of my wits. But enough of such traumas.

The fern boxes—there were two of them—stood on the outer end of the wide railings which flanked our front steps. They were always there, winter and summer, filled with luxuriant ferns, though it was sometimes necessary on the coldest winter days to wrap gunny sacking about them. The ferns were ordinary enough adornments 364 days in the year, but in the darkness of Christmas Eve they marked the utter limits of the known and normal. Beyond them, among the great live oaks in our front yard, and in the fields and the forest beyond, lurked on that night a spine-tingling mystery, the good man who would bring us gifts. There he waited to play his part in our family's own special rite, which was the setting out of a cup of coffee for Santa Claus.

I am sure now that my mother and father intended the coffee ceremony as a lesson in gratitude and reciprocity, though they never said so, and it did please my brother and sister and me to know that we were helping warm the fat saint's innards, especially on the colder Christmas Eve nights. But far more thrilling was the manner of notification to us that all was ready for the putting out of the coffee. It would come within moments after Christmas Eve supper was over. The coffee, home-ground and steaming in the drip pot on the wood stove, waited only the signal from somewhere in the woods, true and clear and incongruous, a cavalry call whose words were known by heart:

> *"Come all that are able and go to the stable*
> *And get your horses some fodder and corn*
> *For if you don't do it the major will know it*
> *And you'll get the devil as sure as you're born."*

This meant only one thing, incontrovertibly, Santa Claus was somewhere in the dark, chilled and thirsting for coffee. Then would begin the scramble over carrying the coffee, and since I was older than my brother and sister, I generally was persuaded to give way; and out on the front gallery we would sally, our parents behind us and urging us on to the fern boxes beside the front steps. Behind one of them— it was always the right-hand one—the cup of coffee would be set down, scalding hot and half-hidden by the fern fronds, and I am sure it was welcomed by Oliver, the Negro tenant and handyman who, because he could blow a bugle and could count upon a stiff drink as his least reward, always stood in for Santa Claus on Christmas Eve. But I didn't know that until years later. I would never dare to look out in tantalizing fear of seeing the old fellow; for in that day before the multitude of store and television Saint Nicks, I believed that an unguarded glimpse of our benefactor could mean a bunch of switches in our stockings as the only reminder that he had passed by.

So, as fast as we could make it, we would scuttle back into the house to perform in the living room the last act of the Christmas Eve drama. Not until then, just before bedtime on Christmas Eve, would the candles be lit on the tree, and for a very good reason. Few Southern farmhouses forty to fifty years ago had electric lights, and ours was not one of them. Our home was illuminated by kerosene lamps, and our Christmas trees by small wax candles which are very dangerous trifles.

Under our parents' watchful eyes we each would light a few of the candles, some slanting crazily so that they dripped onto the tree or the floor, and others precisely upright in the shiny tin clamps that gripped the slim outer branches of the long-leaf pine sapling. And always, as we lit the candles, Santa let us know that he had found and liked the coffee. Once more in the night would float a bugle call, this time Taps, and its keening always made me a little lonely and afraid and sorry in a way for that old man who one night a year must make the rounds of the world alone and encumbered.

But not for long would I feel that way, for the tree was too much a thing of beauty, whose flamed loveliness could be savored in full only for these few moments tonight and again when the candles would burn briefly on Christmas morning and Christmas evening. Our tree lacked the rich exotic baubles that hide the tiredness of today's tamely regimented substitutes. But its redolence filled the living room for it had been freshly cut only the day before, and its boughs were draped in long silvery ropes of tinsel and drooped beneath the mostly homemade ornaments and fruit and Christmas cookies. And, most meaningful of all, the presence of the tree made me and in time my brother feel capable and self-reliant, and fit companions outdoors for the father whose prowess with gun and ax and fishing line we marveled at and sought to emulate.

The getting of the tree was a strictly male affair and one shared in, as soon as we could walk, by my brother and myself. My father's farm was situated in the piney woods land of Southern Louisiana, and such of his acres as were not in cultivation, perhaps half of the total, were shaded by thickets of pine trees, some virginal still but mostly second growth or later; and among these forested acres there were thinned-out areas where the mature trees had been cut away for timber, the random new growth affording such a lavish choice of Christmas trees as to make selection a matter of prolonged debate.

We would ride to one clearing or another in a wagon, our father's man-size ax and our small hatchets bouncing noisily on the floor of the wagon body, my brother or I holding the reins, and Dad, with a shotgun across his knees, alert for the whir of a rising quail that would add extra savor to the adventure. Sometimes the quail obliged and sometimes they didn't, and no matter because the tree was our only objective. On other winter days, his hunting dogs—Don, a setter, and Sport, a pointer—would go wherever the shotgun did. But this day was ours alone and quail shooting was incidental.

Once at our destination, another ritual was resumed, a prescribed process of selection and rejection that went on over and over until we were all satisfied. I know my father had fun with us. He would single out a nice-looking tree and remark upon its proper qualities; but when we would chime in agreement, he would point out a flaw, and we, of course, would agree again and tramp around looking for perfection.

The right tree could not be over eight feet tall nor too thick in the body since our living room was not large. Its top must be straight and true, for upon it the homemade star of Bethlehem would perch. It must not have lost its lowest branches as so many even young pines do; nor among the branches could there be any dead or dying members, for every pine needle must be vibrantly green and aromatic. And it must be symmetrical, or nearly so. We did not spell out these requirements but we knew them, and to meet them consumed a good part of the morning of the day before Christmas Eve. The tree could not be gathered earlier lest its needles become too dry and so make more hazardous the lighting of the candles.

In time a selection would be noisily agreed upon, and my brother and I would fall to with our small hatchets, believing that we would finish the job ourselves; but we were tired long before we had cut through the five- or six-inch base. Our father would complete the felling with one or two strokes, and the tree would lie on its side, quivering, its resinous stump bereft and nakedly white. He would then drive the wagon as close to the fallen tree as he could get it and my brother and I, grasping it by a lower branch, would drag it, base forward—woe to the tenderfoot who forgot and pulled the tree against the upthrusting limbs—to the wagon, and home we would rattle, our faces pink and our bodies warm and tingling from the exertion, to decorate our victim.

But the decorating never meant as much as the getting of the tree. The heady joy of Christmas was mostly represented then, and in memory is yet contained in a bugle call and a cup of coffee and a sapling pine, and all of them to be remembered at the sight of a boxed fern.

We believed, my brother and sister and I, longer than do most children that a very real Santa Claus came each Christmas Eve; for we were country children, living mostly to ourselves and so less likely to be disillusioned than were our knowing town cousins. It was not until we moved to town so that we could more easily be schooled that we were disenchanted. And long after the disenchantment, the ceremony of the finding and the felling of the Christmas tree lived on; through high school and through college when I, home from the East, went out again to the pine thickets, sometimes with my father and sometimes not, as he grew older, and with my brother; and through my first few years as a newspaperman and husband, for my wife and I established our first newspaper in that little Louisiana town near and in which I had grown up. The ceremony lasted until, with our own first son, we removed to a far larger city and newspaper in the alluvial land of the Yazoo-Mississippi Delta. And not since then have I felled a Christmas tree or taught any of my three sons to do so. There are no pine trees in our delta land, nor have there been any to be had for the felling anywhere that war or inclination has brought us at Christmastime.

It is possible, I know, to set too much store in things remembered and to become too sentimental about them. My wife and our three sons and I have our own loved rituals at Christmastime and at other special times of the family. And it is likely that some years from now our lads, fathers by then themselves, will recall the ceremonies of their own childhood and, doubting perhaps that Christmas can ever be so joyous and meaningful again, will proceed to make it so for their own. They may say, as their own youngsters grow older, that things are no longer as they were in the days when they made magic walnuts and enacted the Nativity on Christmas Eve, which are our own specialties today: the walnuts carefully halved, their meat replaced by nickels, dimes, quarters, and, in one, a dollar bill, carefully glued together again with a ribbon inserted for suspension, gilded and hung from the tree as a drawing card for the children of neighbors; and the Nativity play on Christmas Eve with our and our friends' children as actors, wherever we have been since our oldest was five, which is sixteen years gone. Perhaps, remembering the gaudy lot of real and makeshift Holy Land costumes, the homemade manger, the recitations of the ancient story, and the singing of songs of Christmas, they will tell each other that nothing can match such pageantry and fun as they knew at Christmas, which is as it should be, even though they will prove themselves wrong.

Like most older folks anytime and anywhere, I would like Christmas to be as it was when I was young. My wife and I protest that every year at Christmastime, and especially since our two oldest have reached dancing age, we fight a losing battle with a myriad of cotillions and Christmas tea dances and the holiday house parties and delirious flittings back and forth between homes and even between towns throughout Christmastime. No, I say to myself, it's not like it was in the good old days. I feel a little sad about it; something of the sadness that a believing youngster on a Louisiana farm knew a long time ago at the thought of a Santa Claus who would be cold and sleepy and lonely, did not a cup of coffee await him beside a fern box, not stopping to think that if everyone put out a cup for the old fellow, he would have been a very nervous and wakeful Christmas Eve traveler indeed.

4

LITTLE MISS RACHEL AND D. O. VOLENTY
1963

I was very young when curiosity finally got the better of me and I inquired of little Miss Rachel who D. O. Volenty was. What I actually asked was, "Miss Rachel, who is Mr. D. O. Volenty?"

What followed seemed unjust. Little Miss Rachel, who was a sort of great-aunt-in-law-by-inheritance and then in her early and wiry sixties, rapped me over the head with her thimble finger—the thimble was on it. She said, "Child, don't be sacrilegious. As the twig is bent so is the tree inclined." She always put *child* in front of any admonition, and followed it with one or more of the hundreds of homilies stored away in her mind for any occasion.

The thimble rap made me sorry for myself and angry with little Miss Rachel. All I had wanted was identification of the mysterious stranger whom she was constantly bringing up in conversation. I suspected he was a local Hungarian or Sicilian or maybe German farmer or tenant. In our Louisiana truck- and fruit-growing region, there were many such newcomers who leavened and gave exotic contrast to the older settler. But I couldn't understand why Miss Rachel would have to speak the name of one of them so often. D. O. Volenty, I had begun to imagine, was somebody really important to Miss Rachel, like Little Albert, her departed sister's small son who had died many years before I was born, or Captain Witherspoon, whose heroic death in the Army of the Confederacy had left her, so my mother had told me, a spinster forever.

So I raced to my mother and told her little Miss Rachel had thumped me with her thimble for nothing. My mother asked me what the nothing was, so I began telling her about

Mr. Volenty. My mother made me repeat the name several times. And then a look of comprehension gave way to sudden laughter. She told me, as gravely as she could, that D. O. Volenty was no Mr. at all. Deo, she explained, meant God in a language called Latin, and volente meant willing, and when Miss Rachel said *Deo volente,* she meant only that things would turn out as expected or hoped or predicted only if the good Lord approved. My mother instructed me to go back to Miss Rachel and tell her that I wasn't making fun of her or the Lord. And then, as usual, she admonished me, not to be sassy or unkind to little Miss Rachel because she was all alone in the world. My mother always said that about Miss Rachel, and so dolefully that I invariably wanted to weep for her. So I apologized to Miss Rachel, who accepted my explanation with an unthimbled pat on the head this time and one of the lemon drops she always kept in her cavernous bureau.

"Deo volente," I kept saying over and over for days, savoring the awesome new meaning. I still say it, sometimes to myself, sometimes audibly, sometimes with the hurriedly abbreviated D.V., borrowed from my mother, whenever I make a positive comment as to a future act or event. And when I do I think of little Miss Rachel who, as she would say it, has gone to her reward long since.

Southern family relationships can be complex. Little Miss Rachel was the aunt of the first husband, already long dead, of an older sister of my father, and please don't ask me to explain it again. When this other remaining nephew had died, she was left all alone in this world, blood-tie-wise, and it seemed better for her to stay with our family than with the widow. She sometimes spoke of herself as being in the way, but I don't think our house could have functioned without her.

There were many like her in the Southern families of my childhood, a great many more, I suspect, than there ever will be again. Almost every home had some such near or distant elderly kinswomen, who, so they would say, were just waiting for the Lord to carry them home, but who, in the meantime—unless they were hopelessly ailing—made themselves so useful in homemaking as to be anything but useless relicts. Mostly they were the widows of soldiers, in a land left sadly overstocked with women after the Civil War. Some, like Miss Rachel, were widows before they were brides.

She was scarcely more than five feet tall and didn't weigh a hundred pounds. But her vigor was inexhaustible, her domestic talents many, and her willingness to work a shame upon the rest of us. These attributes were all needed in our house; for while there were only three children, never a month passed for years when at least two other cousins or needful children were not part of the family. We took tending too, and little Miss Rachel did much of the tending and a lot more.

Miss Rachel considered it a near-sacrilege to throw away any seed or any cutting that might take root. And with that incredibly green thumb of hers she would plant anything she came across, anywhere in the yard or garden she could find room—and in flower buckets, tin cans which she painted, old cups, and once even a discarded *pot de chambre*. When we teased her about this proclivity, the adage was invariable: "Great oaks from little acorns grow," she would say, adding, of course, "Deo volente." Her room, with its great, dark fourposter in which she must have felt hopelessly lost each night, was a fragrant herbaceous jungle, the windows and furniture tops and even floor crammed with tiny boxes and cans and pots from which peeped all manner of green things in every stage of growth. My father swore she could even cause hardware nuts to take root, and this was almost believable. Lacking other space, she would sometimes push an incongruous avocado nut or lemon seed or onion into any handy flower bed; and almost always the intruder would come up, to my mother's mild vexation and the children's delight. And whatever she couldn't plant she would preserve or pickle or dry, from watermelon seed to sassafras root.

Blackberries were the one thing that Miss Rachel didn't

30

plant, or need to, for they grew wild in profusion; but she would pay us a nickel or so a gallon bucket to gather them for her own use. Little Miss Rachel liked to make and primly to sip blackberry cordial, which she kept tightly corked in a wicker-covered jug, reminding us that there was no sin in a little wine for the stomach's sake.

How she found time for all she did, I do not know. She drove our servants in unrelenting war against dust and food waste. In those days of knee pants and black stockings for boys, my brother's and my clothes ended up as more darn than original garment, for Miss Rachel and her darning egg, her needles and thimble restored every garment. When we complained that our clothes sometimes had a scarecrow look, she would say, "Child, waste not, want not," and continued to keep our wardrobes in being long after most of the apparel should have gone to the ragman.

If she helped the family save on clothes, she was even more versed in ways to hold down the doctor's and druggist's bills. She hoarded everything that might be useful—string, pins, wrapping paper, nails—and especially medicine bottles—no matter how small a residue they contained. She had her own remedies that seemed to do just as well as or better than sto'-bought ones. For sore throat, a swatch of cold water-soaked flannel around the neck; for croup, a spoonful of sugar and coal oil; for a chest cold, a mustard plaster that blistered the skin a bright red; for bleeding wounds, cobwebs; for a bumped forehead, vinegar and brown paper; for a hornet sting, a plastering of mud; for I can't remember what, asafetida in a bag around the neck; for a spring tone-up sulphur and molasses; for indigestion something called nux vomica or a few drops of diluted hydrochloric acid in water; and, for any muscular ache, Sloan's Liniment—if she could catch us—the hottest such concoction ever made, or the milder Dr. Tichenor's antiseptic, which she set especial store by because its label portrayed a nobly charging group of Confederates beneath the Stars and Bars. We all lived.

I am sure she spoke other than in adages, but I find

this difficult to believe; and today I can rattle off literally scores of them that I learned from Miss Rachel's constant use. *Enough is as good as a feast,* she would say when we ate too greedily; and *Handsome is as handsome does,* if we were unruly; and *Children should be seen and not heard; Blessed are the peacemakers; Let dogs delight to bark and bite; Satan finds some mischief for idle hands to do; Man shall not live by bread alone; A stitch in time saves nine; Procrastination is the thief of time,* and so on, and on, from sources Biblical, classical, and folk, a saying for every occasion, and almost all of them making sense. And, whenever it could be worked in, Deo volente was added to the original.

God willed that little Miss Rachel should have perhaps her happiest moment in His temple. She taught a Sunday school class of boys, in the eight- to ten-year group, long before and long after I was a member of it; and in my last year in high school, Miss Rachel stood proudly before the entire Sunday school while the principal praised her devotion and presented her with a little emblem for a record of ten years of teaching without missing a single Sunday. That morning, as she walked happily back to the children who were hers only on Sunday, was one of two times I ever saw tears in Miss Rachel's eyes.

The other and earlier time was my own unintentional doing. She had asked me to go upstairs and find something in her bureau, and rummaging around I came upon a daguerreotype of a young woman who I knew was the long-ago Miss Rachel, a beautiful girl with high-piled blonde hair and wistful eyes. I brought it down with me and handed it over to Miss Rachel, and I said, "Golly, Miss Rachel, if this is you, I bet the Cap'n thought you were pretty." She snatched it away, her bright eyes wet behind her clouding spectacles, and for once she had no homily handy. I said, "I'm sorry, Miss Rachel," and went away and cried a little myself over her romantic sorrow.

Miss Rachel died not long before I was married, but she knew I was going to be and it pleased her. She had no use for wifeless men. When my younger brother, who was her favorite, married a couple of years before me she had taken almost all of her small hoard to give him a Ford automobile. And when I told her that I wouldn't be far behind my brother and that she'd be at my wedding too, she said, of course, "Deo volente," and told me she was sorry she couldn't give me the money for a new car because she loved me too, but that my brother had always kept her in mind of Little Albert, who was her dead, dear sister's only child. She was looking forward, she said, to my wedding, and God bless us. But suddenly, not long afterward, little Miss Rachel died, somewhere in her eighties. I know that my mother and the servants and probably my father also wondered how the house would get along without her. I doubt that it ever quite did. And I don't think God would have been willing for it to.

5

IN THE BUCKBOARD SUMMERTIME
1954

One day this summer, as in all but one summer since the war's ending, we wedged sons and typewriters and suitcases and Thermos jugs and fried chicken into the carefully doled sections of the station wagon and set out from Mississippi to Maine—1722 miles and four days of precarious trending that becomes worth while the very instant, though not usually a moment before, we see Penobscot Bay.

This summer's trip was nicely different. The diary made it so, the diary I kept the Maine summer I was nine, the summer of 1916; not my first in Maine by three years, but the first of personal record. We had found the diary during one of those old-trunk-emptyings, its hard, black back mildew-rotten, its binding glue a forgotten feast for mice, its pages gnawed, and the faithfully penciled daily entries faded but generally legible, each day's accounting beginning: "I woke this morning at seven o'clock, got up and had breakfast and went out to play."

The stories the diary conjured were enough to get us from the Lower Mississippi to the George Washington Bridge with the least fratricidal strife and parental irritation in all the history of cross-country travel. For all I had to do was remember another Maine story out of the diary and tell it. Each story, and the endless and envious questions it prompted, was good for an hour or more of serene traveling. The only pity of it is that my sons now feel that life has cheated them: all they can do in these unglamorous times is sail and fish and square dance and gorge and sleep late and go to the movies and climb Mts. Battie and Megunticook and Bald, and spend their money on fried clams and ice cream, whereas their fantastically blessed father. . . .

Most of the stories, though not the 1913 ones, can be proved by the diary; and they all have as their First Cause my Grandmother Carter's frequent wish to gather about her, for a summer in Maine, her sons and daughters who once numbered eleven, and their wives and husbands and their sons and daughters, and kinfolk unto the third and fourth degrees of removal. These intermittent family reunions had one thing in common, from the first one to the last before she died; Grandmother always had God along, which was a fortunate restraint upon the rest of us.

From the first year on, Maine's air was God's air—she never called it anything else—and Maine's sunshine, God's countenance, and each tingling Maine nightfall, a mandatory time for us to foregather in Grandmother's living room for family prayers. These were evenings in which God's praise sometimes rang out in unseemly ragtime as a venturesome aunt, abetted by the more daring grandchildren, often put into those old Presbyterian hymns a swing and substitute words for which there may yet be forgiveness.

But it was not the tales of the tempting of Providence that I told the boys to keep them quiet, for such goings-on as family prayers are remote to them and incomprehensible. Instead, I tried first to relate what it meant to a youngster from a Louisiana farm to take a four-day train trip—wonderful despite the humiliating if ample dining-car divisions of one adult portion for two children—and to stop over in Washington for the Smithsonian and the monuments, and in New York for the Hippodrome and a baseball game with my father, and in Boston and Cambridge and Concord and Lexington for History in capitals and spun-glass flowers, until it seemed that nothing in Maine could match the reaching of it; and then on to this aromatic land to discover how wrong such a supposition could be; to find that all adventure and fun and insight into the nature of families began and ended here.

There is the story of the tired buckboard. . . .

God, our family friend, had endowed my uncles and aunts with generous proportions. One bright day they hired two buckboards with drivers, there being no more than two or three automobiles in Camden in those days, and set out on the old carriage road up Mount Battie for a day of picnicking and surveillance of Miss Millay's three long mountains. Into one buckboard swarmed a horde of children; into another climbed ten sisters and brothers and wives and husbands, that being the stated limit of passengers for an agreed-upon fee, and up the mountain we started.

Soon the grownups' buckboard halted, for the horses rebelled at the load. The driver said he'd have to fetch another buckboard and split the adult party. One of my more thrifty uncles said that the charge would have to be the same for the ten, no matter how many buckboards were needed. The driver said no, and there matters rested until we children were ordered to climb instead of ride, and five grownups took our places. I learned how Yankee cunning had once again bested the South; for the driver, finally agreeing that he had guaranteed to take ten adults up the mountain for a predetermined fee, said that there was nothing in the contract about how long it would take. If my oversized uncles and aunts and parents insisted, he'd get them up in one buckboard, but it might take a couple of days, what with the hour's rest the horses would need every hundred feet or so. Otherwise, he'd get another buckboard which would be five dollars additional. . . .

There were Uncle John and the seagulls. . . .

Uncle John, a sedate lawyer, came up a little late that first summer. He had taken, for the first time, the overnight Boston boat. The night had been rough, and he was no sailor. When he dragged himself down the gangplank the next morning, and was told by his wife that the family had chartered a boat for a sea outing that very day, he objected and was overruled. An hour later, still a seasick man, he was outward bound on a tossing sea for Mark Island and beyond. About that time he sighted Robinson Rock, a small reef which looked to him to be just the right size for one deliberate castaway. He insisted that he be put ashore on the rock there, to remain until the cruise's end in the afternoon. And so he was, with a blanket and a few provisions.

Uncle John wrapped himself in the blanket, head and all, and stretched out; being tired and weak from the past evening's ordeal, he soon fell asleep. It was a good thing he had the blanket, for Robinson Rock was home to thousands of seagulls. These, looking over my blanketed uncle as he slept, decided he was no threat and continued about their daily business. What happened to the blanket and the exposed areas of my sleeping uncle should not have been discussed, but it was.

And such scandalous behavior. . . .

Looking back, I realize that some of my younger elders must have been Emancipated Thinkers. That's not what the more decorous members of the older generation, including Tante Lulu, a great-aunt, said about them; but I insist that they were not truly evil, only temporarily influenced by the Devil.

One of them was an English girl cousin in her well-formed teens, who one day went in swimming in Lake Megunticook in a one-piece bathing suit—without a skirt. I overheard one shocked aunt say the cousin might as well be Annette Kellerman; and then I knew, for I had seen the movie posters about *Neptune's Daughter*, though the movie itself had been forbidden me. To this day I think of that English cousin as sort of semi-fallen.

There was also the youngest uncle and a giddy aunt by marriage, who, on a Fourth of July, dressed in each other's clothes, being almost of a size, and paraded brazenly not only before the family but also, inconceivably, into downtown Camden where they were not arrested. The next Sunday they were mentioned unfavorably from a Camden pulpit but that, thank God, was all, except for what Grandmother had to say at family prayers.

And there were the two near-grown girl cousins, lithe and long-limbed, who went about in middy blouses and bloomers and sneakers and little else, though they were certainly old enough to be corseted. They must have been amazingly athletic, for it was nothing for them to climb trees with younger cousins clinging to them piggy-back. They were talked about too, which, I'm sure, pleased them.

There was the day of my own unclothing at Hofer's pier. It was a chill morning, but the family had already planned to swim. (I didn't think they did anything except in concert, like the swarming of the lemmings.) So we gathered to disport in Penobscot's icy waters, all in swim suits save my brother and sister and myself. Our mother had decided it was too cold for us. I set up a howl, seeing all my hardy cousins having, or pretending to have, fun in the bay, until I finally won the sympathy—or irritation—of the oldest aunt. She was unmarried, which made her distinctive, and was my Grandmother's executive officer by right of her firm nature. She took me in her lap and told my mother I should be permitted to swim. Thereupon she stripped me down to nothing, waved grandly seaward, and ordered: "Swim!" My cousin Hamilton swears to this day that I picked up two flat rocks to cover myself fore and aft, and leaped shrieking, while the cousins jeered, into six inches of water and began rolling in the general direction of Iceland.

I wouldn't come out when the others did, though my mother threatened direly. Finally she waded out with a towel. I wrapped it around my blue and rigid body and came ashore. Mother, who was angry, told my aunt I would die of pneumonia. My aunt only said, Nonsense, and she was right, though at the time I almost wished she were wrong.

There was the near-drowned cousin. . . .

This time it was a family fishing trip, and we smaller grandchildren were left at home. However, my cousin Hamilton, who was about ten, qualified. The Kazi-Moto hadn't been under way five minutes before he made his way forward where he essayed to stand on thin air and fell overboard. Amid general hysteria the Kazi-Moto began leaving him behind; but as he bobbed past the stern, my mother somehow grabbed him by the hair—which must have loosened it badly for his is becoming bald just where she had a handhold—and yanked him aboard. Mother was a family heroine for the rest of the excursion, though Hamilton insisted he could have made it to shore, which was probable. But Mother faded into the background after Grandmother heard the story, for it was obvious that nothing but the Hand of God had reached out and jerked Ham from a watery death.

Grandmother decreed a special thanksgiving prayer session for the next night, which lasted far too long, with much singing, the repeated likening of Ham to Jonah, and the secret devising of a new verse to our favorite children's hymn. The verse began: "I am Jesus' little lamb, and so is little Cousin Ham."

There was a beauty to that evening which I can appreciate now more than I could then; my lovely, white-haired grandmother, her face rapt with worship of the Living God; and her grown sons and daughters, accepting and marveling at her faith and obeying dutifully her command to give thanks; and the less disciplined younger generation, following some rebellious compulsion to pretend an irreverence we did not truly feel. We must have sung mightily that night, for two days later a note came, unsigned, protesting that the loud noises of that evening had disturbed the whole of Knox County.

My own fall from Grace. . . .

A widowed aunt married again that summer of the diary, and I was a ribbon holder or something else as special in the home wedding. At the reception two kinds of punch were served, one presumably for the clergy, the ladies, the more decorous laymen, and the children, and the other for the unrighteous. Two of my older cousins led me to the second bowl, and there plied me with champagne punch until I careened away, unnoticed, to the solarium where I crawled under a chaise longue and went to sleep.

An hour or so later when I couldn't be found, the culprit cousins confessed their misdeed, and a search party set out in expectation that I had wandered to the beach and, poor boy, drowned while in my cups. The volunteers might have had some casualties themselves, what with that punch and the rocky shore, had they kept at it long. But a maid cleaning up about midnight saw a shoeless foot protruding from the chaise longue and rescued me. For the rest of the summer I was an object lesson in Temperance, which gave me a rakish reputation among the smaller fry.

And the old Yankee soldier. . . .

In a cemetery between Camden and Rockport, not far from my grandmother's home, wild daisies grew abundantly. It was my chore, whenever the family entertained, to gather daisies in a huge basket and lug them home. The first time or two I had scruples and thought myself almost a grave robber although I took care not to approach closely any grave. Then I discovered that a considerable number of the cemetery's interred population were Union veterans. That made me lose my scruples for, remember, the year was 1916, and in every Southern town old men, still vigorous, sat in the sun and instructed the young in the evil ways of Yankee soldiers, all of whom, they maintained, were better at house-burning and silver-stealing than at fighting. Raiding the cemetery for daisies made me feel that I was helping get even with Sherman.

One day, as I gathered the daisies, the cemetery was invaded by a live comrade of those fallen soldiers. He frightened me when he asked what I was doing and why; then he told me not to run because he wasn't going to hurt me. He asked me where I came from and I replied defiantly, even though I was making ready to run, Louisiana. The old man grinned and said he had been there a long time ago. I knew then that he must have been one of hideous old Ben Butler's men. He talked to me a little while and laughed when I told him that my grandfathers had been Confederate soldiers; and he said at the last that slavery was wrong and the war had been wrong too, which confused me. I liked him and never saw him again. . . .

There were the stories of which the diary reminded me, and which at least had usefulness on the long drive to Maine. Telling them to my sons, I decided that the Southern invaders in those long-gone summers must have seemed an odd lot; with Negro servants who had never seen white ones; with the medley of free-wheeling cousins, not forgetting the English one who spent much of his time wastefully pouring maple syrup upon flypaper (the better to trap flies); with the all-family picnics and sightseeing jaunts and tennis tournaments and family devotions and all the other summer diversions of a matriarchal and once-teeming clan which is decimated now and scattered, but with its remnants, I am certain, closeknit still.

6

THE TIME GOD DIDN'T STRIKE US DEAD

1954

Among the twenty or so relatives who with our parents foregathered occasionally in Maine for summertime family reunions, my cousin Anna and I were the closest in age and in scheming for a larger share of life's blessings. My Presbyterian grandmother called her grandchildren the sweet pledges of our parents' devotion and spent most of her waking hours redeeming us.

The summer Anna and I were nine we learned how the lure of Mammon could collide with the glory of God. It was Anna who conceived the sinful trickery; but I can see now that Grandmother was not altogether without fault. She was a truly Christian woman who, during those summers, ruled her matriarchal clan. She had prayed that at least one of her ten sons and daughters would become a minister or missionary. All had disappointed her, so she had redirected her prayers toward the grandchildren. And, possibly because she had learned from harsh experience, she added to prayer a system of bribes.

Except for *"Jesus wept,"* any Bible verse no matter how short was worth a nickel when we had committed it to memory and recited it to her. A proverb brought a dime, a short psalm two bits, a longer one from fifty cents to a dollar. The Ten Commandments commanded a dollar fifty, as did the Beatitudes. The Children's Catechism Grandmother valued at three dollars. This was not overly generous, for while the questions and answers were short, there were 145 of them, beginning with *Who made you?* (God), and ending with *What is Heaven?* (A glorious and happy place . . .). But we did not have too much trouble with the Children's Catechism.

The misnamed Shorter Catechism, a long and tedious set of questions and answers, was something else again—a financial Grail wrapped in a ten-dollar bill. None of us seriously considered trying to earn that incredible sum. We contented ourselves with turning into nickels, dimes, quarters, and dollars much of the Old and New Testaments.

Into this Presbyterian Eden my cousin Anna introduced the serpent, the summer we were nine. We were low in funds, and we had already collected for the Commandments and Beatitudes, the Children's Catechism and other longer recitations. Lying on our fat little bellies beneath Hofer's pier, Anna and I talked of the enormous task and reward which the Shorter Catechism represented.

"The Shorter's too long for us," Anna said. "Let's get Horace," (he was a new stepcousin) "and split it up three ways. We will then go in to Grandmother together. I'll answer the first question and you the second and Horace the third——"

Before the simplicity of Anna's plan I capitulated without a single apprehensive glance heavenward. So later did Horace. We would each learn, in rotation, one third of the Shorter Catechism. We would each receive ten dollars!

That afternoon we went to Grandmother's sitting room. "Grandmother," I said, "we want to learn the Shorter Catechism. Could we have some copies to study?"

Grandmother's happiness almost shamed us. "Blessed children," she said. "How splendid, how noble, how Christian." (She was never content with a single laudatory adjective.) "Of course you may." She dug three Shorters out of a pile of tracts and Sunday-school lessons and handed them to us. "Blessed little darlings!"

"We'll learn just as quickly as we can, Grandmother," Anna said.

And quickly learn it we did, hastened in part by a growing unease that made us want to get the evil deed over and done with. We split the Shorter three ways, marking the questions each would be responsible for, and memorized the answers in ten days. We held final rehearsal in our hideaway near the shore, a lean-to among the birches and firs and raspberry rushes. And then on a fateful afternoon we knocked at Grandmother's door.

She asked if we really had learned the Shorter, and we nodded our lies. I consoled myself with the thought that we had really learned it, all in all, and so were not exactly lying.

"What is the chief end of man?" Grandmother asked the first question, and beamed when Anna answered that man's chief end is to glorify God and to enjoy Him forever. On we went, haltingly but somehow managing, and did not think of our wickedness until the catechizing was nearly over.

"What does every sin deserve?" Grandmother asked, so dramatically that I could smell brimstone. It was my turn.

"Every sin deserveth God's wrath and curse, both in this life and that which is to come," I faltered. Anna and Horace and I looked at each other. Surely Hell, that place of dreadful and endless torment, yawned. But it was too late now. With the hounds of fear yelping behind us, we stumbled to the end.

Grandmother could scarcely contain her delight. She embraced each of us in turn, bestowing kisses of approval between praises to the Lord.

"Think of it!" she glowed. "Only nine, and you have earned ten dollars for doing the Lord's work." She rummaged through the desk until she found her pocketbook, but as she peered into it her radiant face clouded.

"Oh dear," she apologized. "I haven't thirty dollars here. I must give you each a check. But your parents will get the money for you." She wrote mysteriously in her checkbook and handed out the unconvincing pieces of paper. "Now let us pray," she said, and pray she did for three children who of a sudden had begun to believe that they badly needed prayer.

When we reached our hideaway the afternoon was nearing its end. The usually benign Maine sky was turning a baleful black; the trees were beginning to creak and an insistent wind was tugging at the lean-to's roof. Rain started to fall, slowly at first and then faster. A bolt of lightning lanced toward the sea, and the first clap of thunder spoke in God's retributive voice.

We did not wait to confirm the fear that possessed us. God had wasted no time—He was after us. We fled the wood, Horace and I an ungentlemanly distance ahead of Anna, and we didn't stop until we reached the house, where we regrouped in the room that Horace and I shared on the third floor.

I offered a legalistic defense, though not too hopefully, for I knew that God was listening.

"We haven't really taken any money," I pointed out. "It's just checks. We won't cash them."

"But we took them for money," Horace said. "God knows that. Not cashing them won't help." The sounds of the rising storm raged round us. We trembled and drew shuddery breaths that were almost whimpers.

"We've got to learn all the answers that we skipped," Anna whispered. "Real quick. If we don't, God most likely will strike us dead."

Of course He would, unless we made amends. There was nothing else for us to do but learn the entire Shorter, each of us, no matter how impossible it might be.

We found our copies and settled down to the task, grim in the knowledge that we could not possibly memorize two thirds of the answers each, not before supper, not before family prayers, not before bedtime and a lonely facing of God's wrath in the storm-racked night. I groped for a way of salvation.

"Let's each of us learn one answer at a time, and say it to the others and then do the next and the next, one at a time until we finish," I said.

"But we'll forget an answer as soon as we've said it," Horace objected.

"That's all right," I said. "We didn't say we'd remember it. We just said we'd learn it."

Anna agreed. "Later we can learn it all for keeps," she said.

We had no way of knowing whether God would be satisfied, but it was worth trying.

I read over and over the answer to the first question I hadn't learned, then parroted it before the words could vanish from memory. So did Anna. So did Horace. On through the Shorter we galloped. Never was anything so quickly memorized—or so quickly forgotten. But we had repented and we were learning the whole catechism, if only fleetingly—and tomorrow, as Anna said, we would learn it for keeps. Surely God would understand.

And He must have. I listened while Anna and Horace gave the answer to the one question I knew better than the rest: "What does every sin deserve?" "Every sin deserveth God's wrath and curse. . . ."

Nothing happened. Then we were on higher ground, for most of the last questions and answers gave the promise of redemption. We finished before supper, with time to spare.

"Let's don't tell anyone at all about this," Horace cautioned.

"Except God," I amended his motion. "In our prayers."

"He already knows," Anna said.

For the rest of the summer we were singularly studious. We were learning the Shorter with a retentiveness which, I am sure, would have equally satisfied both Grandmother and God. Only after we were sure of every answer did we turn in our checks to our parents to be cashed. In due time we got ten new dollar bills each, and, as we held them, still not too sure of salvation, I had an inspiration.

"We ought to tithe," I said. "Let's each give a dollar for the poor heathen."

We did, and Grandmother accepted our donations joyfully. In return, despite our protestations, she gave us fifty cents apiece and expressed her conviction that one day we would surely provide the church with two new ministers and one missionary.

And there matters rested and still do, except that I must

have failed to transmit those long-ago fears when I told this story to my sons. For Tommy, who also is nine, said that God didn't strike people dead any more, and why hadn't he been paid for learning the Ten Commandments?

PART II

Our People and Our Problems

7

THE LIBERAL ARTS AND THE BILL OF RIGHTS
1955

Return with me to a chilly, multi-hued campus in the Maine autumn of 1923. I was then a sixteen-year-old freshman at Bowdoin College. My Louisiana background was that of almost any rural and small-town youngster of good and orthodox Southern antecedents. What set me apart from my classmates was that I had come from so far away. What set me apart back home was that my parents had decided to send me so far away. And what has since placed me apart at times from some of my fellow Southerners and fellow Americans was the impact of that liberal arts college upon an impressionable student to whom the Bill of Rights had hitherto been something to learn of and fleetingly admire in high school civics and history classes, and file away in the back of the mind.

In that year, 1923, the highways and byways of the United States were infested with robed, murderous men. The Ku Klux Klan was riding high and far that year and for too many years to follow. The American air was tortured with the cries of beaten men and women. Klan violence, Klan killings went unpunished. Americans were afraid because they were Catholics, or Jews, or Negroes, or dissenting Protestants or non-conformists. Ministers of God were driven from their pulpits, editors from their desks. Men dared not speak out because they did not know whether those to whom they spoke gave allegiance to the Klan or to freedom. I remember that I didn't like the Klan in 1923. But it was mainly because I didn't like the hometown people who led it. I did not place the Klan in contradiction to the first article of the Bill of Rights, which guarantees to all Americans freedom of religion and speech and press.

In that year, 1923, thirty-three persons—twenty-nine black and four white—died by the lynch mob's rope and bullet and faggot. In my four college years, 112 human beings were similarly to die, most of them Negroes, most of them in my homeland. Earlier in my boyhood, I had seen the inert body of a lynch victim. The specter has never altogether vanished. But I am sure then the Louisiana freshman at Bowdoin College did not relate that specter or the ghastly total to that article of the Bill of Rights which declares that no American should be deprived of life or liberty without due process of law.

In that year of 1923 we were only beginning to recover from a postwar ideological panic into which the advent of Bolshevism—world communism—had thrown us. The fear that Americans would succumb to the new virus turned unthinking men against many ideas just because they were new, and against many old ideas that did not command majority respect. Organized labor, especially if it were militant; the socialism of even so gentle and peaceable a dreamer as a Norman Thomas; any variant idea however loyal basically—these were sedition, these were un-American, these must be stamped out, even punished by imprisonment. Perhaps in 1923 I had heard some older person warn that the United States Attorney General's witch-hunting was a smirch on the face of free America. But I am certain that I did not link the scare headlines, the persecutions of the unlike with Article IV's promise that "the right of the people to be secure in their persons, houses, papers, and effects, against unreasonable searches and seizures, shall not be violated."

In that year of 1923, the American electorate wondered whether the Republican, Calvin Coolidge, or the Democrat, John W. Davis, would be elected President of the United States of America. That November, less than fifty per cent of those eligible to vote did so. In the South fewer than two white citizens in five voted and fewer than one Negro in 100 voted. It is probable that I was unaware of the low national vote total. It is more than probable that I accepted the fact of Negro disenfranchisement as altogether proper. It is altogether certain that I was not concerned over the flaunting of the Fifteenth Amendment, that addition to the original Bill of Rights which extended the voting privilege to all Americans without regard to race, color, or previous condition of servitude.

And in that year of 1923, an obscure Austrian war veteran named Adolf Hitler led a Beer Putsch in Munich against established authority. I did not know, nor did any American foresee, that the bloody brawling in a German street had as its ultimate objective the human rights of free men everywhere. It didn't bother us. Only five years before we had made the world safe for democracy. Let the silly Europeans stew in their own juice.

It would be an exaggeration to say that such unhappy events dominated my freshman world of 1923. Actually, even in sum total, the challenges to American freedoms, to human freedoms, did not loom large in self-satisfied 1923. Certainly, they did not intrude greatly upon my horizon. Not, that is, until my pliant mind had received, in a little New England liberal arts college, its first healthy jolts.

I would be unfair to my family, to my church, and to my earlier teachers were I to say that until that memorable fall I was unaware of ethical values, democratic values, spiritual values, or of right and wrong. But my pity, or scorn, or loyalties were mainly for individuals, not for ideas. Never before had folklore, mores, inherited certainties been really challenged. And so it is that my greatest and lasting intellectual debt is to the faculty—and to some fellow students —of a small Maine college. They made me think. They introduced me to divine reason. In that school of Longfellow and Hawthorne and Coffin, a campus editor or even poet could rank with football captains. There, the heretic could have his say. There patient, gifted men welcomed the students to their homes for afternoons and evenings of talk and coffee— even tea. There I first discovered the humanities, the eternal, ever-identical struggle between good and evil. And the meaning of the Bill of Rights. There I found that a teen-ager could with impunity march in protest against the legal murder of a Sacco and Vanzetti or picket the dean's office; that he could editorially take the president, or even the football coach, to task; that he could attend a class with a darker-skinned fellow student without having the color rub off on him. And there I first came into contact and sometimes in primordial conflict with that tough, town-meeting mind of New England, discovering that a man who differs with you—in ideas, in race, in politics, in creed—is not necessarily or even likely to be a scoundrel. That is in part what the liberal arts meant to me when I first encountered them.

Here we will take leave of that school which will be forever dear and vastly important to me. I hope I have not kept you there overlong.

Perhaps, before we move ahead, some definitions are in order. We should try to define the purposes of the liberal arts education and condense into a fitting phrase or two the meaning of the Bill of Rights. We should identify the products of the liberal arts colleges—their graduates—with the democratic purposefulness of the American Constitution, amendments and all.

I do not feel equal to these tasks. But, playing by ear, as newspapermen generally must do, and borrowing freely from the wisdom of others, I can put forth these rough definitions and identifications, sufficient and accurate enough, I hope, for present requirements.

The liberal arts college recognizes primarily that "the proper study of mankind is man," his past, his behavior, his aspirations, his achievements, his accumulated knowledge. It seeks to make the student at home with the ages, or, more properly, at home with man through the ages; and to distill from this general knowledge some wisdom about himself and his directions. The scientific specialist is not excluded, but he is not encouraged in his over-specialization. Perhaps we can say that in the liberal arts the spiritual or abstract verity has pre-eminence over the exact, material science, or the laboratory truth. It gives impetus to learning. It does not offer an end to learning.

The Bill of Rights also deals with man. It recognizes the dignity of the individual man, and the political requirements for such dignity in organized society. In the tradition of the liberal arts it is concerned with spiritual values in applied form. We cannot imagine the liberal arts flourishing in an atmosphere in which was lacking the spirit of Western democracy, that our Bill of Rights bespeaks. It would be just as hard to imagine the Bill of Rights as being created, defended, and maintained in an atmosphere where the humanist tradition had died or had never lived. Our Constitution was the work of political philosophers, social students, practical historians. They borrowed from their English past; from that earlier Bill of Rights which their stubborn forebears had presented, a century before, to William and Mary of Orange, and which in turn went back to the Declaration of Rights, to Magna Carta. Its authors, though they may not have so described themselves, were in the liberal arts tradition.

And so also have been many the principal latter-day interpreters and defenders of the Bill of Rights. I do not say that one segment in the population is more patriotic or in general more perceptive than another. I do say that men who have learned how the past flows into the present and how the present can ebb toward the past have a deeper love and a vaster anxiety for the Bill of Rights than do others.

I believe also that four occupational groups have been chiefly so concerned, and that each has been principally molded directly or indirectly by the liberal arts colleges. These groups are the clergy, the teachers of the humanities and the social sciences, the creative writers and journalists, and the judiciary. Their impact is all about us. This has been especially true in the South, in its proud, near incredible progress during the quarter century past.

So let us now journey from a freshman's New England of 1923 to the South today. There is no need to detail the achievements of the South, in agriculture, in industry, and, most of all, in democracy, in these intervening years. The evidence of material growth is everywhere: in the diversified fields and the modern, mechanized farms; in the rising schoolhouses and the spreading campuses; in the industrial smokestacks, the gleaming highways, the trim new homes. So too is the evidence of spiritual progress, the workings of the democratic conscience. Little remains today of those not exclusively Southern evils with which my schoolmates once mocked me. The lynch mobs have been dispersed—let us hope forever; the ancient inequalities, though not yet remedied in full, are being dealt with; the right to differ seems no more insecure in the South than anywhere else in our nation. It is no exaggeration to say that nowhere else in our tormented world has a region made the material, social, political, and spiritual gains in a like period as has the South of the last twenty-five years. And the upward surging is all the more remarkble because it has come in one of humanity's darkest eras.

This moral progress, rare in our seemingly hell-bent century, has been paced by a fourfold leadership: by the clergyman in his pulpit, urging the responsible brotherhood of man under the fatherhood of God; by the teacher in the classroom, sweeping away the cobwebs of ignorance and superstition and self-satisfaction; by the editor at his desk, summoning the cleansing forces of informed public opinion; by the jurist on his bench, insisting that justice triumph in all its beauty and morality and might. And behind them all, the force of the liberal arts tradition, hammering, hammering at the eternal theme: the proper study of mankind is man.

It would be happier to stop here than to proceed. And it would be reassuring if we could assume that the only threats to these interacting guarantors of American freedom come from outside our borders. We are a strong nation, unlikely to go down to military defeat.

But there are also domestic perils to the liberal arts and

to the Bill of Rights. Some of them are created out of the
foreign threat. Some are indigenous.

I am no alarmist. All of us, I am sure, share that American
spirit of optimism, the frontier certainty that we will win
through all along the line. But it cannot be amiss to remind
my readers of domestic perils to the liberal arts and to the
Bill of Rights. I can do no more than simply to list in outline the more obvious ones. Nor will I try to distinguish in
every case between those which imperil the liberal arts and
those which chop away at the structure of the Bill of Rights.
They are interacting threats.

We live in a time of increasing specialization. We require
specialists. Our civilization and our self-protection demand
them. But a specialization that begins in the high school
and continues unendingly to the specialist's rendezvous with
his laboratory neither adds much to our national culture nor
to the internal safeguarding of democracy. A nuclear phy-
sicist, if undisturbed, could conceivably adjust himself to
the police state. A teacher of American government could
not.

The liberal arts can flourish only in an atmosphere of
intellectual freedom. One requirement for institutional freedom is a degree of financial security as a buttress against
pressures political and ideological. The present hard-pressed
condition of so many of our private, non-denominational
liberal arts colleges is not reassuring. Greater alumni support and a broader concept of corporate giving appear the
only practical alternatives to reduction of our liberal arts
colleges in number, scope, and importance.

But financial problems are not the only or even the
greatest obstacle to the continuation of the liberal arts tradition. The no-quarter warfare that is being waged against
the unfettered intellect may partly be explained, though not
forgiven, as the tendency of threatened people to demand
utter conformity within the group. The examples are many.
I need cite only two—the relentless libeling of Harvard, the
greatest American university, as a seed bed of communism;
and the fantastic indictment of the nation's most notable

research and philanthropic foundations by a buffoon majority of a House committee.

The attacks upon the Bill of Rights today are not always as direct. But certainly those guarantees are menaced by the book burners, the faceless informers, the warping of senatorial investigative procedures so that the master inquisitor functions also as judge, jury, publicity man, and personal savior of America.

And the Bill of Rights is menaced in our South today because of inevitable disquiet over a near-revolutionary decision of the Supreme Court in the matter of public schools integration. It is my belief that time must and will be granted for orderly adjustment; that most decisions as to integration will be made at local levels; that the equal schools which we so long promised without fulfillment will temper any demand for biracial enrollment; and that migration will in time reduce the pressure of numbers which is the principal determinant in the most disturbed of the Southern areas.

But in the interim the South is threatened in some areas by the spirit and the near fact of anarchy. In my own state, a questionable organization, the Citizens' Councils, is gaining thousands of members. The initial objective of the Council was to prevent integration in the public schools by economic pressures and—I quote—"without violence if possible." Its secondary objectives are a reduction in the number of Negro voters, the screening of all political candidates, and social and political reprisal against white citizens who oppose the Councils. This is the Klan spirit if not the Klan in fact. The growth of this organization in Mississippi, and its spread into some of our neighboring states, is the most alarming—if not unexpected—result of the Court's decision. For here are explosive ingredients—the threat of violence, attempted thought control, disenfranchisement, and economic suffocation—that in the affected areas can make meaningless the Bill of Rights.

It is certain that every effort, in Washington or Mississippi, at thought control endangers internally our democratic structure. Every indication of racial discrimination

makes more effective the charge of our Communist enemies
abroad that Western democracy bears a label: "Reserved
for white patrons only." This is no fantasy. Within the past
few years I have spent some five months in Asia and the
Pacific. Two questions I encountered everywhere, among
friends of the United States and among Communist and
pro-Communist hecklers alike. What of McCarthyism? they
would ask. And what about the Negro in America?

Here are visible threats. But they do not mean destruction
for the liberal arts tradition, for the Bill of Rights, or for the
nation in which they thrive. We recognize them, and recognition insures that we will deal with them.

I do not have the gift of prophecy, but I know that there
is more to be seen ahead than blood upon the face of the
moon. There is more to be heard than the rumble of disin-
tegrating cities. What we have created out of man's accumulated knowledge cannot die. There are other visions. I
choose gladly to fasten eye and spirit upon these. We can
and must believe in the everlastingness of the liberal arts
idea, an idea for which a great Virginian once gave immortal definition.

"This institution," said Thomas Jefferson of the University
of Virginia, his creation, "will be based on the illimitable
freedom of the human mind. For here we are not afraid to
follow the truth wherever it may lead, not to tolerate any
error so long as reason is left free to combat it."

8

SOUTHERN CONTRADICTIONS

1959

Among American stereotypes, none is more derided than the professional Southerner and none less understood. Most of us know all about Colonel Claghorn and Miss Dixie Rose Honeychile. Most of us know little of why they got that way or even if they are really that way.

I am not a professional Southerner, nor do I profess to be a scholarly authority on the South. I do happen to be Southern by ancestry, by birth, by residence, and by choice, all tempered by what some of my Mississippi neighbors think was an overexposure in my college days to the New England inquisitive conscience. And, as a newspaperman and free-lance writer, my interests and concerns have been largely though not entirely limited to the Southern scene. I am not going to talk about the profound changes in that scene in my lifetime. They are many and heartening, even if some of them required prodding by outsiders. If you are not familiar with them, you might well become so, if only to reassure yourselves about a vital American region.

In respect to these changes, the South is something like the old lady who ran afoul of three determined Boy Scouts. These resolute youths had promised to do a good turn daily. But on Scout meeting night they turned up without a good deed for that day. The Scoutmaster gave them five minutes to go out and do their good turns. They returned within the time limit and were asked by the Scoutmaster what they had accomplished.

"We helped an old lady cross the street," the first Scout said.

"And you?" the Scoutmaster asked the second, after warmly commending Scout Number 1.

"I helped him help the old lady across the street."

The Scoutmaster looked a little puzzled, but accepted the good deed, and asked the third what he had done.

"I helped those two help the lady across the street," the third Scout said.

The Scoutmaster shook his head angrily. "Do you mean to tell me that it took three boys to help one old lady across the street?"

"Yessir," said the first Boy Scout. "She didn't want to cross."

The South is crossing the street, with and without assistance, forcible or otherwise. But instead of telling you more about this venture I want to discuss the principal contradictions—or seeming ones—in the emerging and historic South, to resolve some of them, and to look especially at two of the most provocative and encouraging. These two are public education in the South and the state of Southern letters. Certainly the goals of the one and the achievements of the other contradict the stereotype of Southern tolerance or indifference to illiteracy, and of the South as a region whose

"Books have grown fewer——
She never cared much for literature."

But first let us consider briefly the conflicts and contradictions that must be perceived for proper understanding.

1. The South is the seat of an early, almost the earliest, American culture. It is a long-settled region. Yet today it is the principal American frontier.

2. The South contains the nation's most homogeneous people. They have shared a common language, common tenure, common occupations, and common tongue longer than have any other regional group. Yet it holds also the largest unassimilated and still unassimilable racial group in the United States.

3. In common with all people of predominantly agricultural background, Southerners have a strong love of the land, a deep affection for the homeplace. Yet a larger pro-

portion of its farm workers are landless than elsewhere, and its land has been the most cruelly wasted in the nation.

4. The South can probably count more churchgoers proportionately than can any other region. Organized religion plays a wholesome and unusually significant part in the Southern mores. But the basic implication of Christianity as bespeaking the brotherhood of man under the fatherhood of God is in general lost sight of within the Southern church memberships.

5. The Southerner is an individualist. Nowhere else is the citizen as likely to stand up fiercely and physically for his personal rights, his personal honor, and his personal opinions. Yet, politically and in certain aspects of his social thinking, the Southerner is also the nation's most regimented man, who finds it inexpedient or disloyal to differ from his neighbor.

6. The South is a kindly land to the stranger. Southern courtesies and hospitality have been overemphasized and exaggerated, yet it is true, I believe from long observation, that we are more likely than are others to welcome and share with the visitor whatever we have. Yet we, above all Americans, are suspicious of the stranger who challenges and criticizes our social and economic and political patterns.

7. The Southerner is proverbially gentle in manner. It has been said that until he is angered enough to kill you he will treat you politely. Yet the South's statistics for violence top the rest of the country's.

8. It is not wise to try to sectionalize patriotism. Nevertheless, the South, for the past seventy-five years, has voluntarily responded to the calls to battle in greater numbers than has any other section. If only because the South knows what it is to be a defeated and overrun land, its national spokesmen have been leaders in urging a strong nation. Yet the Southerner is more defiant of the national authority than is any other American.

9. The South has more have-nots in proportion to the haves, and the have-nots are more destitute than are submarginal citizens anywhere else in the nation. Yet the South

has fewer Communists and fellow travelers than does any other American region.

10. The South takes its politics more intensely, perhaps, than does any other area, yet relatively fewer of its citizens vote, and more obstacles are put in the way of voting than anywhere else in the United States.

There are two other contradictions which are especially germane, namely, education in the South and Southern letters. We will examine these later, and more closely. It is in order now to try to resolve the ten basic contradictions which I have just listed. In attempting this bit of sociological legerdemain, I am aware—from painful experience—that the Southerner who tries must duck brickbats from both sides of the street. But here goes.

The presence of the Negro in the South in great numbers and under long-continuing patterns is the key to these social, political, and moral conflicts and seeming contradictions. I do not propose to present the Negro here as the victim of manifest injustice, which he is, nor as the unwilling and unwitting villain in the piece, though he might also be so described. Here he is simply a fact, made up of some 10,000,-000 dark-skinned human facts who frequently are in numerically superior juxtaposition to 25,000,000 light-skinned human facts. So let's go over those contradictions once more.

1. The South is a frontier today because for nearly 300 years it geared itself to a primitively agricultural economy, resting on the back of unskilled black men, slave and free. Its technological potential and its industrial balance were delayed until it was overtaken by the inevitable failure of a cheap-labor, one-crop economic system.

2. Even though the enslaved, imported Negro adopted the white folkways of the homogeneous South, he did not share in that homogeneity because of the conditions of his presence, the cultural lags, and the recognizable if superficial physical differences.

3. Cheap-labor and one-crop agriculture is the most wasteful of all. The slave Negro had no other course save to

lay waste the land. The defeated white landowner had no other course after the Civil War than to continue the old ways under a system of landless tenantry for the freed black and the submarginal white man.

4. Most Christians make special reservations in the South, because fundamentalist interpretation of the Old Testament, tradition, emotion, custom, and even law combine to exclude the Negro from the Protestant's Christian fellowship.

5. The otherwise independent-minded white Southerner is a frequent prisoner of rigid social and even political conformity because of a folk insistence upon racially based unity. This unity was forged in war, in Reconstruction, and in a long and continuing determination that the white South should guide the entire South.

6. Southern animosity and suspicion of the critical stranger go back at least as far as the days of the underground railroads through which slaves were spirited to freedom. It has encompassed in turn the Reconstruction carpetbagger, the free-lance writer, and the sociologist for whom the Negro in the South has been an irresistible and often a remunerative magnet.

7. The Southern practice and tolerance of violence has two principles.

Southern predilection or tolerance of violence is at least partially caused by racial considerations. We cannot omit the distorted notions of personal honor and the historic necessity for the frontiersman and the farmer and the small-town citizen to be his own policeman. But the Negro commits most of the South's crimes of violence. As long as those crimes are committed against other Negroes, the white Southerner has been relatively indifferent to them. On the other hand, the white Southerner has reacted savagely when the white man has been the Negro's victim. Race has been the determining factor both in crime and punishment.

8. The rebellious Southerner of today is a rebel only when the racial patterns he has established are threatened by the federal authority. Fear of Negro domination was the

chief reason for the formation of the old Ku Klux Klan immediately after the Civil War. Antagonism toward the racial policies of the Roosevelt and Truman administrations was almost the only reason for the States' Rights revolt of 1948. Southern discontent today arises only from the Supreme Court's historic school-segregation decision.

9. The economic status of the South gave unfounded hope to the Communist party in the thirties and forties that here would be the Communists' most fertile American ground. Of the South's poor the Negro has been the worst off; for while poverty is no respecter of race and while there are Southern whites as desperately impoverished as are any Southern Negroes, the Negro is the bottom rail. Yet Communism has made almost no headway in the South or among Southern Negroes. The FBI lists one Communist in Mississippi and he is white. I think—and like to think—that the Negro's rejection of Communism comes from personal identification with Christianity and the native American's long-rooted distrust of distant panaceas.

10. The otherwise political Southerner is willing to make voting difficult because up to now the restrictive devices kept far more Negroes from voting than whites. Similarly, Southern rejection of a two-party system continues principally for fear that the Negro could otherwise hold the balance of political power.

What I have just said runs the risk of criticism because of oversimplification and generalities. Nevertheless, I believe the outline holds. It is impossible to do other than skim the surface, preliminary to some more extended comments on education and letters in the South.

Prior to the Civil War the South had more college graduates per capita than did New England.

Today the South has the nation's highest rate of illiteracy. Yet the South spends a greater part of its tax dollar on education than does the rest of the nation. What it spends is not enough to bring us abreast of the rest of the country because we have the lowest per capita income and hence the fewest tax dollars; we have the nation's highest birth rate, and we have been committed for nearly a hundred years to a biracial public school system. Our Negroes furnish most of our illiterates, but they number only five Negroes in 100 today as against ninety in 100 only seventy-five years ago. With more schoolchildren per family and less tax contribution per family, it has been financially impossible until now for the South to provide equal school facilities for white and Negro children without reducing its general level of public school education. In permitting inequalities in its segregated school system, the South has been more human than moral. The white parent, in political control of his community, has been acutely aware that it is largely his tax money and not the low-income Negro parents' taxes which support the school. He favored his own children at the expense of the children of the politically and economically subordinate race. I wish such selfishness were unique in the world's annals. It isn't.

Yet the story has been different in the past decade. Slowly, too slowly, but surely the South has progressed toward equality of facilities for all its own children. The movement has been propelled partly by the proverbial Boy Scouts—in Congress, on the Supreme Court, and also in the South. But the old lady wouldn't have been able to budge or be budged, had not an industrial and agricultural revolution swelled the Southern incomes. We are spending more money on schools because we have more money to spend. We have lately been spending it more equitably because our collective conscience has been jolted.

Now the Supreme Court has ruled that racially separate public schools are unconstitutional no matter how equal they may be, and the South has reacted to that decision in a way, though not with the intensity, that any informed person expected. The states with the greatest number of Negroes in proportion to whites are those who show most determination to circumvent the decision. In such states as Alabama, Georgia, South Carolina, Mississippi, and Louisiana, such expedients as gerrymandering, resort to the state's police power under the Tenth Amendment, economic pressures, local agreements, and even the abolition of public schools have been employed or threatened. In such states I doubt that there will be anything more than token integration for many, many years. And I say, fearfully, that the public school systems in at least three of these states, including my own, are in real danger if Negro children somehow do gain admission in proportionate numbers to hitherto white public schools.

It is easier for the non-Southerner to enjoy moral superiority in this matter than to understand it. I have said before and say again that the Court's democratic motivations and its awareness of world considerations were sounder and better based than was its legal reasoning. It must also be said that no court decision can wipe out immediately old biases, established patterns, or the very real cultural gaps between the average Negro and white child in the South. Our hope—yours and mine and the nation's—lies in the long run here, not the short haul. And, once again, the key to a Southern contradiction, indeed a contradiction between democratic ideal and human misgivings and biases, is the presence of the Negro in large numbers.

It is not my purpose here to moralize but only to point out. Perhaps if I were more a creative writer than a newspaperman I would pursue a different course. But as I turn to a last Southern conflict—the writer's love and frequently contrasting criticism of a region and the resultant effect on Southern letters—let me remind you that I am simply a newspaperman who does some creative carpentry in his spare time.

Nevertheless, perhaps I have a special claim to your attention. In our little town of Greenville we have some unique literary distinctions. One is a small publishing house which two friends and I operate as a pleasure, and quite apart from my newspaper. This venture has published limited fine editions of original work by such Southern writers as William Faulkner, Eudora Welty, William A. Percy (in a posthumous edition of his lyrics), David Cohn, and Shelby Foote.

In the same town of some 35,000 people (of whom half

are Negroes) we have now eight publishing authors—some of them of considerable repute. I have on my own little paper two novelists. I sometimes complain that they spend more time writing novels than they do news stories, but they tell me I do the same thing—so there we are.

In the state of Mississippi we have had so many excellent writers that I can name only a handful of them: William Faulkner, Eudora Welty, Thomas Hal Phillips, several Williamses (even Tennessee Williams is a Mississippian), Edward Kimbrough, Elizabeth Spencer.

It seems worth noting that three of the four recipients of Guggenheim awards for creative writing in 1958 were Mississippians.

Those of you from other states in the South, of course, can match my list of Mississippi writers with lists of authors from your states. They may be equally long, and for the most part they may represent equal talent. It is certainly true that writing has flourished to a much greater extent than have the other creative arts in the South. I am sure that one reason writing has such a position in the South is that we have had almost no centers where it was possible to acquire those disciplines and formal training that are almost mandatory for music, for painting, and for sculpture. Even now ours is largely an agricultural society, and in the absence of great centers of other creative arts, the spoken and written word is the most important creative medium that such societies can have.

The word has been extraordinarily important to our Southern people—the word as it pertains to religion, the word as it pertains to political oratory, to the pamphleteer, to the poet, to the social critic, and to the novelist. This is understandable both because of the lack of formal means of schooling in the other creative arts and because a relatively primitive, predominantly rural people respond to the stimulus of the spoken and written word more readily than to that of any other art. Perhaps we are so responsive to words because on a frontier we are more combative, and words are a far stronger combative weapon than are the brush or the chisel or the scale.

We in the South further distinguish ourselves from the rest of the nation because we have made our literature a means of expressing our sense of being a people apart.

Here again race enters: the institution of slavery itself, the one-crop slave system, the persistent colonial overtones of our culture, and then—most important of all—the experience of a destructive lost war and Reconstruction. And both before and after that war, but particularly after it, the unending racial pressures and racial prejudices.

So it is that for more than a hundred years the South has been almost a nation within a nation, with the experience of certain tragedies that are almost un-American to the American who is not a Southerner. The tragedy of being a defeated people. It is not in the American tradition to lose. We in the South know better.

Even before the supreme clash between opposing regions, our way of life served to shape up the Southernness of our writing. We had little mercantile activity in the pre-Civil War South. And so it was that the Southerner was largely conditioned by and largely confined to the plantation and the small town. He was neither a widely traveled man, unless he was a rarity, nor was he too greatly influenced by outside literary trends. There were no grand tours for the average Southerner of intellect; there were no principal centers of culture or of trade where he could rub shoulders with people from not only the rest of the United States but from elsewhere in the world.

The national result of all this is that Southern literature, and particularly our fiction, has been sectionalized and self-centered to a greater degree than is true, I am sure, of any other geographical or social area. And because of this centering upon essentially Southern problems, we have had a division in Southern literature, and particularly in fiction, that exists to a degree to this day: the division between the defender of an order and the critic of that order.

The early literary defenders of the South were romanticists, as are some of the contemporary ones who evoke a never-never world of chivalry and moonlight and white pillars, roses, honeysuckle, dueling at dawn, and of gallant, chivalrous men riding off to war. The fictional critics, on the other hand, have conjured up nightmares that have accented the grotesque, the evil, and the decadent in Southern life. So we have had two creative spirits largely hostile to each other and largely partisan, concerned with social phenomena that are basically regional. The Negro, the poor white, the demagogue, the acute social and political problems of the South have taken precedence over more universal subjects. In the antebellum South we found our writers and our spokesmen resentful of and answering the Northern critics of our institutions, our cultural institutions, our economic institutions. They demanded as one proof of loyalty that the South must remain blindly true in its writings, in its words, in every way to these beleaguered and attacked institutions. So it was that we remained aloof from one of the great movements in American literature, the New England humanitarianism which in a metaphysical sense approximates something that has been developing in the South today.

When the war was over, the South, in the period of transition, of recovery, of Reconstruction, found itself still defensive in its letters, bitter over the war and particularly its aftermath, and, as defeated people will do, trying to draw some happiness and solace out of the past. Thus romanticism continued in the South. But with it there came something else that was the salvation of that romanticism—the rise of the local color (to use a hackneyed phrase) school of writing. Within that theme of wistful longing and of pride in being on the losing side, we did have in this postbellum South our first approach to what might be called realistic writing as against propagandistic writing. We were discovering ourselves. We still kept out of the mainstream.

I think it is significant that at the century's turn our writers in the South stayed aloof from one of the really significant periods in American writing: the muckraking period

when the nation's writers were challenging the social conscience. Whatever the Southerner's conscience said to him,
he did not take part as a writer in this muckraking. I am sure
that it was because we felt, subconsiously or otherwise, that
this approach endangered what was left of our so-called
cultural institutions.

A great change took place in the post-World War I period,
when two movements that were significant to Southerners,
and significant to the rest of the nation, flowered. On the
national scene, there was the development of naturalism,
in which Southern writers did join. They began to talk of
the South as they saw it, often in very critical terms. We
had many other propagandists for change in the South.

At the same time there was born in Nashville another
movement. It was generated by a group of metaphysical
poets who called themselves fugitives and then agrarians.
They didn't go along with the Southern naturalists. The
agrarians in the twenties and early thirties protested not
against Southern institutions that they thought evil but
against a blind imitation, as they saw it, of certain Northern institutions: against technology, mechanism, industrialism. In a book called *I'll Take My Stand* they said they
would side with the old agrarian culture of the South. The
impact of these men, arriving as they did almost simultaneously with the challengers, in incalculable.

These two groups were not necessarily and not completely in conflict at all, but they point up the inner struggle
that characterizes the Southern writer. In him there lives
the traditionalism, the love of and loyalty to the past, and at
the same time the awareness of wrong and evil that flourished in that past and continues on into the present. This
inner struggle perpetuates rather than destroys the regionalism from which the South has both profited and suffered.
We have profited from that regionalism in many ways. To
me there is something hopeful and heartening in a region
that is rooted in the past. The South is traditional, it does
have a unity of suffering, of great and still unreconciled
problems, a unity of faith. But we Southerners like to talk of

how dear and strong and deep running are our regional traditions and our allegiance to them. Too often we are not willing to accept, outside of literature, the other side of this cultural inheritance, the other side that is not noble, the other side that, particularly in our political and economic life, refuses to recognize wrong. In our reaction to the Supreme Court decision it is not simply a coincidence that on the one hand you find creative Southerners, the educators, and men of God admitting that the issue is a moral one and that no other step could have been taken; and on the other hand the economic and political South reacting adversely and strongly to the Court's interpretation of the Constitution. The conflicts go on in this creatively fruitful region of ours; the long struggle between old and new, between frontier and urban society, between black and white, between democracy and paternal dictatorship, between violence and order, between agriculture and industry, between good and evil, if you will.

Ours is a region of conflict. It is bound to produce writers as it does because it is a region in transition, a region that is subject to strange and often sudden change and that challenges.

We, more than any other part of our nation, have subjected ourselves and have been subjected to constant examination and constant criticism. No other region in the United States has for as long a period been examined as closely by as many of its own people and so critically and often so blindly from the outside. That in itself has produced relations which help explain why Southerners write. We have the tools, we have the inspiration at hand, we have the challenge to write about this still disorderly region of ours.

And now to tie up, if possible, some of the loose ends of this extended hodgepodge. I would think that your principal question would be: "Will these contradictions and conflicts last forever?"

Some Southerners—a diminishing number—would probably answer yes. I differ. I believe some of the contradictions will last longer than others, even as far into the future as we can presently ascertain. But their impact is decreasing, and for the most part they will continue to decrease. There are today fewer areas of justifiable democratic challenge to unjustifiable and undemocratic contradictions. The Southern Negro is catching up. So is the Southern white. Time is on the Negro's side and on the white man's side too in the South—time translated into education and increased income, into extended suffrage, into wider acceptance of the Christian ethic. Time and also space—the American space into which the Negro is increasingly moving. Perhaps it is admitting defeat to say that a more evenly distributed Negro population would lessen Southern tensions and reduce the Southern contradictions. But this is so; and it is also so that the Negro is moving out of the South in dramatically great numbers to what may be more promising lands. I hope the promise is fulfilled.

Time and space—and also the spirit of a younger South are on the Negro's side. The young today are not generally willing to live by the fears and biases of their elders. And this is the most hopeful aspect of all.

Integrated public school education in the Southern localities where live large numbers of Negroes is still distant. But in state universities, in parochial schools, and Catholic and Protestant seminaries in the South, in schools operated by the military establishments, young people are going to school together and the roof hasn't fallen in.

What is happening is affecting and will continue to affect Southern letters no less than all other aspects of our lives. Southern regionalism in letters will persist, but not with such one-sided preoccupation with the South's sociological problems. Our writers will become increasingly more concerned with the inner man and the universal man than with the Southern man and his restricted environment. And this is just another way of saying something that I truly and hopefully believe: the South is at long last entering the American mainstream.

9

FAULKNER AND HIS FOLK

1957

As preface to some informal observations on a genius, I would like to relate a bit of modern literary and journalistic history. It is not offered with the arrogance commonly associated with Texas, nor defensively as would speak some Mississippians today, but with the modest conviction that by their works ye shall know them.

So, let us go back to late April of 1955, when, as a member of the Pulitzer Advisory Board, I met at Columbia University with my ten omniscient fellows to select the annual assortment of Fortune's favorites. This we did with assurance and dispatch. By nightfall we had picked, unerringly, the proper winners of the fourteen awards for the year's best American newspapermen, historians, poets, musicians, novelists, biographers, and playwrights. As a self-perpetuating body, we had also picked a successor to a Board member who was retiring after many years of service.

I will not name every winner of the Pulitzer Prize in 1955. I will name four of them, and the new Board member as well. The winner of the Pulitzer Prize for local reporting for the exposure of land frauds in Texas was Roland Kenneth Towery, editor of the Cuero, Texas, *Record,* and a Mississippian. The winner of the Pulitzer Prize for disinterested public service, to wit the exposure of vice and lawlessness in Phoenix City, Alabama, was the Columbus, Georgia, *Ledger,* and the man responsible was the executive editor, Robert Brown, a Mississippian. The winner of the Pulitzer Prize for the best play, *Cat on a Hot Tin Roof,* was Tennessee Williams, who, despite his assumed first name, is a Mississippian. The winner of the Pulitzer Prize for the best novel, *A Fable,* was William Faulkner, a Mississippian. And the new Board member we chose was the managing editor of the New York *Times*, Turner Catledge, a Mississippian.

As I've already said, in all humility, by their works ye shall know them, individuals and the states alike.

It would be better if this bit of history could be bitten off here. But there is another aspect, less happy and more significant. Of these five Mississippians, four had to go elsewhere, or thought they had to, to achieve. This is the worst of the curses which affect us, that our young continue to be our principal export, primarily because we have not yet attuned our society to the necessitous clangor of industrial balance or to the American clamor for the recognition of the rights and the dignity of all men.

Four left Mississippi's soil. Only William Faulkner remained, and he to withdraw, in spirit, for so long a time, into the dark tarns of the world of the Sartorises and the Snopeses, of Popeye and Temple Drake, of Addie Bundren and Quentin Compson, of Lucas Beauchamp and the rest of his tortured, torturing, ineradicable legacies of man's inhumanities and man's endurance of them.

But I am not here to talk of William Faulkner's self-created world, the imaginative dwelling place which has angered and bewildered and frightened many among those of his fellow Mississippians who have come upon it either through hearsay or by investigation of his printed word. These fellow citizens, and others in the South, took pride in him, or they did until he began speaking to us warningly in words we could all understand, about an ancient conflict that plagues our souls. The pride was awed and even resentful, but it was nonetheless real; for we rejoiced that Mississippi seemingly produces at least as many writers of books as readers of them, and that at the head of our authors was William Faulkner, whose writing, which we comprehended the least, commanded mankind's attention.

What I speak of, instead, is of William Faulkner in his Mississippi setting, which means his relationship to Mississippi and the South. That relationship was different in the

latter years from what it was in the early time of his ec-
centricity or in the later hour of recognition.

It is Faulkner as prodder of the Southern conscience—
albeit not the only nor even the most persistent one—that
concerns me here, though not to the exclusion of Faulkner
the legend, Faulkner the citizen of Oxford, and Faulkner
the authentic Southerner. As legend he was known to many
of us in Mississippi. Vastly fewer among us knew him as
friend and citizen, and fewer still comprehended the au-
thenticity of his Southernness. But he pricked the consciences of his widest Southern audience in the last meaningful days; not as an unforgiving castigator, as does the
impatient outsider whom he has also warned, but as one
of us, feeling more strongly than most the ancient pull between our love and our anger at our region.

In this Southern land, Faulkner was legend before he became goad. The legend had been in the making for more
than a quarter of a century; first for the few of Oxford and
Lafayette County and later for the state and for the South.
William Faulkner was the bearded, barefoot Count No-
Count of Oxford, Mississippi, squatting beside a drugstore's
magazine rack, loitering in the courthouse square, listening,
looking, and not giving a damn. He was the dishwashing,
wing-walking, rumrunning so-and-so, who would one day
tell a fancy-dancing foreign woman that he couldn't see her
because he had a previous engagement to hunt a coon. He
was the ex-postmaster of the University, displaced because
of an artistic inability to distribute properly the mail; an in-
voluntarily retired public servant who, when a friend commiserated over his jobless status, assured him that he was
tired, anyway, of being at the beck and call of any son-of-a-
bitch with two cents in his pocket. He was the uniquely
secluded Oxfordian whose ways of discouraging the unin-
vited and unwanted tourist could be indescribably Rabelai-
sian. He was the whiskey-drinkingest, Hollywood-baitingest,
contrariest man Mississippi had produced since Jones
County refused to go along with the Confederacy. He was
the sot-in-his-ways Mississippian who thought it over several

days before deciding to go to Sweden to accept the Nobel Prize, and then only because it would be a nice trip for his daughter, Jill.

Mississippians rejoiced in William Faulkner, the legend, for we like to think of ourselves as independent and individualistic folk. And so we are, but only up to a point. That point is where independence runs into the Great Taboo which reads: "White man, don't step out of line when the opposing line is black or Yankee or both." Which is what William Faulkner did, so that he made of himself a different kind of legend; so that a Faulkner letter in the Memphis *Commercial Appeal* could destroy, for many if not most of his fellow Mississippians, the aura of greatness; so that the great-grandson of the Old Colonel and the grandson of the Young Colonel was called scalawag in his state.

So much for the older legends and the beginning of the newer substitution. There also was Faulkner the Oxford citizen. He was innately a courteous man, though he could be rude to the point of cruelty for he cherished his solitude. The people of Oxford knew him as a man interested in at least some of the affairs of his community and state long before he became engaged in the basic Southern contest.

Putting together this scattered evidence of community identification, we find that once, long ago and briefly, he was a scoutmaster; and that during World War II he was, incongruously, an air-raid warden. He had a countryman's love of fishing and fish fries. Oxford entertained him at one such when he returned home from receiving the Nobel Prize. He was a hunter, especially of coons, and a good camper among better ones. He could have been a passable farmer, and his farm, though it contributed almost nothing to his livelihood, added greatly to his love of living. He could use his hands for fixing up a house, and formerly he had to, by necessity. And it is not accidental that the occasion for one of his first public talks in Mississippi was the high school graduation of his daughter, Jill.

"So, never be afraid," he then told the young students. "Never be afraid to raise your voice for honesty and truth

and compassion, against injustice and lying and greed."
And it was these young people of Oxford and Lafayette
County whom he had in mind after he received the Nobel
Prize; for he set up a trust fund, with the $30,000 prize
money, to be used for good causes in the town and county;
and the first prize dollars were spent on college scholarships
for talented, needy high school graduates.

This was the Faulkner whom his more discerning neighbors found reassuring, even though his letters to the papers—to the Oxford *Eagle*, the Memphis *Commercial Appeal*, the New York *Times*—sometimes disturbed or irritated
them. Some might grumble at his public protest against a
decision not to put the names of Negro soldiers killed in
World War II on the local memorial, but there were many
who sided with him and were glad when the names did go
on, though separated from the dead young white men. Those
who were not fanatical drys could laugh over the beer controversy in which Faulkner, in a broadside addressed to the
voters of Oxford, took on three local preachers and prohi-
bitionists during a beer-legalization election. The broadside
and a letter to the *Eagle* are too good to pass up here.

"To the Voters of Oxford
"Correction to paid printed statement of Private Citizens
H. E. Finger, Jr., John K. Johnson, and Frank Moody
Purser.

(1) *'Beer was voted out in 1944 because of its obnoxious-
ness.'*
"Beer was voted out in 1944 because too many voters who
drank beer or didn't object to other people drinking it, were
absent in Europe and Asia defending Oxford where voters
who preferred home to war could vote on beer in 1944.

(2) *'A bottle of 4 percent beer contains twice as much
alcohol as a jigger of whiskey.'*
"A 12 ounce bottle of four percent beer contains forty-
eight one hundredths of one ounce of alcohol. A jigger holds
one and one-half ounces (see Dictionary). Whiskey ranges

from 30 to 45 percent alcohol. A jigger of 30 percent whiskey contains forty-five one hundredth of one ounce of alcohol. A bottle of 4 percent beer doesn't contain twice as much alcohol as a jigger of whiskey. Unless the whiskey is less than 32 percent alcohol, the bottle of beer doesn't even contain as much.

(3) *'Money spent for beer should be spent for food, clothing and other essential consumer goods.'*
"By this precedent, we will have to hold another election to vote on whether or not the florists, the picture shows, the radio shops and the pleasure car dealers will be permitted in Oxford.

(4) *'Starkville and Water Valley voted beer out; why not Oxford?'*
Since Starkville is the home of Mississippi State, and Mississippi State beat the University of Mississippi at football, maybe Oxford, which is the home of the University of Mississippi, is right in taking Starkville for a model. But why must we imitate Water Valley? Our high school team beat theirs, didn't it?

"Yours for a freer Oxford, where publicans can be law abiding publicans six days a week, and Ministers of God can be Ministers of God all seven days in the week, as the Founder of their Ministry commanded them to when He ordered them to keep out of temporal politics in His own words: 'Render unto Caesar the things that are Caesar's and to God the things that are God's.'

William Faulkner
Private Citizen"

"The Editors,
Oxford Eagle,
City

Sept. 8, 1950

Dear Sirs:
"I notice that your paper has listed me among the proponents of legal beer. I resent that. I am every inch as

much an enemy of liberty and enlightenment and progress as any voting or drinking dry either in Oxford.

"Our town is already overcrowded. If we had legal beer and liquor here where you could buy it for only half of what we pay bootleggers, not to mention the playgrounds—tennis courts and swimming pools—and the high school gymnasiums and the public libraries which we could have with the proceeds and profits from one four-year term of county-owned and operated beer and liquor stores, we would have such an influx of people, businesses and industries with thirty and forty thousand dollar payrolls, that we old inhabitants could hardly move on the streets; our merchants couldn't sleep in the afternoon for the clashing and jangling of cash registers, and we older citizens couldn't even get into the stores to read a free magazine or borrow the telephone.

"No; let us stick to the old ways. Our teen-age children have cars or their friends do; they can always drive up to Tennessee or to Quitman County for beer or whiskey, and us gray-beards who don't like travel can telephone for it, as we always have done. Of course, it costs twice as much when it is delivered to your door, and you usually drink too much of it, than if you had to get up and go to town to get it, but better [that] than to break up the long and happy marriage between dry voters and illicit sellers, for which our fair state supplies one of the last sanctuaries and strong-holds.

"In fact, my effort in the recent election was only secondarily concerned with beer. I was making a protest. I object to anyone making a public statement which any fourth grade child with a pencil and paper, can disprove. I object more to a priest so insulting the intelligence of his hearers as to assume that he can make any statement, regardless of its falsity, and because of respect for his cloth, not one of them will try or dare to check up on it. But most of all,—and those ministers of sects which are not autonomous, who have synods or boards of bishops or other bodies of authority and control over them, might give a thought to this—I object to

ministers of God violating the canons and ethics of their
sacred and holy avocation by using, either openly or under-
hand, the weight and power of their office to try to influence a civil election.

William Faulkner"

His fellow citizens could grieve with him when he wrote
about Pete, Jill's fifteen-month-old pointer puppy, run down
and killed by a careless motorist. They could grow uncomfortable when he ridiculed progress in a letter congratulat-
ing the *Eagle* editor on a piece urging the preservation of the
old courthouse and ending:

"Your cause is doomed. They [the courthouse landmarks]
will go the way of the old Cumberland church. It was here
in 1861; it was the only building on or near the square still
standing in 1865. It was tougher than war, tougher than the
Yankee Brigadier Chalmers and his artillery and all his sap-
pers with dynamite and crowbars and cans of kerosene. But
it wasn't tougher than the ringing of a cash register bell.
It had to go—obliterated, effaced, no trace left—so that a
sprawling octopus covering the country from Portland,
Maine to Oregon can dispense in cut-rate bargain lots, bananas and toilet paper.

"They call this progress. But they don't say where it's
going; also there are some of us who would like the chance
to say whether or not we want the ride."

Such Faulknerian taunts and protests were not anathema.
In Mississippi a man can be an antiquarian, a beer drinker,
a lover of dogs, a believer that Negroes who died in the
service of their country should have their names on a monument, and still not be suspect. In Mississippi a man can
urge high school students to speak for honesty and truth
and compassion against injustice and lying and greed. A
Mississippian can chide his fellow citizens, as Faulkner did,
in his address at the annual meeting in 1952 of the Delta
Council, whose membership is made up mostly of cotton
farmers, mocking the paternalistic federal handout system
which was responsible for the new suits most of them wore:

"I decline to believe that the only true heirs of Boone and Franklin and George and Booker T. Washington and Lincoln and Jefferson and Adams and John Henry and Paul Bunyan and Johnny Appleseed and Lee and Crockett and Hale and Helen Keller, are the ones denying and protesting in the newspaper headlines over mink coats and oil tankers and federal indictments for corruption in public office. I believe that the true heirs of the old tough durable fathers are still capable of responsibility and self-respect, if only they can remember them again. What we need is not fewer people, but more room between them, where those who would stand on their own feet, could, and those who won't, might have to. Then the welfare, the relief, the compensation, instead of being nationally sponsored cash prizes for idleness and ineptitude, could go where the old independent uncompromising fathers themselves would have intended it and blessed it: to those who still cannot, until the day when even the last of them except the sick and the old, would also be among them who not only can, but will."

All these things he could be and do, as legend, citizen, and prodder of conscience in certain acceptable directions. But then years ago William Faulkner ventured beyond the ultimate Southern pale; and nothing, not even the initial Oxford reaction to *Sanctuary*, could match what happened to him since. For he wrote a more or less connected series of letters to the Memphis *Commercial Appeal*, and two magazine articles, and he gave a number of interviews, all in a few months, and all related to the Supreme Court's decision on public school integration.

Of the letters Faulkner wrote in support of integration in the schools, four must be quoted, at least in part. Here is the first (in the issue of March 20, 1955):[1]

---

[1] The text has been corrected according to the version of the letter included in Faulkner's article "On Fear: The South in Labor," *Harper's* Magazine, CCXII, No. 1273 (June 1956), pp. 29-34.

"To The Commercial Appeal:

"We Mississippians already know that our present schools are not good enough. Our young men and women themselves prove that to us every year by the fact that, when the best of them want the best of education which they are entitled to and competent for, not only in humanities but in professions and crafts—law and medicine and engineering—too, they must go out of the state to get it. And quite often, too often, they don't come back.

"So our present schools are not even good enough for white people; our present state reservoir of education is not of high enough quality to assuage the thirst of even our white young men and women. In which case, how can it possibly assuage the thirst and need of the Negro, who obviously is thirstier, needs it worse, else the federal government would not have had to pass a law compelling Mississippi (among others of course) to make the best of our education available to him.

"That is, our present schools are not even good enough for white people. So what do we do? Make them good enough, improve them to the best possible? No. We beat the bushes, rake and scrape to raise additional taxes to establish another system at best only equal to that one which is already not good enough, which therefore won't be good enough for Negroes either; we will have two identical systems neither of which are good enough for anybody. The question is not how foolish can people get, because apparently there is no limit to that. The question is, how foolish in simple dollars and cents, let alone wasted men and women, can we afford to be?

William Faulkner
Oxford, Mississippi"

Here is the second (April 3, 1955):
"To The Commercial Appeal:

"I have just read the letters of Mr. Neill, Mr. Martin and Mr. Womack in your issue of March 27, in reply to my letter in your issue of March 20.

"To Mr. Martin, and Mr. Womack's first question: Whatever the cost of our present state-wide school system is, we will have to raise that much again to establish another system equal to it. Let us take some of that new fund and make our present schools, from kindergarten up through the humanities and sciences and professions, not just the best in America but the best schools can be; then the schools themselves will take care of the candidates, white and Negro both, who had no business in them in the first place.

"Though I agree that this only solves integration: not the impasse of the emotional conflict over it. But at least it observes one of the oldest and soundest maxims: If you can't beat 'em, join 'em.

"To Mr. Womack's last question: I have no degrees nor diplomas from any school. I am an old veteran six-grader. Maybe that's why I have too much respect for education that I seem unable to sit quiet and watch it held subordinate in importance to the color of the pupil's skin.

William Faulkner
Oxford, Mississippi"

Here in part is the third (April 10, 1955):
"Instead of holding the educational standard down to the lowest common denominator of the class or grade group, let us raise it to that of the highest.

"Let us give every would-be pupil and student the equality and right to education in the terms in which our forefathers used the words equality and freedom and right: not equal right to charity, but equal right to do what he is capable of doing, freedom to attain the highest of standards —provided he is capable of it; or if he is not competent or will not work, let us learn early, before he has done much harm, that he is in the wrong occupation.

"If we are to have two school systems, let the second one be for pupils ineligible not because of color but because they either can't or won't do the work of the first one."

And here in great part is the fourth (April 17, 1955):
"We in the South are faced by two apparently irrecon-

cilable facts: one, that the National Government has decreed absolute equality in education among all races; the other, the people in the South who say that it shall never happen.

"These two facts must be reconciled. I believe there are many young people, too, in Mississippi who believe they can be, who love our state—not love white people specifically nor Negroes specifically, but our land; our climate and geography, the qualities in our people, white and Negro both, for honesty and tolerance and fair play, the splendors in our traditions and the glories in our past—enough to try to reconcile them, even at the risk which the young writer from Dorsey took, despite the fact that he didn't sign his name. And what a commentary that is on us; that in Mississippi communal adult opinion can reach such emotional pitch that our young sons and daughters dare not, from probably a very justified physical fear, sign their name to an opinion adverse to it."

And a year later, in June 1956, he spoke out in *Harper's* magazine:

"If we had given him [the Negro] this equality ninety or fifty or even ten years ago, there would have been no Supreme Court ruling about segregation in 1954.

"But we didn't. We dare not; it is our Southern white man's shame that in our present economy the Negro must not have economic equality; our double shame that we fear that giving him more social equality will jeopardize his present economic status; our triple shame that even then, to justify our stand, we must becloud the issue with the bugaboo of miscegenation. What a commentary that the one remaining place on earth where the white man can flee and have his uncorrupted blood protected and defended by law, is in Africa—Africa: the source and origin of the threat whose present presence in America will have driven the white man to flee it."

Then in conclusion:

"We must be free not because we claim freedom, but because we practice it; our freedom must be buttressed by a homogeny equally and unchallengeably free, no matter what color they are, so that all the other inimical forces everywhere—systems political or religious or racial or national—will not just respect us because we practice freedom, they will fear us because we do."

The ruminations were much too much for most Mississippians and for many other Southerners. Not even his warning in *Life* magazine—an admonition which turned against him the professional liberals elsewhere—lessened the Southern shock and anger.

"Stop now for a moment" [he wrote in *Life,* March 5, 1956]. "You have shown the Southerner what you can do and what you will do if necessary; give him a space in which to get his breath and assimilate that knowledge; to look about and see that (1) Nobody is going to force integration on him from the outside; (2) That he himself faces an obsolescence in his own land which only he can cure; a moral condition which not only must be cured but a physical condition which has got to be cured if he, the white Southerner, is to have any peace, is not to be faced with another legal process or maneuver every year, year after year, for the rest of his life."

And so William Faulkner became for the majority of his Mississippi contemporaries a renegade in his homeland. What was doubted most of all was his Southernness, and this is ironical because William Faulkner was as Southern and as Mississippian as was the late, odious Senator Theodore G. Bilbo. This is so because the South, the white South, is today and has long been at war with itself in a struggle as old as mankind. Faulkner was on the side of today's minority, which is not necessarily the losing side.

By every standard, Faulkner was Southern. The town in which he lived by choice is an epitome of Southernness. So is the faded majesty of the ante-bellum home in which he dwelt there. He was Southern in his pride in the past, in his adoration of the courageous, violent, doomed predecessors who also made legendary the name of Faulkner. He was Southern in his clannishness; in his unposed love of the land, and in the ambivalent love and outrage with which he confronted the South. Only his Southernness can account for the otherwise inexplicable lapse into old prejudice and fear—whatever its immediate motivation—as when he told a London *Times* correspondent that when the chips were down he might find himself gun in hand on the side of his fellow white. It was the Southerner's belief in decent local leadership that led him to try, briefly and with no success, to hold the then embryo white Citizens' Council of his town in the keeping of the moderates. And he was Southern, so we Southerners like to think, in his willingness to face up to odds.

But to the Mississippi and Southern majority, because he aligned himself at the last with the soul of the nation rather than with the meaner spirited in his own land, he became Weeping Willie Faulkner, nigger-lover, purveyor of filthy books, a sixth grader who would give lessons in running our schools, a would-be destroyer of the Southern way of life. I suspect that he reacted in several ways to this newer and pitifully uncomplex characterization; angry that his intent and his identification should be challenged; amused at the wryly comic turn of events which made a Mississippi writer, once shrugged off by his Mississippi peers as incomprehensible, now understood all too well; and determined that the fight must go on. It is a fight we have been waging in the South a long time, and it is not as one-sided as some would have us believe.

And this regional struggle has a certain cosmic quality, not pessimistic. William Faulkner, in Stockholm, might have been talking to his neighbors and fellow Mississippians, when he ended thus one of the grandest messages of man to man:

"I believe that man will not merely endure: he will prevail. He is immortal, not because he alone among creatures has an inexhaustible voice, but because he has a soul, a spirit capable of compassion and sacrifice and endurance. The poet's, the writer's duty is to write about things. It is his privilege to help man endure by lifting his heart, by reminding him of the courage and honor and hope and pride and compassion and pity and sacrifice which have been the glory of his past. The poet's voice need not merely be the record of man, it can be one of the props, the pillars to help him endure and prevail."

10

STATUES IN THE SQUARES

Given enough money and sculptors and the consent
of the states and the communities concerned, I could spend
a pleasurable and useful lifetime placing new statues in a
multitude of Southern town and courthouse squares.

They would not replace but only supplement the marble
figures, like as like, with their broad-brimmed campaign
hats and blanket rolls and grounded muskets, brooding beneath the catalpas and live oaks, the elms and magnolias
and sycamores that shadow the public lawns. These
weather-stained guardians, doing sentry duty above the in-
scriptions to the beloved dead, have earned the right to
unending vigil. Each is an idealization of the vanished, tat-
terdemalion legions of the Lost Cause, the typical and the
untypical men of a homogeneous region who, most of them,
made a poor man's fight of what the rank and file jibed at
as "a rich man's war"; who, poor and affluent, gentleman
and yeoman and redneck alike, etched with their lifeblood
a record of courage and perseverance and fealty to homeland so unique as to have earned for it in defeat a brighter
page in the annals of combative man than has been allotted
to the victors of a myriad of wars.

But the statues in the squares are more than symbols of
gallantry in defeat, or the defeat of gallantry. They are also
the reminders of, and, in an unstated way, a kind of rec-
ompense for, the inexcusable aftermath of military subjugation; for they supplanted the plunderers of Reconstruction,
whose memory still brought in my boyhood ready curses
from the aging veterans of whom we were so proud and
not a little afraid. And it was these old men and their ancient womenfolk, unreconstructed and unforgiving, who

passed on to sons and grandsons the truth and legends of
wrongs which, in the commission and the remembering,
make up the saddest of our nation's multiple legacies.

And statues are reminders, lastly, of the true nature of the
Southern past and of the South's folk heritage; for beneath
the romantic overlay so greatly inspired by a Scots novelist's
tales of knightly derring-do was a frontier land, the stamping ground of Davy Crockett and Mike Fink, of Andy Jackson and Sam Houston, of Nolichucky Jack Sevier and
Oglethorpe's paupers and the unsubdued sons of the clans-
men who fought at Culloden. The warriors in marble bespeak that frontier whose hallmarks are the ready rifle and
the white-hot temper, the violent workings of a code of
honor, a mistrust of the intruder, and the feudal unity of a
people whose fields were bounded all around by wilderness.

Because this is so, because the chiseled sentinels of the
Confederacy evoke the frontier as surely as they recall a war
and a defeat and a needless, consequential humiliation, I
would choose first as their companion figures the likenesses
of men whose abilities the frontiersmen respect above all
others, or whom they could identify with themselves. They
should come, or so I think, from the rosters of warring man
and political man, man the singer of songs and teller of
tales and preacher of sermons, man the underdog, and the
unregimented, maverick man.

Not that the men of other talents—the scientists and the
artists and the scholars and the builders of cities—are not
as useful or do not require more exacting apprenticeships.
They too belong in the courthouse squares. But the others
have prior place.

The fighting man . . .

It is understandable, since the vanquished always remember the longest, that the South should have so lavishly
memorialized her Confederate dead. They died in a war
that their survivors lost. Above their graves a nation-in-being
was pounded to nothingness. Understandable, and sad. For
before and after them were other Southerners who fought in

other wars. While some among these have been remembered, few of them have been honored enough.

What of Nathaniel Bacon of the Colony of Virginia who tested with his life the tyranny which was once the divine right of kings? What of the New Orleans Creoles who died resisting the empire of Spain? What of South Carolina's Sergeant Jasper, the pirates and the backwoodsmen who destroyed the British at the Battle of New Orleans, and the Southern adventurers who made the War for Texas Independence their jubilant cause? Where are the statues of Jeff Davis' Mississippians and those other soldiers of the Deep South who principally fought the Mexican War?

There should be places for them in many a square which has neglected to honor them; places for the men of San Juan Hill and the fever swamps of Cuba, and of Château-Thierry and Tarawa and Bastogne and the Chosen Reservoir. These Southerners battled as bravely for their country as did their ancestors for the nation that did not live. They belong in the company of Bedford Forrest, the Confederate Jehu, and rollicking Beauty Stuart and young Pelham and dour Stonewall Jackson. It would be better for us all if they stood together in the squares.

And the spellbinders . . .

The argument can be made successfully, I believe, that the English and Scots and Scots-Irish have a peculiar genius for political philosophy and political action, and that a notable characteristic of Protestantism is its evangelical concern with the social order. The frontier South was settled mostly by Protestant migrants from England and Scotland and the north of Ireland and their sons. No wonder, then, that the South has produced and that its people—sometimes to their own detriment—have listened so attentively to the spellbinders of the hustings and the pulpit.

We have honored fully the Southern giants who were our nation's political architects—Jefferson and Madison and Monroe who helped put the colonial jigsaw pieces together, and Henry Clay who strove to keep the pieces joined, and gaunt John Calhoun who made his compatriots willing to

take them apart again. But we have not recognized suffi-
ciently the less successful and the later statesmen. It should
not be forgotten that for every five men who spoke for seces-
sion in the Congress of the United States and in the legislatures of the South, at least one other spoke for moderation
and the preservation of the Union. We could do worse than
recall them now, and with them the obscure pleaders for
the little man in the day of domination by the great landowner and the railroaders. They were in the Southern tradition, the frontier tradition.

So, too, the preachers. The churchmen were among the
South's builders; they were the founders of such colleges as
Randolph-Macon and Hampden-Sydney, Wofford and Mer-
cer and many another, largely guiding them and staffing
their faculties. The preachers of the Second Awakening, inspired by tough James McCready, the South Carolina Presbyterian; Louisiana's Benjamin Morgan Palmer, another
Presbyterian, who fought the infamous Louisiana Lottery to
a standstill; the circuit riders of Methodism, who brought
the gospel to outcasts and renegades and doubters; the ministers who died by the hundreds nursing believers and scof-
fers alike in the terrible century of Yellow Jack—surely they
are as worthy of the South's recognition as of God's. They
too should be enshrined in the communities where they were
born or where they worked and lived and died.

And the writers . . .

The orator and the preacher have ever thrived best among
frontier and rural folk whose pleasures are simple and few
and whose hearts and minds are easily captured by the political debaters' thrust and parry, and by the ministers'
warnings of sins of the flesh. Greatly welcome too are the
ballad makers and the tellers of folk tales. But this has not
been as true of the dealer in words that are written instead of spoken or sung; for book learning was not as easily
come by in the frontier South nor was as much store set by
it as in the cities of the settled Eastern seaboard. A suspicion
of scribblers or an indifference to what they write, coupled
with the extraordinary contribution of the South to Ameri-

can literature, has given rise to the wry jest that more Southerners write books than read them, an exaggeration that may make the point better than does unadorned fact.

Because of this oversight, I would erect many a statue to remind region and nation of the South's writers, so diverse in their output, so numerous, and so studded with the brilliance of genius as to dwarf even New England in the time of her flowering. Save for a handful, among whom Edgar Allan Poe and Sidney Lanier alone surmounted regionalism, they arrived late on the scene, rising from the ashes of the Confederacy to plead its cause in verse and story, and to discover for themselves and thereby to reveal to the nation the many-faceted South of mountaineer and lowlander, seafarer and former slave and an aristocracy in travail. Their patriarchs were William Gilmore Simms and Robert Y. Hayne, and the frontier satirist Joseph C. Baldwin. But they escaped in part from the mold. The South could and did inspire and accommodate a host of local-color writers: Joel Chandler Harris, James Lane Allen, Irwin Russell, and Lafcadio Hearn; and such historical novelists as Mary Johnson and Thomas Nelson Page, romanticists who had little save talent in common with those Southerners who came later and who today all but dominate the American literary scene. Though most of them wrote, then and now, of the frontier South, the South has looked upon them with a wonder that is not always friendly. Prophets more honored beyond their region than in it are Ellen Glasgow, the precise Virginia realist, and Thomas S. Stribling, Thomas Wolfe, Erskine Caldwell, and William Faulkner. Yet some day, they and others will be spoken of with understanding and pride in the land they wrote of and loved. The South may yet recognize its creative critics, whose barbs are needful if only because they prick.

And the mavericks . . .

It is a Southern contradiction that a region which prides itself, and rightfully, upon the individualism and independence of its people has nevertheless demanded of them a nearly blind conformity in matters having to do with regional loyalty, political preferences, and racial attitudes. As even the most casual reader of history knows, this disciplinary demand was the result of the presence of the Negro as a slave, the war which freed him, his utilization as a political pawn after that war, and the determination of the white South, once the end of Reconstruction had been brought about, never again to permit any threat to its political and economic dominance. So it is that the non-conformist, especially if his apostasy is a challenge to this determination, is a rare and a brave person and one against whom the pressures of the entire community are usually exerted. But a democracy requires mavericks; so, in our region which looks upon the challenger with suspicion, I would pay homage to the sincere and visionary minority who have stood up throughout the tormented generations and said, "But on the other hand——"

There were more of them than might be supposed. They were among the hardiest of Southerners, they not only walked almost alone but were easy targets as they walked. No Southern memorial has been raised to the little New Orleanian, George Washington Cable, who in the seventies and eighties ranked as author and lecturer with Mark Twain and whose characterizations of the Louisiana French remain unsurpassed in our regional literature. The reason for this neglect is that Cable's conscience impelled him to speak against injustice to the Negro, and to criticize certain Southern shibboleths that to his fellows were sacrosanct. George Washington Cable deserved better treatment. So did Walter Hines Page, the North Carolina newspaper editor who likewise protested inequities and dared to lampoon the professional Southern veteran. Two courageous professors of ante-bellum Virginia, George Wythe and St. George Tucker, must have been even more vulnerable than these, for a generation before the war they dared, as members of the William and Mary faculty, to denounce the institution of slavery.

There were dissenters in matters other than race. I would single out men like Charles W. Macune, the Texan who accomplished seventy years ago the consolidation of the small, badly organized farmer groups and with his Farmers' Alliance brought at least passing benefit to desperate men, and unease to the interests that despoiled them.

Above all Southern mavericks I would recognize stubborn Andrew Johnson of Tennessee who loved the South but not its aristocratic secessionists; who, as a Union Democrat, won the Vice-Presidency under Lincoln in 1864; and who, coming to the Presidency when the Great Emancipator was assassinated, suffered and weathered the efforts of his vengeful political foemen to impeach him because they thought him too lenient toward his native South.

And the underdogs . . .

The frontier has ever been lodestar and refuge for the outcast, the dispossessed, and the underdogs, for its forests offer sanctuary and its fertility another chance; its indifference to antecedents gives a man the right to prove himself on his own. There were more underdogs than gentry among the pioneers and the landseekers who thrust southward and westward from the Atlantic periphery. Some of them found on the Southern frontier what they were looking for; many did not.

But of all the underdogs of the unfolding South, none had the cards so stacked against them as those who came as slaves. Surely there should be statues here and there to some of the Negroes of the South who in the time of slavery, and in the after-years which were often little better, won honor for themselves and their race and region and nation. The free Negroes of the ante-bellum South—there were 250,000 of them on the eve of the War Between the States —numbered such men as Henry Evans whose North Carolina Methodist congregation was biracial; Austin Dabney, veteran of the Revolution whose farm was a gift of the Georgia legislature and who had been the guest of the governor of his state; rich John Jones, whose Charleston Hotel was among the South's most popular; and Thomy Lafon, New Orleans merchant, money-lender, and philanthropist whose charities knew no color line.

In the near century since Emancipation the list of meritorious Negroes has become so long, and the achievements represented thereon so varied, as to win the prideful admiration of most of their fellow Southerners and fellow Americans. We would deny an accolade to Booker T. Washington, foremost of his people's spokesmen in the early years of freedom; or George Washington Carver, who wrought scientific miracles with the products of the South's farms; or William C. Handy, the music master to whom the city of Memphis is rearing a monument; or the poets, James Weldon Johnson, Countee Cullen, Langston Hughes? It is good today for all of us to know that in every field of human endeavor—the arts, science, government, and the rest—can be counted Southern Negroes who for 300 years have given dignity to the name Underdog.

And the fighters not in uniform . . .

Lastly, I would erect somewhere in the South, preferably deep in the Lower Mississippi Valley, another statue, as anonymous and as representative as the graven Confederates of the courthouse squares, but, unlike these, neither armed nor uniformed. This figure would be clad in the work clothes of a farmer or the rough garb of a riverman or the unstylish everyday suit of a small-town citizen. His face would reflect the toil, the frustrations, and the sufferings of a people who have passed through a succession of ordeals of military defeat and of political grinding-down and agricultural ruin and long poverty. The eyes of this unknown and unsoldierly warrior would be fixed upon the far horizon of the frontiersman; and in the set of the shoulders a sensitive observer would perceive the glory of an indestructible people whose struggle for their rightful place in the sun is all but ended.

11

THE YOUNG NEGRO IS A NEW NEGRO

1960

The middle-aged Negro porter in a downtown Baton Rouge store shook his head at the demonstrating students from state-supported, all-Negro Southern University.

"I jes' don't understand what's gettin' into people these days."

His incomprehension is shared by many hitherto relatively complacent white Southerners and by not a few older Negroes who are disturbed lest the wave of student "sit-ins" and the general disaffection of younger Southern Negroes get—to use a euphemism—out of hand.

But, in terms of the old racial conventions, the new generation of Negroes is already out of hand. That fact is arresting enough to those who approve or passively accept the enforced tranquillity of the old order. What is more alarming to the thinking whites and Negroes of the South, and to many outside the South, is the near-total breakdown of communication which might provide insight into "what's getting into people." We are not talking much to each other these days. We never really did, not man to man.

I do not profess to have a unique pipeline to the collective mind of the young Negro; and it may be that I am subconsciously influenced by two contradictory Southern white clichés. One of them has it that among American whites only the Southerner understands the Negro; the other asserts that no one can really tell what is going on in the minds of the children of Africa.

By reason of time and place and a long concern, however, I do believe that I am aware of some aspects of the Negro in transition and some of the factors that discourage and frustrate him, and encourage him and keep him going. I wonder whether the Southerners of my sons' generation will have even my advantage; for time and even place have changed and relationships have become vastly different.

For that next generation, and to a lesser extent for my own contemporaries, North and South, I want to recall two Negroes whom I knew long ago: the first in my boyhood, intimately, in the vanishing tradition of rural and small-town, inter-racial companionship on well-defined lines; the second, a fellow student in a New England college, whom I knew neither well nor favorably.

The first was the much younger brother of our cook in the rural Louisiana of my childhood; I once wrote a story about him and our companionship. I will not repeat it here. He is now in his early fifties and since we live in different states I see him only occasionally; but, save for a rather cautious interest in voting rights, his attitudes are outwardly little changed from our boyhood days. Our relationship remains what it was, warmly personal and stratified in a world in which everyone once knew his place.

I don't know whatever happened to the lone Negro student in the liberal arts college where I was almost the lone Southerner. Steeped in a traditional aversion to racial intermingling except on the white man's own terms, I avoided him. He represented to me an undesirable novelty, a Negro admitted to a sort of equality with whites.

I know now that it was a spurious equality—he had no roommate, he was one of a handful of non-fraternity pariahs, and his fellow members of the glee club, his only campus activity, seemed to me to be a little self-conscious about what to do with him on club trips. He was almost sullenly quiet, and well he might have been. But from what other students told me he was apparently unconcerned either with the inequities existing in the town where much of *Uncle Tom's Cabin* had been written, or with the grosser abuses directed against his contemporaries in my part of the country.

The difference between this Negro student and others, North or South, was, I believe, a matter of degree only.

Among young Negroes in the 1920s there was no great sense of unity in a cause, no cohesive purposefulness aimed at an ending of wrongs.

I think these two Negroes, the all-but-illiterate Louisiana boy who was my playmate and the college student whom I shunned, would be almost equally condemned or derided by the angry young Negro students of today—the one as a subservient "Uncle Tommer," the other because he was only mildly concerned, if at all, with his disabilities or those of his less fortunate fellows elsewhere.

This is the primary distinction of the young Negro today. He is aggressively concerned. His interest has made him the victim of understandable short-term frustration. It has also imbued him with a long-term confidence that is not always realistic. Moreover, contemporary events and the quality and quantity of his education have combined to create a new dimension in his thinking.

For lack of a more precise phrase, the educated young Negro of today might be called a black nationalist; he identifies the cause of other dark people elsewhere with his own and his own with theirs. He is proud of politically adroit Negro leadership everywhere. This being so, it is a national blessing, though not an unmixed one, that his heroes are men like Gandhi and the Rev. Dr. Martin Luther King, Jr.

Dr. King resorted to non-violent protest in the shape of a Negro boycott of the Montgomery, Alabama, bus lines. Gandhi triumphed through passive resistance plus non-violent civil disobedience. Today's Negro students are advocating these approaches; and the danger is that when state or local laws are violated, as in the sit-in demonstrations, the temptation on the one side to commit violence and on the other to counter it actively can become irresistible.

What I will say from now on and what conclusions I may draw are not the result of what is called scientific sampling. But it so happens that I have talked with hundreds of better-educated young Negroes in the last ten years in all sections of our country: high school and college students, North and South; men in uniform and men not long out of uniform; theologians and professional men and government employees, representatives of the Negro intellectual and of the middle and upper economic groups.

Their common denominator is that they are uniformly dissatisfied. All would agree that most of them enjoy economic and even political rights undreamed of by their fathers and, within narrow limits, social acceptance by some white associates. But none of them considers for a moment that the Negro has arrived; and with each victory their resentment of the remaining barriers grows stronger.

The short-term frustration the young Negro feels and freely expresses derives from disappointments political, material, psychological, and, perhaps, spiritual.

Many educated Southern Negroes assumed in 1954 that Jericho's walls would come tumbling down with the Supreme Court's decision. Then they discovered that the Deep South could and would employ a variety of means, from violence to threats and even the reality of school closures, to render the decision all but meaningless.

These Negroes feel betrayed by the Court's subsequent apparent approval of the "token integration" device, through which Southern school boards can sidestep any real integration by admitting a few Negro students and rejecting the mass through screening processes not ostensibly racial.

Politically, they exult over the emergence in key Northern states of the Negro as a balance power and in the tumultuous advent of self-government in much of Africa; but they rage at the low incidence of Negro voting in areas so important to them at home, and in the failure of the federal government to arrive at any formula that can really assure that the Negroes of the Deep South can vote in accordance with their qualifications and numbers.

They speak pridefully of the Negroes on the assembly lines, the athletes and entertainers, the craftsmen and the practitioners in the courts and hospitals of America; but they know that the Negro is still the "last hired and the first fired," and they reserve a special contempt for the union leadership and rank-and-file which proffer the shadow but not the substance of job equality.

They acutely resent all outward symbols of second-class citizenship. Whatever satisfaction they get out of the continuing, generally quiet, and orderly desegregation of transportation facilities—and it is going on at an astonishingly rapid rate—they are more aware of the persistence of Jim Crow's shadow in most of the South.

And more than anything else they are embittered by the absence of color blindness in Southern courtrooms, by the failure of too many white juries to indict or convict white murderers, lynchers, bombers, and other major offenders.

It is my own unhappy observation that as a result of these conflicts the educated Negro in the South dislikes the Southern white man en masse as never before in our history.

This mounting antipathy—which is mutual—is psychologically complicated by the Negroes' inner resentment and outward defense of those among their fellows who neither do credit to their race nor impel white allies to enlist on their side. It is a resentment not often openly expressed but it is there.

Speak to them of the tragically disproportionate rate of major Negro crime, or the relatively low state of Negro morality in America, and they respond that this, too, is the white man's doing—as indeed in considerable part it is. They insist that victory must be achieved over the white opponents before they move broadly against their own worse elements.

While this may be the proper strategy, it does not make for understanding. I have often found myself wishing that young Southern Negroes had more inclination for home missionary work.

The Negro of the slave quarters and the plantation cabin could find solace and hope in the old-time religion as expressed in the spirituals and the pulpit oratory of a more primitive Christianity. But their children are not waiting for the sweet chariot to swing low and carry them to a better life above. They have not forsaken Christianity, but the churchmen whom they heed are the socially militant, well-educated ministers whose pulpits form the core of the Southern Negro's opposition to the status quo.

The determination to alter drastically and soon the patterns of segregation had a dramatic expression on Sunday, April 17, 1960. On that day 140-odd Southern and Northern Negro college students, plus several whites, formed in Raleigh, North Carolina, a temporary organization to supervise student anti-segregation activities throughout the South. It was a milestone in the civil-disobedience movement that began with a sit-in at a Greensboro, North Carolina, chain-store lunch counter on February 1, 1960, and that subsequently spread, with varying degrees of violence, usually white-provoked, into every Southern state.

The organization, which plans to remain closely identified with Dr. King's Southern Christian Leadership Conference, was named the Student Non-Violence Coordination Committee. The student delegates not only discussed further sit-in demonstrations but also tentatively planned "selective buying programs," a phrase less provocative perhaps than "boycott." They postponed any action pending a study of the proposal.

The delegates then went on record as encouraging students arrested in non-violent protest activities to go to jail instead of making bail before their trials. Adult Negroes, probably members of the King organization, counseled with the students during their sessions.

The civil-disobedience movement, the present and proposed boycotts, and the emphasis upon non-violence in each tactic express much of what is in the minds of younger Negroes today. Rarely, during the epidemic sit-ins, have the Negro demonstrators resorted to force even when attacked. The whites almost invariably have been the assailants. Of one encounter between young Negroes and whites, the Richmond *News-Leader,* no proponent of integration, said editorially on February 22, 1960:

"Many a Virginian must have felt a tinge of wry regret at the state of things as they are, in reading of Saturday's 'sit-

downs' by Negro students in Richmond stores. Here were
the colored students, in coats, white shirts, ties, and one of
them was reading Goethe, and one was taking notes from
a biology text. And here, on the sidewalk outside, was a
gang of white boys come to heckle, a ragtail rabble, slack-
jawed, black-jacketed, grinning fit to kill, and some of them,
God save the mark, were waving the proud and honored
flag of the Southern states in the last war fought by gentlemen. *Eheu!* It gives one pause."

Whether the sit-ins will result in net gains or losses for
the Negro cause is debatable. Basically, under the laws of
the various Southern states, they are illegal; the National Association for the Advancement of Colored People has employed only legal approaches in its successful assaults on
the South's white citadel. And even former President Harry
Truman, whose championship of Negro rights won him the
hostility of much of the white South and brought about the
States' Rights vote in 1948, has commented that if, as a businessman, he was the target of a sit-in, he would run the
demonstrators out.

In its recent report on the student protest movement, the
Southern Regional Council had this to say, in part:

"What has happened these last few weeks, and what may
lie ahead, has worried and dismayed many Southerners.
These include not only the persons who are the everyday
enemies of Negro equality, but those others who see in each
new Negro demand a 'setback to race relations.' There are
Southerners friendly to the Negro cause who have doubts
as to the practical wisdom of the student protests, and the
turn toward violent conflict has deepened their concern.

"This is not a point of view to be shrugged off. At the
very least, it is an indication of a segment of Southern opinion. More basically, it is an expression of a view, which has
been implied in some of the Negro press as well, that the
student protests will hurt other more important objectives,
especially school desegregation."

In the same report the Southern Regional Council commented on the potential of Negro economic pressure. It is

already being used. The *Wall Street Journal* of February 21, 1960, reported that the volume in four S. H. Kress stores in the South had dropped fifteen to eighteen per cent. It was also reported that a variety store in Charlotte had had a sixty-five per cent drop and a Greensboro store thirty-five per cent. More than incidentally, Negroes in Charlotte spend $150,000,000 annually, and Negroes account for some twenty per cent of all Southern retail sales.

The militant young Negro today reads these figures. In them and in other statistics and events he thinks he can also read a handwriting on the wall. And it is this vision that contributes to the long-term confidence which perhaps offsets his short-term frustrations.

He is aware that strong forces, most of them greatly resented by the white South, work in his behalf: the N.A.A.C.P.; the racial policies of the federal government; the several race-related decisions of the United States Supreme Court since 1954; the moral dilemma plaguing many Southerners and aptly expressed by former Governor LeRoy Collins of Florida who, while not challenging the legal right of merchants to serve whom they choose, questioned the morality of such selectiveness; and, perhaps most important of all, the potentialities of militantly non-violent action, especially in the economic sphere.

But, however unreal or justified the optimism, however real or exaggerated the immediate frustrations, this much is true: the young Southern Negro of today is far more dissatisfied and determined than most white Southerners believe. Whether these white Southerners are as determined to resist the changes implicit in the student attack on segregation is as yet unclear.

I am not hopeful about a region-wide solution satisfactory to all sides. I do know that there is now being created a climate in which my Negro childhood friend and my Negro fellow collegian would have been, in the time I knew them, vastly uncomfortable. And so, too, am I. For there is little of amiability among us today.

12

A MISSISSIPPI DOCTOR COMES HOME
1961

This may be too quiet a tale for some who think of contact between black man and white only in terms of convulsive conflict or impersonal change. To others, who carry chips on their shoulders, it may sound patronizing on the one hand, or, on the other, too intimate to suit Southern convention. But if the story of Dr. Matthew Page and of a personal friendship between a young Negro and an older white man seems out of joint with our times, then it is the times which are wrong.

I am not sure how best to begin. I first met Matthew Page thirteen years ago when he was eighteen and newly graduated in the class of 1948 from Coleman High School, the Negro high school in Greenville, Mississippi. I might start with a November morning in 1959, eleven years later, when Captain Matthew Page, United States Air Force Medical Corps, stood at attention at a wing review of the Greenville Air Force Base while the commanding officer pinned the Air Force Commendation Medal on his tunic and read to the assembled airmen, graduating cadets, parents, and other civilians of both races the citation which accompanied the medal. It was Matthew Page's first visit to the base located just outside of his home town. We will get to that citation later.

Or I might begin a month after this occasion, when Dr. Matthew Page, ending a thirteen-year round trip, put up his shingle in front of a small frame building on Clay Street in Greenville. A good many Greenvillians had doubted that he would ever make it back or that, having done so, he would choose to stay for as long as six months. Only Matthew never seemed to share this general dubiety.

Now a year has gone by, and Dr. Matthew Page is still with us in Greenville, which he left at eighteen. And, all things considered, I think it fitting to begin now with his leave-taking and the part our newspaper had in it.

At the end of World War II, the *Democrat-Times* established three annual prizes of $100—one each for the outstanding graduates of Greenville High School and Coleman High School and the third for the best among the graduates of the county's other high schools. Two of the awards were to be given in memory of two young men of our town who had lost their lives in the war. The third was named the George Washington Carver Award in tribute to the late, noted Negro scientist.

In 1948 Matthew Page was the third winner of the Carver Award. How he earned it can be easiest told by the clipping from the *Democrat-Times* with which his scrapbook begins:

MATTHEW PAGE
NAMED WINNER
OF CARVER AWARD

The third annual George Washington Carver Award of $100 to the outstanding Negro high school graduate, given by the Delta Democrat-Times, was presented this year to Matthew Page of Coleman High School in Greenville. Salutatorian of his class, Matthew received a total of 18 units with 9 A's and 9 B's and was considered "excellent in citizenship" by Principal G. P. Maddox.

Class President

Other achievements which the principal included in his recommendation are: class president for four years, sports reporter for school athletics, senior Boy Scout patrol leader for three years, assistant Scoutmaster this year, "Mr. Coleman High School" for three years, Hi-Y club officer, member of the dramatics club, a letter man in football, as well as an active participant in tennis, softball and basketball.

A day or so later my secretary told me that a young Negro student wanted to see me. When he came in I didn't connect him with the winner of the Carver Award until he gave me his name, for I had never seen him before. I was considerably surprised, for while every youngster who has received one of these prizes throughout the years has thanked me, almost all of them have done so by letter. Matthew was the first to make a personal call.

The boy who came into the office was slight and under medium height, with remarkably intelligent eyes which seemed to be laughing at some inner joke. After he had identified himself, I asked him to sit down, and there began the first of a good many conversations. I asked him to tell me about himself and what he wanted to do. He was born in Greenville, he said, the son of John and Mollie Page. His plantation-reared mother and father, the latter born in the same house that the family still lived in, had fifth-grade educations. His family was Baptist. His father operated a leveling machine in the manufacture of concrete mats used in the flood-control program of the United States Army Engineers, a seasonal job of seven to eight months a year, with odd jobs in between. His mother was a domestic. He had one sister, Mary, two years younger. Yes, he planned to go to Tougaloo College in Mississippi. Tougaloo is one of some twenty Negro colleges established soon after the Civil War by church and missionary groups from the North. Its faculty is biracial and its support still comes largely from the American Missionary Association and the Congregational Church.

I asked then the usually perfunctory question: What did he want to be? I was taken aback by the answer.

"I'm going to be a doctor," Matthew Page said, casually, as if it would be as easy as pie. He had taken all the math and science available at Coleman, he said, and though he felt handicapped because the school's so-called laboratory was simply a broom closet with a few test tubes and a minimum of other dilapidated equipment, he felt that he could catch up. I had an unhappy vision of a boy with $100 and whatever help a laboring father could give him, and a broom-closet chemistry course. Why did he want to be a doctor?

"I guess the main reason is that I have a sickly sister," Matthew said. "Sometimes she is real sick. I can remember one time when she was having a bad spell. My mother and father were very upset and I was scared to death. And then the doctor came and I could see the changes that came over my mother and my father and my sister. Everything seemed to get better all at once. I said to myself then, I want to be a doctor. I am going to be one."

I tried to get Matthew a job that summer but with no success. Eventually he found one, with his father's help, as an unskilled laborer with the U. S. Engineers.

That September Matthew Page came in to tell me good-by. He was off to Tougaloo. It cost then about $500 a year, including food, lodging, and books, to go to Tougaloo. Matthew had about half that amount, made up from his summer savings, the extra dollars his parents and relatives had scraped up, and the Carver Award money. But he didn't seem at all worried.

Matthew dropped in during the Christmas and Easter vacations, as he was to do every vacation from then on. He told me that soon after entering Tougaloo he had been awarded a first prize scholarship, amounting to $110. He also had a job waiting on tables and he was sure about making it through the first year. He stood second in his class and had the promise of an undergraduate instructorship for the next year. He also expected to get another unskilled labor job for the summer. And he still intended to be a doctor.

That June, a few days after I talked to Matthew, the *Democrat-Times* had this to say editorially:

HE WANTS TO BE A DOCTOR

Last year's winner of the George Washington Carver Award, given each year by this newspaper to the outstanding Negro high school senior, was Matthew Page of Greenville.

Matthew has finished his first year at Tougaloo. He won the first prize scholarship of $110, which is a tribute not only to his own ability but to the instruction he received at Coleman High School. He waited on tables to help put him through his first year. Now he hopes to work this summer to earn money for next year.

He intends to go four years to Tougaloo and then attend Meharry College to study medicine. Then he wants to come back to Greenville to practice. He's off to a good start. And we know that if Matthew has difficulty in continuing his education, there will be citizens of Greenville who will recognize that his future is a good investment.

Not once in his first three years at Tougaloo did Matthew ask me for any help, save in endorsing job applications and the like. He was making it alone on his own, moving up to waiter for the teachers, assisting in biology and mathematics, winning additional small student prizes at Tougaloo, and working in the summers.

But at the end of his junior year Matthew did ask me to give him a hand. A few years earlier the state of Mississippi, which had no medical school, adopted a program which was to be widely applauded. It offered, on a competitive basis, a sizable number of four-year, $1250 per annum medical scholarships to Mississippi college students. Divided between the races, the scholarships would be good at any recognized medical school to which the applicant could gain admission. The scholarships are in the form of loans. The students agree to pay off the loans by returning to the state after graduation and to practice medicine for five years in areas where their services are most needed. As a frowned-upon alternative, they can pay off in cash. Would it be just possible . . . ?

I thought so. Matthew still ranked second in his class and had an admirable extra-curricular record. Moreover, at the time, I had considerably more friends in high places in the state government than I do now. Some of them had quite a bit to do with the selection of the medical scholarship winners. It is likely that Matthew, on his record, would have received one; but we are both sure that the supporting letters and telephone calls helped. Matthew got his scholarship.

Matthew worked again that summer. At the beginning of his senior year he applied for entrance the next year in Meharry Medical College in Nashville, Tennessee. Meharry, whose faculty, like Tougaloo's, is biracial, is the nation's only all-Negro medical college and had produced more than half of the Negro doctors and dentists in the United States. Established in 1876, Meharry had its inception, during Civil War battlefield truces for exchanging wounded soldiers, in conversations between Dr. William Sneed of Nashville and George Hubbard, a Union medical corpsman from New Hampshire. The initial $10,000 to establish the college was contributed by another Nashvillian, Samuel Meharry, who, having become lost many years before when returning to his home in the Indiana territory with a load of salt from Kentucky, was given food and shelter and direction by an aged Negro freedman. He never forgot.

Meharry can admit only about sixty-five students to its freshman medical class. Applications run from 500 to 600 a year. Among others, I wrote supporting letters for Matthew.

In February of his senior year, Matthew Page was notified that he had been accepted as a member of Meharry's freshman medical class for the following autumn. That summer Matthew served as an instructor in chemistry at Tougaloo. His summer stipend, in addition to the grant of $1250 and some family and other aid, made it unnecessary for him to seek an outside job during the difficult first year at Meharry. But when he came to see me at the end of the first term, elated over having successfully completed it, we agreed that he would need additional money the next year. It was then that one of the most heart-warming and amusing experiences of my life began.

I asked Matthew what summer job, if he had his choice, would he prefer above all others.

"The best paying summer job is a dining-car waiter,"

Matthew said. "That's what any Negro male student would like more than anything else."

I told Matthew I would try to pass a miracle. I didn't tell him its intended nature because I didn't want to raise his hopes with little to go on.

Not long before, Greenville had declared war on the Illinois Central Railroad, which, like other lines throughout the nation, was ridding itself as fast as it could of unprofitable passenger service. The I.C.'s passenger trains on its subsidiary river route between Memphis and New Orleans, which served Greenville, were undoubtedly unprofitable. As a result, we finally had only one passenger train a day from Memphis, 150 miles to the north, and it made the distance in a leisurely, unpredictable, and indifferent six hours or so. As our contribution to civic guerrilla warfare against the I.C., we had hit upon the idea of staging a race from Cleveland, Mississippi, forty miles away, to Greenville, between the lone passenger train and relays of plantation mules to be ridden by distinguished local gentry as jockeys. Let it suffice here to say that (1) the mules won; (2) the race was fixed; (3) the news magazines, the newspapers, and the newsreels gave spectacular notoriety to the Illinois Central, Greenville, and the mules; (4) the Illinois Central didn't like it; and (5) the train service didn't improve.

So after Matthew left I wrote President Wayne Johnston of the Illinois Central Railroad, a courteous gentleman for whom I already had high personal regard and was soon to have higher. In effect, I promised Wayne Johnston that if he would do me a favor, namely to find one Matthew Page, a medical student, a job as a dining-car waiter for the next three summers, I would never again sponsor a race between the I.C. and our fleet Delta mules.

In a few days came President Johnston's delightful reply. He wrote that he couldn't resist the bargain I had offered; and accordingly he was asking the chief of the I.C.'s dining-car service to do something for Matthew. The something was the coveted waiter's job, not with the Illinois Central which had no summer job vacancies left, but with the

Chicago, Burlington and Quincy, which has about 14,000 miles of track west of the Mississippi River. Matthew worked for the next three summers for the Chicago, Burlington and Quincy. It was a never-to-be-forgotten experience.

"I traveled over most of those 14,000 miles," Matthew told me later. "It took me into practically every state west of the Mississippi on out to the Pacific Coast. I made more money than I ever thought I could; but aside from that my experiences were valuable from a cultural and educational point of view, mainly because I had the opportunity to come in contact with just about every kind of human being in this country or in the world for that matter. The experience I had with them made me a much broader person."

He worked every possible minute of time and overtime. While the average college student serving as extra hand on the dining cars averages about $900 to $1000 a summer, Matthew earned $1200 the first summer, $1500 the second summer, and an amazing $1700 the last. Those earnings insured him plenty of time for study without worrying about part-time jobs. In 1951 he graduated in the top half of his class. Tucked away was a tidy sum which would go far toward the purchase of the medical equipment in his office today.

I would not want it thought that the only times that I saw Matthew were when he was about to take another important step, or that we talked only of his immediate requirements. As he grew older and his horizons widened and he became more and more sure of himself, the development of his mind fascinated me. We would talk of many things; of the common problems that beset his people and mine; of what was happening in a world concerning whose upheavals he had a sensitive grasp; of why he did and did not want to come back to Greenville one day. I especially remember one of his later recollections, while he was in the Air Force, that is illustrative of so much. In their high school days he and four friends had toured the until then unknown North one summer in a wheezy jalopy. They were, Matthew said matter-of-factly, the best students in the school. All planned to go to college and then return to Greenville. All of them did go to college. But the others are "up North"—three with academic doctor's degrees, and one a highly placed civil servant. But always with Matthew and me, that degree of Doctor of Medicine was uppermost in our minds.

After Matthew was graduated from Meharry, he participated in what is called the Intern Matching Program. Under it a medical school graduate selects several hospitals that qualify for an internship program. He makes applications to these hospitals. When he has completed his applications, he rates them in the order of his choice. The hospitals which receive applications from medical school graduates also rate the applicants as to their desirability. The graduate is appointed to the hospital which he has rated the highest or nearest to it, and which also rates him relatively high. Matthew was matched with the George W. Hubbard Hospital in Nashville which is associated with Meharry.

At the end of a year of internship at Hubbard Hospital where he specialized in pediatrics, young Dr. Page was faced with a decision. In good health and without prior military service he was eligible for the draft. As an alternative he could become a medical officer in one of the armed services. He decided upon entering the Air Force Medical Corps and, during his internship, was commissioned in the Air Force Reserve. When he came home after his year as an intern he told me that he had requested that he be called into the service as soon as possible. And so he was, in September of 1957, as a captain in the Air Force Medical Corps.

I did not learn all that began almost immediately afterward until Matthew was home again for keeps. After entering upon active service that September, he attended for three short, dazed weeks a Medical Officer Indoctrination Course at Gunter Air Force Base in Montgomery, Alabama. Then he was assigned to Ernest Harmon Air Force Base in Newfoundland; and there Captain Matthew Page, fresh out of his internship in a Negro hospital in Nashville, was appointed chief of the pediatric service in the 100-bed hospital whose staff ranged from ten to sixteen doctors. In addition, because of his interest is obstetrics and gynecology, he was made assistant in this division. He spent two years at Harmon Air Force Base, and in his last year he was appointed chief of the obstetrical and gynecological service, a position he held until he was rotated home in August 1959.

"That tour of duty in Newfoundland meant everything to me," Dr. Page says now. "First of all, the experience that the assignment gave me could not have been gained in three times as many years elsewhere. And it was important to me personally that I came in contact with people about whom I had only read (he meant white people), and it cleared up a lot of things in my mind simply by talking with them."

To his knowledge he was the first Negro doctor to be stationed at Harmon. He says that he had felt some personal apprehension about being there and about the work he was assigned to do, and that there were a few minor incidents in the beginning. "But I am happy to say that none of my fears ever materialized," Matthew told me. "After a few weeks I got the impression that I was just as welcome and appreciated as any other doctor on the staff. For the most part I was treated very, very well and I had no trouble at all as far as my work was concerned."

Captain Page delivered more than 150 babies while chief of the obstetrical and gynecological division and he didn't lose one that came to full term. He was so happy with the life and associations as a medical officer in the Air Force that he seriously considered staying in the service. As an alternative he also thought of accepting an offer from a small town in Iowa, which came in his last year of service. Lacking a doctor, the community offered to build a clinic to his specifications free of charge, and a $20,000 home on which he would only have to pay two per cent interest beginning the fourth year.

There were other, similar opportunities too. Under the terms of his scholarship grant he did not have to return to Mississippi if he chose instead to repay the $5000 loan. But Matthew Page decided to come home.

"One reason was my feeling that I had obligated myself to the state by taking the scholarship even though I could have got out of it by repaying the loan," Matthew says. "The second reason was another more or less moral obligation. During my college and medical school days I promised a good many people and groups that I would return to Mississippi, specifically to my own home town. It wasn't a matter so much of making a living but of what contribution I could make to the area in which I would practice. Mississippi has many, many needs. There is so much that can be done that is not done yet in our state. And this is true especially among my own people. Maybe it's because I used to be a Scout leader but I am most interested of all in the young folks who have not yet finished high school. I would like to do as much as possible to help channel their minds into productive directions. It's productiveness that can make them better Mississippians and better Americans." From some people, this kind of comment might sound corny. It isn't when you hear it from Matthew Page.

So my friend came home in October 1959. When he called at my office he was still in uniform for his period of service would not end for a few more weeks. He told me that he had just rented a small building on Clay Street for his offices and that he planned to marry a Tougaloo classmate, a prospective member of the Coleman High School faculty, as soon as his practice got under way. Then he told me the big secret. He was to receive a commendation medal from the Air Force and it would be given to him on the occasion of the next of the periodic wing reviews which are held at the base in conjunction with the graduation ceremonies for the cadets who take basic training there. He asked me to attend.

I promised him that my wife and I would be there. I also suggested that before he even had his office swept out, he ought to go to the courthouse and register as a voter. He did, that very day, and the registrar told us later that he had never had a more comprehensive set of answers to the questions in the voter-qualification test which, in our county, is administered fairly regardless of race.

It is unlikely that my wife and I, or any others with a knowledge of what lay behind the event, will forget that November morning when Captain Matthew Page received his commendation medal. On the parade ground behind him the airmen and cadets of the Greenville Air Force Base stood at attention. Directly before him were the commanding officer and his staff. In the stands behind the officers waited the parents and other relatives of cadets, a few other interested white persons, and a cluster of Negroes, among them John Page, who has been seasonably occupied as a leveling-machine operator for the United States Engineers for twenty-five years, his wife, Mrs. Mollie Page, who cooks, and the attractive young Negro woman whose name was then Vivian Patton, daughter of a Tougaloo carpenter and herself a teacher-to-be in Greenville, who would become Dr. Page's wife the next spring.

I have purposely saved the text of the Air Force citation until nearly the end of this story. This is what Colonel Jasper Bell, commanding officer of GAFB, read into the microphone so that all present could hear and others later could read:

CITATION TO ACCOMPANY THE AWARD OF THE AIR FORCE COMMENDATION MEDAL TO MATTHEW J. PAGE

Captain Matthew J. Page distinguished himself by meritorious service as Chief of the Pediatrics Service and later as Chief of the Obstetrics and Gynecology Service, Harmon Air Force Base, from 15 October, 1957, to 6 July, 1959. During this period, he gained outstanding recognition and respect from his patients and fellow physicians, demonstrating tact, patience and concern in his relationship with patients and instilling in them a feeling of confidence and trust. Through his diligent study and exceptional application, he was able to solve all problem cases encountered during this period with a knowledge and

technique far above that which would normally be expected of a physician of Captain Page's training and
experience. For his exemplary devotion to duty and un-
tiring efforts, he has reflected great credit upon himself
and the United States Air Force.

When it was over, and the base squadrons began to pass
in review, the jaunty little GAFB band swung into "When
the Saints Go Marching In." Under her breath my wife said,
"Hallelujah," and not to be funny. I couldn't think of anything by way of answer. I was looking at Captain Matthew
Page's mother and father and fiancée, a couple of rows
over, and I don't think they could have said anything either.

I have talked with Greenville's newest doctor perhaps a
dozen times since he opened his practice and on a variety
of subjects; sometimes in his office, sometimes in mine or
in my home. From a variety of sources I have learned that
Dr. Matthew Page is doing well in the community which is
served by some forty white doctors who treat anybody and
four other and older Negro doctors who treat Negroes. As
one friend of his father's put it: "That boy's sure spreading
himself out; they're even coming in from across the river in
Arkansas and Louisiana." And neighboring planters and
other white employers of Negroes have also told me that
they and their employees are more than satisfied with his
services.

Matthew himself is optimistic; and if he is not entirely
happy, I suspect that he is happier than he expected to be.

"I can only describe my reception in Greenville as being
very cordial and helpful," he told me near summer's end.
"I've received much help from members of both races. I've
been especially surprised at the treatment which I have received from the white doctors of Greenville. It is 200 to 300
per cent more than my original expectation.

"What is surprising to some of my friends elsewhere is the
fact that, like other qualified Negro physicians here, I am
eligible to be and am a member of the staff of the General

Hospital. A Negro doctor can admit his patients to the hospital and treat them there. To my knowledge, within whatever limitations he may have, he can do whatever he is qualified to do. As far as the hospital privileges are concerned, I have general practice privileges along with minor surgery privileges. This is the extent of my professional education and capabilities now."

After a year Matthew says that returning home and staying has not been the easiest decision he ever made. "I have been so busy getting my practice established that I haven't had too much time to think about anything else," he said. "However, work is just a part of living and having just left a different set of conditions in the Air Force and elsewhere, the adjustment hasn't been too easy.

"The biggest question that I keep asking myself is what do I want as a person. For a short answer I can say only that I want to be a full American citizen. I would like to be able to enjoy the privileges that full citizenship gives. I also want to share the responsibilities that citizenship demands."

He said that he has found his life, away from his work, restricted and in a sense repressive.

"I like to play golf when I have time, to bowl and to go to some decent place for dinner, to take part in civic events, but there's not much opportunity," he says, not morbidly or with rancor but as a plain matter of fact. "But at the Greenville Air Force Base, as a reserve officer, I can play golf and bowl and be a member of the Officers' Club, and that does make a lot of difference. Not that I've had much time to do very much beside work and settle down."

Most of his energy outside of his practice goes into working with young Negroes. He meets often with gatherings of young people, some of whom are still in high school and some in college, and he feels that he is giving them something out of his own experience that they can use in becoming better citizens. He is also turning again to a boyhood love of hunting and fishing.

Will he stay in Greenville for as far ahead as he can see? He is not too sure but just now it seems likely. He is aware that he is in the unusual and useful position of being a medical and social missionary in his own land and among his own people, and that he can spend a lifetime here without running out of something needful to do.

As for myself, looking back upon these thirteen years, I cannot help but think of one aspect which Dr. Matthew Page, in his zeal to help his people, and because of those frustrations which today are still inevitable, may overlook. Tougaloo, the college which Matthew attended, arose out of the determination of men and women of different races to bring light to the darkness of ignorance; and the white instructors who helped teach Matthew Page at Tougaloo are not unaware of stigma and ostracism. The medical scholarship which Matthew Page won on merit was established by the legislature of a state which white men completely dominate. Out of the battlefield dream of a Northern and Southern white man and the lasting gratitude of another white Southerner was born Meharry, the medical school from which he graduated. The good-humored and thoughtful response of a railroad president most certainly smoothed his path through that medical school; and, as he readily says, the helping hands which have been extended since he returned home have been both white-skinned and dark.

We are not entirely islands of black and white.

13

THE HEGIRA OF ALEXANDER SMITH
1956

During a hot week in August 1950, a mysterious delegation arrived in our town of Greenville, Mississippi. We knew only that the strangers represented a reputable industry up North which was interested in locating a branch plant somewhere in the South. One man, however, wore a tie clasp which commemorated twenty years of faithful service to Alexander Smith, Inc. A few minutes of checking revealed that we were dealing with one of the biggest carpet manufacturers in the United States.

We kept the secret and so did they. We knew that we could expect rough competition from other Southern communities if they learned too soon that we had a new industry nibbling at our civic bait. And the Alexander Smith people knew what would happen back home in Yonkers, New York, if it became known that they were seeking a Southern location, even for what was then envisioned only as a secondary branch. As it developed, about a year after the branch factory opened in 1953, Alexander Smith, Inc., shut down the Yonkers plant and moved the entire Axminster carpet operation to Greenville.

For several years the South has been criticized for "industrial pirating" by political leaders, particularly in New England. The American Federation of Labor has demanded punitive federal laws to prevent "subsidized migration" because it leaves in its wake "poverty, unemployment and industrial chaos."

These criticisms worried me. Would Greenville's gain bring poverty and industrial chaos to Yonkers? What happens when one city acquires a new industry at the expense of another city? What does the industry gain? Why did it want to move in the first place? And now, what about Yonkers, New York, which has lost its biggest industry? How bad had the city been hurt?

Yonkers and Greenville are about as different as two cities can be within the same nation. Yonkers, with an estimated 170,000 people, is a metropolis; its 300 industries make it representative of the concentration of industry in the Northeast. Greenville is primarily a cotton-and-cattle town, a Mississippi river port, with less than 40,000 people, even today. The average family income of Yonkers is $7181, one of the highest in the United States; Greenville's is higher than the Mississippi average of $3132, but still less than half that of Yonkers.

Greenville was already a prosperous community, but we had only two fairly sizable industries—one making wall-board and the other packing cases—with a total peak employment of about 1200 workers. We had never participated in Mississippi's controversial "Balance Agriculture with Industry" plan because, prior to World War II, Greenville leaders didn't fancy our cotton kingdom as an industrial region. Under Mississippi's BAWI program, the city or county, by holding a special election, can authorize a bond issue and use the proceeds to build a plant for an acceptable industry. The industry then pays rent sufficient to retire the bonds within twenty years. Meanwhile, since ownership is vested in the municipality or county, industry pays no property taxes.

This plan, which has brought more than 100 new industries to Mississippi, is the principal means by which the state's industry-hungry towns can lift themselves by their own bootstraps. And so, in 1948, Greenville too decided to go industry-hunting. The friendly group from Yonkers, brought in by a paid industry-locating service, seemed like the answer to our community prayer.

Alexander Smith, Inc., found Greenville no less attractive. The century-old company had to establish another plant somewhere. On its thirty-five acres in Yonkers stood some sixty buildings of all ages, sizes, and descriptions which formed a generally outmoded industrial rabbit warren. For example, the raw wool coming into the plant journeyed nearly fifteen miles before it emerged as a rug, in contrast to the two- or three-mile trip in a modern carpet factory.

Moreover, the company had been caught in a postwar squeeze. Wool prices had risen fantastically; inevitably, the price of rugs soared, and the market diminished, Alexander Smith had to compete with other kinds of floor coverings, and with more modern mills. Also, the company was having labor troubles in Yonkers.

Greenville looked good to Alexander Smith because our water was abundant and chemically suited for scouring and dyeing. The supply of natural gas was virtually unlimited and labor was plentiful.

With preliminaries settled, our Chamber of Commerce persuaded the citizens to authorize a $4,750,000 bond issue to build the nation's most modern carpet mill. Late in 1951, Alexander Smith supervisors and trainers began arriving. They taught rug-making to new employees in a converted warehouse, while on the outskirts of Greenville a functionally beautiful plant began rising. It was nearly two years a-building; then, in March 1953, the first Axminster carpet came off the looms.

Greenville Mills, Inc., as the subsidiary was called, employed some 300 people. Back in Yonkers about 4000 Alexander Smith workers continued at their jobs. There was some grumbling, principally from politicians and union spokesmen, but the proportionately small shift of production to Greenville wasn't greatly noticeable in Yonkers. It was certainly noticeable in Greenville!

In June 1954, when Alexander Smith decided to move everything to Greenville, the Yonkers mill was on strike because of inability to agree on a new union contract. The Alexander Smith spokesman said the company could not meet the union's wage and other demands. The union blamed inefficient management, obsolete techniques, and failure to keep up with the times.

In the year that followed, the Greenville mill's labor force rose to nearly 1000 workers, and Alexander Smith executive, supervisory, and clerical personnel came to settle in our town. Within a year 500 new homes were built and sold. Five new subdivisions opened, a new grammar school, three new churches, and three shopping centers were constructed —two of the last-mentioned in what formerly was the outskirts of town. Our newspaper circulation rose from 10,000 to nearly 14,000.

Greenville's population in the 1950 census was 30,000; today, according to an interim survey, it's over 34,900. Alexander Smith didn't bring all these people, but the company's arrival and growth were the primary reason for an influx of new business, new distribution agencies, new people. Less than thirty miles east of Greenville, in the little town of Indianola, the Ludlow Manufacturing and Sales Company built a plant that turns out jute and cotton twine for the backing of Alexander Smith's carpets. That alone meant 300 more jobs in our trading area.

There were human gains, too. With the arrival of the Northerners, Greenville High School got an outstanding football player; the Presbyterian church got a talented pianist; the garden club ladies discovered that ideas from Yonkers could be applied nicely in Greenville. The civic clubs gained new members, the country club got some exceptional golfers, and Greenville's voting rolls acquired some Republicans. We have profited in many ways from these new neighbors whose backgrounds, experience, and thinking are often so different from our own.

Meanwhile, what happened in Yonkers? A week after the decision to close the plant in 1954, the CIO Textile Workers' Union ran advertisements in New York papers headed: "A Lesson in Failure—That's the Story of Alexander Smith, Inc." It described the closure as a tragedy to the workers, denied that union demands had anything to do with the move to Greenville, and called for federal tax laws that would penalize "runaway" industry. Later, an AFL survey reported that the "pirating" of plants caused "unemployment, un-economic dislocation and sectional bitterness."

Last summer I went to Yonkers to discover for myself how the city had been affected. I talked to editors, industrialists, labor leaders, cab drivers, housewives, bartenders, and the proverbial man-in-the-street, but I could find no evidence of "tragedy, unemployment, or sectional bitterness." Instead, I found a heart-warming story of community co-operation to minimize the economic shock of the plant's shutdown. I also learned that Alexander Smith's departure had brought about some healthy changes in the behavior of labor, management, and government in Yonkers.

The city hadn't wasted time on trying to fix the blame. A few days after the plant closed, a civic committee was formed to find jobs for the displaced workers, seek new tenants for the old Smith buildings, and otherwise temper the wind in a town shorn of its wool. This Community Council for Economic Development was made up of industrial, labor, business, and professional leaders.

The council was extraordinarily effective. Most of the displaced workers found jobs in Yonkers or near-by communities, and hundreds were trained for new jobs. (Workers fifty-seven years old or older were pensioned by the company or taken care of under union plans.)

Then, in May 1955, a Yonkers syndicate contracted to purchase the old Smith property and buildings, renamed it the Westchester County Industrial Center, and offered space for sale or lease to assorted small industries. By December the first "replacements" were moving in. Yonkers is confident that every building soon will be fully occupied. When that happens, more workers will be employed on the old site than during the wartime peak of Alexander Smith operations.

But if the Smith departure had no serious economic impact on Yonkers, it undeniably caused other changes. There was fear that other industries would follow the carpet company's lead and seek greener pastures. The Otis Elevator Company, now the city's biggest single employer, was able to make new agreements with the unions and the municipality. Otis asked the union to surrender certain pay systems. The union agreed. The city has agreed to more lenient tax valuation, and negotiations are under way to give the company the use of four streets adjoining the plant.

With labor, management, and government working together on behalf of local industry, a different climate exists in Yonkers today. And that new climate may spread. For the exodus of these small and diversified industries from metropolitan New York City is a part of a national movement that is taking smaller industries into the suburban areas and larger industries to less thickly populated parts of the country. What's happening is the slow breaking up of the huge and unsound concentrations of people in the big cities. The change is of real significance in connection with national defense, and as an aid toward more equitable distribution of industrial wages.

The South, in this expanding nation, is not endangering other regions by attracting industry. We are simply getting a bit nearer to our fair share of the national income. There are still fewer industrial workers among Mississippi's 2,000,000 citizens than there are within a ten-mile radius of Yonkers. This won't always be true. Somewhere in the South a new industry is being established every twenty-four hours. This means that some day Mississippi will no longer have to stand by helplessly while sixty-five out of every 100 of its college graduates leave the state for employment elsewhere.

Meanwhile, we in Greenville have more than 1000 new carpetmakers who are earning wages they never dreamed of making, even if the pay does not equal the Northern scale. So if anyone knows of a worth-while industry that wants a shiny new factory, plenty of workers, a variety of raw materials, and a fine regional market—well, the address is simply Greenville, Mississippi.

14

YES, *TENNESSEE, THERE ARE SOUTHERN BELLES* *1962*

If a United Association of Southern Belles existed in the general pattern of the United Daughters of the Confederacy, I'm right sure that it would be meeting in special session about now. The one happy purpose would be to draw up and endorse unanimously a resolution of appreciation directed to my fellow Mississippian—admit it, lad—Tennessee Williams.

The resolution might read something like this:

"BE IT RESOLVED, that we, the United Association of Southern Belles, do herewith express our heartfelt appreciation to Mr. Tennessee Williams for deciding not to write about us in future, as revealed in an interview in London, England, when he said: 'I don't feel inclined to write any more about the so-called Southern belle. You might find what I call mysticism coming into things I write from now on.'

"BE IT FURTHER RESOLVED, that we, the members of the U.A.S.B., now quietly return to our desirable little old streetcars and hot tin roofs and there wait for Mr. Williams' milk-train not to stop."

Of course, this can't happen—if only because Southern belles can't possibly afford to unite in a region where the ladies outnumber the menfolk and it's every girl for herself and Lord bless the honeysuckle. Also, Mr. Williams can't *stop* writing about Southern belles because he really never *started* to write about them, leastways about none of the kind to whose defense I now bring all my artillery to bear. While I like Mr. Williams' plays even better than anything out of the Grand Guignol, I just don't recognize his Southern womenfolk. Besides, his slightly epochal decision has raised doubts in some mighty high quarters that our belles ever existed or do exist, or will continue to exist, or ought to exist; and we are not going to put up with such badmouthing down here among the magnolias and missile centers. If there is one thing we are still confederated on, it's our belles. And, let it be graciously added so that Tennessee won't be affronted, also our *belles lettres.*

So, in the name of a long line of admirers and defenders, from John Rolfe of Virginia, who married the first one of record—name of Pocahontas—to Governor John Patterson of Alabama, who wouldn't have approved, I wish to answer resoundingly that our belles did, do, will, and ought to exist. And I will make our case on geographical, historic, economic, social, educational, hereditary, and personal grounds.

The geographical proof: Let me start this one off by asking if anyone has ever seen many beautiful Eskimos, Laplanders, or Northern Mongolians (if there is a Northern Mongolia). No. And why not? The answer is simple: the weather—which is an accident of geography. The Far Northern females of the species have to work so hard to keep warm, to keep their husbands fed, and even to keep alive, that they don't have time to work on their faces, their figures, their small talk, or their men. On the other hand, our temperate Southern climate, with its perfumed nights and greenly gracious days, is just right for belles. (Memo to prospective industrialists: mean year-round temperature of seventy degrees, ample power, water, and raw materials; willing labor supply.) But why rub it in?

The historical proof: Not since the dawn of our nation has a trained observer ever referred to a Southern woman as just a Southern woman—not even Charles Dickens, who didn't think so much of us. Most of them take their pick from such prefatory adjectives as "beautiful," "lovely," "charming," "patrician," "vivacious," "coquettish," and the like (with the exception of General Ben Butler during the occupation of New Orleans, circa 1862; and if we had caught him, we'd have shot him, the cad). And did you ever hear anyone speak of the beautiful Harriet Beecher Stowe, for instance?

The economic proof: The leisure class may not be all it's cracked up to be but its women have a better chance to stay beautiful, or become beautiful, than do most others. And, as almost every Southerner knows, in the days befo' the war, almost every Southerner was waited upon by a faithful and ever-lovin' retinue—juleps for the men, hairdos for the women, and don't worry, sugar, about making up your bed. It takes more than a hundred years to lose an advantage like that and there are still parts of the South where you can get mighty fine help for twelve dollars a week. (I'm not saying where because the emerging nations might take the matter to the U.N.).

The social proof: At almost any party you go to, especially in the North, an at least reasonably attractive, flirtatious, intelligent, and purposeful Southern girl is wondering aloud why "you all are being so nice to poor little me, I declare." This comes right out of the Fair Rowena school of literature, which gives the lie to those who deny the South's cultural past. And did you dance with her?

The educational proof: I can handle this one quite simply. Whoever heard of a university that produced two Miss Americas in a row? Well, Ole Miss did, just a while back. If that isn't enough, let me tell you about the time my wife went to her first meeting of Harvard Dames. (Those are dames who meet at Harvard and my wife was one because I was holding a fellowship there at the time.) She dressed as if she were going to a meeting of the Greenville Garden Club: nylons, a sort of sassy hat, high shoes, and a rustly dress—nothing fancy, but I thought she looked cute. She came back in tears. All the other Dames were in flat shoes, lisle stockings, tweed suits, and all-weather hats. And no one even asked her if she were Phi Beta Kappa.

The hereditary proof: I have never known a Southern man who didn't want a pretty wife. If she was also talented and could find her way around the kitchen, so much the better. But looks and personality come first, and, natural selection being what it is, pretty wives have pretty daughters who get married in the South and have pretty daughters who get married in the South, et cetera, et sequitur. The others either go North to marry or turn to writing novels.

The personal proof: I know that the Southern belle did exist because I married one. I know they still exist because two of my sons have followed suit. I know they will continue to exist because I have two small granddaughters who already show their grandmother a thing or two when it comes to handling the men.

So much for unassailable documentation.

And I'm glad that the belles are still with us in the South and wherever they go beyond the South. What's wrong with femininity? What's wrong with a girl soft-pedaling her mental capacity when she wants a man who wouldn't like to find out that she's smarter than he is—which nine times out of ten she is. Attention is fun and dancing is fun. One of life's great objectives for a gal should be to make men like her, and another is to make a home for the man she decides will do.

What's wrong with a belle who wants to dress up fit to kill after working hours and go out with the boys instead of settling down with a good book? What's wrong with coquetry and flirtation and whatever gifts the Lord endows a girl with? What's wrong with pretending helplessness and being wide-eyed and bearing down on an accent which a great many men prefer to the clipped or the twanged or the detachedly English tones of lovely women elsewhere?

What's wrong with it all? Nothing, honey. You just keep right on the way you are.

And now, permit me a few serious moments. No type is as easy to parody on the stage or in literature as the Southern belle. That's all right if it's recognized as parody or satire or an expression of individual or artistic distaste. But it is unfortunate, even unfair, that some of the women characters of Tennessee Williams and lesser writers are thought by the audience or the reader to be typical or representative of a considerable segment of the population or of the sex itself.

Tennessee Williams' Southern women are vividly, memorably presented, but for my money they are untypical, sicklied, abnormal caricatures of a group and a society which, for his own good reasons, he surely must despise or pity or condemn, or all three. So I am very happy that he intends to leave them alone.

Again seriously, it wouldn't hurt for the rest of the country to know more about the real women of the South than they can learn from Southern writers. Regionalism isn't cured by ridicule. And to the extent that the so-called Southern belle reflects regionalism, I hope it is never cured at all.

At this juncture, I would like to quote from a piece by another of my favorite Southern authors:

"The mistress of the Southern manor was required to act like a lady and work like a drudge. Her lord, who never became quite civilized, remained largely outdoors, riding his fields, fishing, hunting, drinking (but like a gentleman), and on occasion paying calls motivated solely by interest in the physical well-being of his slaves. The chatelaine herself stayed close to home where the real life of the plantation was centered. It was her responsibility to supervise the kitchen, to direct the endless baking and curing and preserving, to exercise over-all care of the sick . . . The production of feedstuffs, foodstuffs and the cyclical money crop rested with the planter, the overseer and God. But the lady's duties were not so delimited. She was childbearer, supervisor of the home, hostess, nurse . . . and spiritual comforter—and she had to fill all such roles while living out the most difficult role of all, that of the beautiful, innocent, incapable, devoted and obedient wife, the exemplar of all virtues and forgiver of all vices.

"It is no wonder that the feminine turnover—or turnunder —was high. But those devoted ladies who survived were, behind their drawing room manners and engaging adoration, a tough and resourceful breed. So were their daughters and so are their granddaughters; and what I like best and am most awed by is their ability to make their menfolks think otherwise.

"And then, the war. If the plantation housewife's existence was strenuous in the halcyon ante-bellum days of chivalry, it was a nightmare during the war and throughout the dark aftermath. While battle and invasion swirled around them, Southern women lived for the most part alone, in threatened mansion and split-log cabin alike, sharing lonely fear, the agony of loss, and a drab concern with the elemental problem of survival itself. The make-believe of chivalry gave way to the drearier pretense that parched corn and hogback made a fine meal. And out of those harrowing years of the Southern ordeal, the artificiality of the past was reinforced by a true chivalry of sorrow, by the affection and respect of man for grieving woman, and woman for broken man.

". . . while the Civil War intensified the self-reliance of the Southern woman, the Reconstruction period that followed made it imperative for her to hide that self-reliance even more effectively behind a mask of appealing femininity. The self-respect of the homecoming, defeated Confederate demanded that manliness be thus buttressed; moreover, in a very primitive sense, Southern women had to compete with each other for the men they outnumbered. Coquetry, charm, the ability to attract became practical necessities for the woman who sought a mate or would heal a husband's wounds of the body and the spirit. And, because of these imperatives, the South slipped into an elsewhere archaic matriarchy: a competitive, coquettish society which set great store upon the feminine and in which the true role of woman as the pursuer instead of the ostensibly pursued is still enacted with a purposeful skill that is unmatched anywhere else."

I wrote that thirteen years ago, which was before *A Streetcar Named Desire* came along, or at least before I saw it. What it says about Southern women may be as romantic a collection of notions as ever came out of Sir Walter Scott. But if this is so, don't blame the belles. Blame the men who like to think of them this way.

Come spur along, Ivanhoe. Let no man sully the name or deny the reality of Fair Rowena.

15

THE AMAZING GENTLEMAN FROM SEWANEE

1953

On top of the Mountain—a wooded, waterfall-laced plateau in the Tennessee Cumberlands—lies the tranquilly beautiful village of Sewanee. It is the spiritual and educational capital of the twenty-two Southern and Southwestern dioceses of the Protestant Episcopal Church, which together own the 10,000-acre domain. The name of the village is also the loved, short substitution for the Church's University of the South, which dominates it.

Among the villagers are a number of indomitable little old ladies, relicts or relatives of Confederate generals and Episcopal bishops and Sewanee professors. In the late spring of 1952, so a newer legend goes, one of them guided a visitor around the serene stronghold of Southern Episcopacy. They stopped first at a shrine to a noted son of the Confederacy, General Edmund Kirby-Smith, whose surrender in Texas was considerably later than Appomattox, and who came to Sewanee to teach mathematics and botany only after an angry, self-imposed exile in Mexico.

Impressed by a bronze bas-relief plaque of the general, the visitor asked who was the artist.

"Lovely, isn't it?" answered the little lady. "Edward McCrady, the sculptor, did it a few years back. But you should see his oils, especially the portraits, and his wood carving."

A little later the pair paused to view a magnificent glen. On the far side cascaded a sixty-foot waterfall. Beside it clambered a group of students, behind an older leader who seemed to be the only one taking the climb with ease.

"Who's that?" asked the visitor. "Isn't he a little old for such goings-on?"

"Oh, that one," said the lady. "That's Edward McCrady,

the explorer. He's always taking the Sewanee boys out climbing and looking for caves and bones and things."

At dusk the little old lady of Sewanee suggested, "We'll drop in at President McCrady's for a cup of tea."

She parked her car, decorated with a small Confederate flag, in front of a rambling white house set far back from the road. From the tree-shaded house floated a harmony of stringed instruments, flute, and piano.

"Listen," said the lady. "The president and his family are practicing some of his chamber music."

At their knock, the front door was opened and they were ushered to a study. Around the walls ran bookshelves and against a front window stood Atlas, carved in wood, bearing a globe, and on one wall hung an oil portrait of a gowned, elderly man with a gray mustache. On the mantel rested what the visitor decided was the skull of some wild animal.

"That's the skull of a wildcat or tiger or something. It's awfully prehistoric. He found it in a cave."

A suspicious look came into the visitor's eyes. "Who found——" the visitor began. She was interrupted by a blond, smiling woman who entered the study with a viola in her hand. Behind her trailed three boys in their teens, bearing flute, violin, and cello, and an eight-year-old girl. Bringing up the rear was a wiry, heavy-browed man, youthful-looking and high of forehead, holding a violin.

"This is my guest, Mrs. Jefferson Lee Stuart," said the little old lady of the mountains. "Mrs. Stuart, this is President and Mrs. McCrady, and their children, John, Edward, Waring, and Sarah."

Mrs. Stuart, so the story has it, murmured, "Everybody is McCrady," and fainted dead away.

When she came to, Doctor McCrady had disappeared. The visitor to Sewanee rose shakily.

"Doctor McCrady is so sorry he had to leave," explained his wife. "But if you're a biologist, and especially if you've been mixed up with that atomic business at Oak Ridge, folks won't leave you alone."

"Biologist," whispered the visitor. Again she fainted.

You can take that story or leave it alone. But to the sons of Sewanee, Edward McCrady, confirmed at forty-six as vice-chancellor and president, after a year as acting head of the university, is the South's answer to the confining over-specialization of our times. Thomas Jefferson, with his many interests, was his prototype in colonial days. McCrady's multiple interests in the world about him, as biologist, explorer, composer, musician, artist, and theologian, attest to his conviction that man need not be the creature of this technical, specialized age. And to thousands of Episcopalian laymen and clergy, his conviction that science and Christian beliefs are not exclusive of each other answers their question as to whether there is room in the atomic age for the believer.

The University of the South is the only remaining men's institution of higher learning, save for seminaries, completely owned and operated by the Episcopal Church. It offers to its some 650 undergraduates a liberal arts education, with bachelor degrees in arts and sciences, in an academic tradition that is reminiscent of the small New England colleges.

Down from the Mountain to death in battle rode its first president, Leonidas Polk, the fighting bishop of Louisiana, who, as a young West Point graduate, had turned from the military life to the Church and who donned a Confederate general's uniform when the Civil War began. Behind him the little mountain college, whose cornerstone had been laid only in 1860, became also a victim of war. Union troops, angrily mindful of Polk as an adversary, burned the few college buildings to the ground and even dynamited the cornerstone to bits for souvenirs.

English friends, principally within the closely identified Anglican communion, contributed largely to the rebuilding of Sewanee. Because Polk admired the English universities, Sewanee's scholastic flavor is distinctly reminiscent of faraway Oxford. Upperclassmen who make the scholastic grade wear academic gowns, short and ragged, to class and throughout the day. The chapel is entirely English in its interior appearance, and many of its furnishings and gifts came from England. Among its relics is a stone from the monastery at Iona, off the coast of Scotland, mounted with a silver cross and set in the top of the main altar. Its inscription reads in part: "This fragment of Iona marble serves as a connecting link between the American church and the beginnings of Christianity in Scotland." In the south wall is a Canterbury stone reading, "This stone from Ethelbert's Tower of St. Augustine's Abbey at Canterbury, England, founded in A.D. 597, was presented by St. Augustine's College to the University of the South in 1925, as a bond of unity with the first foundation of English Christianity." Set in the north wall is the Painswick stone from the Henry VII Chapel, dating back to 1503, the gift of the Dean and Chapter of Westminster Abbey.

From Sewanee have gone out more than 500 Episcopalian ministers, and more than 100 of its graduates are listed in Who's Who. Included are such assorted Americans as Surgeon General William Crawford Gorgas, who made possible the building of the Panama Canal by stamping out yellow fever there, and who was knighted by the King of England for his work in World War I; Archibald Butt, presidential aide to Theodore Roosevelt; Cary T. Grayson, onetime chairman of the American Red Cross; William Alexander Percy, the Mississippi poet; Huger W. Jervey, of Columbia University; Bishop William T. Manning of New York.

A Sewanee president and vice-chancellor must be versatile. His authority approaches the feudal except that he and his actions are subject to final approval by a Board of Trustees. He decides who can be buried in the domain and what the speed limits can be. He is a landlord; none of the 10,000 acres can be sold, but private homes can be built and owned under long-term leases of the sites. He fills the role of mayor. He is chief of police of the domain. His force consists of one man, a veteran of many moonshine raids, who in twenty-nine years as the domain's peace officer cannot remember having come to blows with a student. The president is also director of the University Press, which publishes the *Sewanee Review*, the oldest literary quarterly in America, with more subscribers in London than in any city in Tennessee. He must know something of farming and dairying, for the university owns a 250-acre farm, a herd of Jerseys, and a modern milk-processing plant. He is the over-all administrative head of the university's Emerald-Hodgson sixty-bed hospital, caring not only for the Sewanee students but for the village citizens and for mountain people for many miles around.

Besides directing the affairs of the university itself, the vice-chancellor is also administrative head of the Sewanee Military Academy, with 240 students, and the Sewanee Theological Seminary, where about eighty seminarians study for the ministry.

It would be impossible to think of any other background or position into which Edward McCrady—his friends call him Ned—would fit as naturally. He belongs to Sewanee by association, by ancestry, and by preference.

Because Ned's father, an Episcopal minister, had a parish in Mississippi at the time of his birth, he is not a South Carolinian by nativity; but in all other respects he and all the McCradys are as proudly Charlestonian as St. Cecilia's ball, as traditionally Episcopalian as eighteenth-century Virginia, and as closely associated with Sewanee as any family in the Church's history. His grandfather, John McCrady, was the first teacher of biology at the war-wrecked little institution. Ned McCrady's father, who was the rector in my boyhood Louisiana home town, was born in Charleston, went through Sewanee Military Academy, and was graduated from the University of the South and the Sewanee Theological Seminary.

Ned McCrady recalls now how his father once differed with Einstein on a metaphysical-mathematical conclusion and entered upon a debate with him by letter.

"Papa," recalls the president of Sewanee, "well, Papa just tied Professor Einstein in knots."

Whether or not Doctor Einstein would have agreed, the

comment is revealing; for no McCrady has ever been reluctant to dispute any man's idea when the idea is different from his own. Ned was also good at tying opponents into knots. He startled one fundamentalist high school teacher by telling the class that while Darwin's theory had its weak points, there was another, propounded by some McCrady ancestor, which made evolution a verity.

As an early-teen biologist, he secured snake specimens by diving for water moccasins, which are poisonous, and kept it up even after he had recovered from the bite of one moccasin that was a little quicker than was he. He wore short pants into his senior year in high school. Even then, when it suited him, he came barefoot to school. The smallest quarterback in his school's history, he had difficulty going through a line, so he developed a technique of diving high in the air, somersaulting in mid-air and then landing on the back of his neck to come up running.

His senior year in high school was his last in Louisiana. In 1923 he entered the ancient College of Charleston. There he majored in Greek and Latin, and, because his father had said no man is educated without calculus, he took up calculus. While a student at the college he bought a cheap violin and a book of instructions and taught himself to play. Later he learned more from various violinists with whom he played, and most of all while rehearsing when he played with the Oak Ridge Symphony, years afterward. He took up painting, too, while at the College of Charleston—also on his own—and was good enough while a student to win a scholarship to the Gibbes Art Gallery, which he couldn't use because he was immersed in his regular studies. It was years later that he learned professional techniques from his younger brother, John McCrady, one of the outstanding artists of the South.

But biology remained his principal interest, and after graduation and a summer at Columbia, where he studied Japanese, among other subjects, he became assistant curator of the Charleston Museum of Natural History. A year later he entered the University of Pittsburgh to earn his Master of Science degree in genetics and comparative anatomy.

In 1929 on a biological expedition to Woods Hole, Massachusetts, he met and within a year married Edith Dowling, New York born and Boston bred.

Then the University of Pennsylvania offered him a coveted Wistar Institute Fellowship, and to Philadelphia he went, enrolling in the medical school to study human anatomy and embryology on the side. He received his doctorate from Pennsylvania in 1932.

Ned McCrady remained at Wistar until Sewanee summoned him to teach biology in 1937.

At Wistar, thanks to the opossum, he became an authority on the mechanism of human hearing. Fascinated by the opossum's embryology—the opossum is one of the most primitive of mammals and is born prematurely—he spent three years inducing the opossum to breed in captivity. Previous studies of opossum embryology had been limited by the animal's refusal to reproduce as a captive. Observing that captive opossums were all having rickets despite plenty of sunlight, vitamin-D concentrate, milk, and eggs, Ned looked into a wild opossum's stomach and discovered from its heavy consumption of small vertebrates, bones and all, that bone was what was lacking in the tame opossum's diet. Adding bone meal to the diet made the opossums grow to full, normal adult stature and proportions. But they still did not breed.

There was some suggestion that lack of exercise was the trouble. So Ned enlarged the pens, hung the nest boxes on racks on the walls, and placed the food pans on the floor. "The animals now had to climb down to feed during the night, and with the return of daylight, if they wanted a dark hole in which to hide, they had to climb back up," he reported. "This they invariably did, rather than sleep on the floor in open daylight, so a certain amount of exercise was forced upon them, but they took advantage of their opportunities to a greater extent than that, and at night I often found them chasing each other up and down the tree branches which led to the nest boxes." The exercises apparently provided the needed stimulation, and the opossums soon provided baby opossums. During the spring and summer of 1935 a total of 250 were born in the colony, and by 1937 the laboratory was the proud possessor of third-generation, captive-born young.

There wasn't much more to learn about opossums by the time Ned got through with them. He showed that the lungs of the opossum are very precocious. They begin to function at a much earlier stage than do the lungs of other animals, even including the chick. He found that the opossum's ear, however, is unfinished at birth and not yet in working order. By a delicate operation on these living embryos he was able to wire them for sound, using their ears as microphones, which he hooked up to radio equipment so that as the embryo grew older and began to hear, whatever it heard came out of the loud-speaker.

This enabled him to find out when the opossum could first hear and what, and to correlate these facts with changes in the developing ear. Since the opossum's inner ear, when finished, is very much like man's, these discoveries also applied to human hearing.

In between, he learned conversational as well as academic German and French, and lectured over the nation and Canada and at the Sorbonne on the mechanism of hearing. Finding time heavy on his hands, he also wrote music for string quartets, and piano, violin, and cello trios.

Though all these years Ned came home to the Mountain whenever he could. He explored many known Cumberland caves and discovered new ones with his friend, Doctor Kirby-Smith, six-foot-four-inch grandson of the general, and director of the Sewanee hospital. And as new McCradys appeared, they in turn became sure-footed as mountain lynxes.

Meanwhile, Sewanee had kept its administrative eye on Edward McCrady, the biologist; and in 1937, without advance notice, the university elected him head of the department of biology. To accept meant financial sacrifice, but it meant also a year-round life on the Mountain and the opportunity to serve Sewanee.

The next eight years were happy, varied, and productive. Ned kept after the opossum, but he found time also to write papers on Courbet and the naturalist movement in art, begin a symphony, continue his work on the mechanism of hearing with Rockefeller Foundation equipment, and serve a term as president of the Tennessee Academy of Science. Whenever he could, he kept exploring caves.

What he missed at Sewanee was enough equipment and time for research, for it is not a rich school and cannot afford enough teachers to give researchers time to work in their fields.

"Teaching should permit time for teachers to extend the frontiers of knowledge as well as to transmit it," he says today, "and it is in this phase of higher education that the smaller, privately endowed, and denominational schools are deficient, particularly in the South." That is one of the challenges of Sewanee, where higher salaries should be the reward, he thinks, for a devoted faculty.

Ned remained at Sewanee throughout the war years, teaching biology to a diminished student body, and physics to the cadets of the V-12 unit which was established there. Those were difficult years for the little college, but for the McCradys, whose family at war's end had grown to three sons and a daughter, it was as happy a time as any such period could be.

It was during this period that he and Doctor Kirby-Smith and a friend, Harvey Templeton, made their notable discovery, in 1944, of a Pleistocene jaguar skeleton. They came upon it in Little Salt River cave near the Alabama border, a half mile back from the dank entrance, where sometime in the last ice age, perhaps 20,000 years ago, the animal apparently had crept in to die. They discovered a second skeleton in 1947, including nearly every bone in the extinct cat's body. Previously, only six bones and a tooth of the Pleistocene jaguar had been found. If anyone doubts that this find was important, go to the Smithsonian Institution's publication, *Proceedings of the U.S. National Museum,* Vol. 101, Art. 3287, 1951, in which the three discoverers, working under a Carnegie grant, report for fifteen illustrated pages their measurements, contrasts, and conclusions.

After the atomic bomb had been exploded, the AEC designated Ned as the Sewanee scientist who would receive such restricted information as would be made available to the nation's college scientists. His interest must have been challenging, for in 1948 he was summoned to Oak Ridge to become chief of the biology division, with a staff of some 150 and an annual budget of $2,000,000 to be devoted to peacetime biological and medical applications of atomic energy.

At Oak Ridge, as a lay reader of the Episcopal Church, he occupied for six months an Episcopal pulpit vacated by a resignation. During those months more than one skeptical scientist came to share his conviction of a meaningful God. He brought to scores of campuses and adult audiences throughout the South the story of the peacetime miracles which surely could be wrought by a force which they looked on only as destructive; challenging and comforting disturbed people with the serenity of a faith which knowledge only buttressed. He believed then and believes now that nothing is so important to man as the full exploration of the peacetime uses of the incredible power of atomic energy; and that its presence both underscores man's needs for spiritual values and argues for the existence of a supernatural creative force which can be scientifically demonstrated as well as accepted by faith alone.

In the summer of 1951 Sewanee called Ned McCrady back to the Mountain. Behind him he left the seclusion and facilities that are the dream of the research scientist. Ahead lay the harassing problems of the small-college president; the requirement to be fund raiser as well as scholar, businessman as well as teacher, official greeter as well as introspective thinker. But also ahead lay the greatest challenge of his lifetime—the opportunity to help answer for young Americans the two questions which plague man of the machine age: (1) How can the liberal arts tradition of the well-versed man be preserved in a time of increasing technical specialization, and (2) How can we reconcile religion and science?

The answers he gives are straightforward. He believes that the man who knows a great deal about one thing and little or nothing about anything else isn't educated. And he is sure through personal proof that man can discover and enjoy most of the fruits of learning.

He tells his students that knowledge can come from an inner spiritual source no less than from the test tube; that life is wasted if it is not used to examine and appreciate the multitude of man's achievements, and not simply in the mastering of one achievement. His familiarity with atomic energy itself, the vastest force ever known to man, made him feel all the more a need for religious guidance in its uses.

"There are recurrent periods in history when men imagine they are too wise to believe in God," he says. "Instead, by some strange miracle of faith, they permit themselves to believe the most incredible improbabilities of coincidence under the impression that they thereby rise above the superstitions of their forebears."

Today is such a disbelieving time, Ned McCrady thinks. The world's "valiant effort to avoid religion in education" is one of these symptoms. He points out that one of his son's public school history textbooks fails to mention even the historical presence of Jesus Christ on earth, although the impact of Christianity, however it is interpreted, has been one of the most important in all the history of the world.

"It is a labored distortion of history to write it as if Christianity had nothing to do with man's destiny," he says. "And it is a deadly blow to integrity in public and private life when the educational system is detached from religion."

Ned McCrady's happiness at returning to Sewanee was tempered in June 1952 by the beginning of a Church and academic controversy concerning the proposed admission of Negro students to the school of theology. The incident, which suffered from considerable misinterpretation in the lay press, was climaxed by the decision of eight out of ten of the members of the divinity school's faculty to resign in protest against the failure of Sewanee's trustees to recommend admission of Negroes.

The controversy began soon after a committee of the Synod of Sewanee, which included fifteen of the twenty-two dioceses owning the university, recommended in 1951 that existing Episcopal seminaries in the South should be opened to students of all races. The report was approved by the synod in convention, but in June 1952 the trustees, while pointing out that there was nothing in the university's ordinances to prevent the admission of Negroes, decided by a vote of forty-five to twelve that the encouragement of such enrollment was at present inadvisable (1) because the action would be in violation of Tennessee's segregation statutes; and (2) because the school of theology was not separate and self-controlled, but a part of the social life of the university community "which is located on an isolated domain."

The divinity faculty members thereupon announced their decision to resign and the issue was joined in the Church and public press. In the following months, effort at compromise failed.

Ironically, only a relative handful of Negro students a year enter all Episcopal seminaries in the United States, and ten of these seminaries are ready to admit them. But the protesting faculty members think it imperative that the university go on record as being willing to admit students to the theology school regardless of race, even though no Negro ever applies.

It was a hot potato for McCrady. He sided with the trustees in agreeing that it did not seem advisable to encourage Negro enrollment *now,* pointing out that the university had no segregation regulations, but that the state of Tennessee did, and that the trustees' decision was the fairest and kindest they could make at the time. He asked for forebearance while the trustees further studied the issue.

"With respect to the Christian principles involved," he

commented later, "I have never had any uncertainty about the fact that the salvation of any Negro soul is as important to God as is the salvation of any other man's soul; also, that as children of God we have a real brotherhood and men of all races should work for what is best for all. But judgments as to what is best for all at particular times and under particular circumstances may be so difficult to make as to lead to complete disagreements. They should not, however, lead to bitterness or enmity if we are really Christian in our intention."

And there the incident rests for the moment. In the words of one Sewanee alumnus: "The university is indulging in its own brand of self-mutilation by publicly airing a fruitless controversy over the hypothetical admission of theoretical Negro seminarians." Most of the lay graduates of Sewanee probably agree. Most of the Episcopal clergy probably do not.

Each season on the Mountain has its advocates; some like best the gay, mad riot of autumn, and others the green, fecund spring. But there are still others, just as discerning, to whom the Christmas season has a deeper beauty that is more than nature's own coloration.

Perhaps at Christmastime the purpose of Bishop Polk's mountain university seems to be more apparent to its sons.

In the study of the rambling white house, Edward McCrady of the Mountain closes the book he has been reading. He is joined in the hall by his wife, the three McCrady boys, two of them in the uniform of the military academy, and little Sally. Together they walk from the president's home to the candlelit, richly bedecked chapel. It is eight o'clock on the Sunday night before the closing of Sewanee for the Christmas holidays, and the magnificently trained university choir is about to give the traditional Christmas service of choral music. The McCradys and their house guests fill half the second row.

The service begins with the solemn, beautiful ritual of the Protestant Episcopal Church, and then the choir offers to the packed chapel the best of the world's holy music—

Bach's "Christians, Mark Ye Well This Day," and Andriessen's Latin chant, "Magnificat"; the beautiful Catalan folk song, "The Song of the Birds"; the old Slovakian "Carol of the Sheep Bells" and the ancient Welsh "Dark the Night," Reger's "The Virgin's Slumber Song" and Jacob Handl's "Lo, I Reveal Unto Thee." And then there floats out on the mountain night the Alleluia.

Out of Sewanee's chapel file students, town folk, guests who have come for miles around to hear the service. In the light of the entrance, the McCradys exchange Christmas wishes and holiday farewells with friends and students. High on the western brow of the plateau shines the great, lighted cross of Sewanee, visible for scores of miles around. It is not hard on this night and in this place to believe with Ned McCrady, purposeful man of the Mountain, that behind all purposefulness are divine plan and perfection and eternal verity.

16

WE NEVER FELT MORE AT HOME

1960

The Johannesburg immigration officer, noting from my entrance papers that I was a newspaper publisher, looked up and said not unkindly but with a familiar resignation: "I suppose you'll be doing a book about us, too." Many a time I had heard that said in my own land; more than once I had said it to a visitor myself. From that moment we felt at home in South Africa.

At home from the beginning . . . At home that first day on the streets of pulsating Johannesburg because of the presence everywhere of great numbers of black men and women, unnoted and all but unseen by the whites with whom they rubbed shoulders; resignedly at home when we read in our first South African newspaper that two Elvis Presley renditions and "The Chipmunk Song" were among the first four of South Africa's ten top tunes; at home when, upon our arrival three days later at the suburban Cape Town house we had rented, our young neighbors across the street greeted us with a platter of cakes and fruit.

And from first to last, and overriding and underlying all else, we felt at home throughout our stay because the determination of the majority of South Africa's whites is precisely that of the majority of whites in the American South: to maintain white political and economic control and as complete a separation of the races as is possible. There is, for the South African, an all-important difference. The American Negro is only one man in ten. The nonwhites in South Africa number three out of four. Because of this ratio, the South African whites believe that at stake is their very survival under the only terms which most of them are willing to accept. Most of them would talk freely

to us because we were from the South. Most of the educated non-whites whom we met were just as frank because
we were Americans.

We had not expected such cordiality. Before our departure for South Africa we had listened to many a warning. Had we heeded them we would never have come to
know that singularly rich and lovely land and its divided,
beset, and greatly uncomprehended people. We had been
told repeatedly that we were in for a bad time. South
Africa was united in name only. It was the home of
apartheid—to American ears a far more sinister-sounding
word than segregation. Its racial animosities and fears were
the strongest to be found anywhere. It was a land angrily
suspicious of strangers, an all but friendless nation in a
world which is wooing the emerging black man of the new
Africa. All this we heard and more.

But we went anyway, in part because South Africa did
not seem altogether alien to me although I had never been
there before. Two brothers of my Louisiana-reared father
had gone out as young mining engineers, and in my childhood and later I had heard their stories. During World
War II, I had met in North Africa some of the gallant
South African volunteers who more than offset the sorry
record of those of their fellow countrymen who were Nazi
sympathizers. Frequently since the war a variety of questioning South Africans, drawn to Mississippi principally
because of our own racial problems, had visited our home
town.

So we knew something of the good along with the bad
in what is probably the most fractionalized nation on earth.
No visit to South Africa was required to discover that its
white minority of 1,800,000 Afrikaners, who once were
called Boers—descendants of early Dutch and Huguenot
settlers—and 1,200,000 other resident whites known collectively as "English-speaking" are cleft by deep economic,
political, and religious differences. We were aware that
South Africa's 11,500,000 non-whites are compartmentalized
by law and custom into 1,400,000 mixed bloods known of-

ficially as Coloreds; 440,000 Asiatic Indians; 9,600,000 black Africans and 60,000 Malays. We knew that the black Africans were further subdivided into linguistic and tribal groups, each with a history of bloody inter-tribal hostility. We had learned that the people of this vast land, nearly a third as large as our own, had, like the South, greatly wasted its soil; that, the people, like ourselves, were now making restitution, and that the country contained great and yet undeveloped resources. Our minds were crammed with statistics about South Africa's cattle and sheep and grain and fruit, its gold, diamonds, uranium, and coal. And we were to be constantly reminded of what we had been told in advance: that South Africa is a lonely, hated, white-dominated outpost of Western civilization on a continent whose 200,000,000 blacks no longer willingly accept white overlordship.

And of these overlords, we were especially at home among the Afrikaners, the sons of the Boers, whose English is generally better than their English-speaking compatriots' Dutch. In background and behavior and outlook, the Afrikaners are more nearly like Southerners, I am certain, than are any other people anywhere on earth. They are much less reserved than their British-descended fellow citizens, quicker to offer the hand in friendship and hospitality— and quicker to close and clench the fist in anger. It was important for our understanding of their country that we did become friends with so many Afrikaners; for, principally because they outnumber their fellow whites, they will have the last say, or at least the white man's last say, in South Africa.

What we found out first of all was that the Afrikaners are as proud of their long record as fighters against odds as are the most ardent sons or daughters of the Confederacy. We talked with still vigorous old men who in their youth had fought the English in the Anglo-Boer War more than half a century ago. We listened to unforgetting women in their seventies who had survived the British concentration camps which finally broke the back of Boer resistance. One

of these militant veterans spoke for most of his generation when he answered me, in response to a question about
race relations: "Yes, I do think we get along better with the
English now." The Boers of 1900 were the outnumbered
Confederates of the 1860s. The English were the Yankees;
and, as with us, the English-Yankees still have most of the
money in the land that the Boer-Southerners run. Young
and old talked of that war as, in my youth, we talked of the
War Between the States, and of undeniable, long-ago
wrongs. Even if they did not, their politicians would no
more let them forget the old humiliations than do ours.
They spoke often too of another and tragic relationship
which has no counterpart in the South, the 200-year-old
record of warfare between white man and black. Mostly
they are certain that the present marks only an uneasy truce
and that the conflict will some day be resumed.

Like Southerners, the Afrikaners are greatly resentful of
the critic who will not see that there is anything right,
historically or otherwise, on their side. And they are quick
to tell you that South Africa is unique in Africa because
it is not a colonial possession but a nation, built by Eu-
ropean white men who settled there almost as early as did
the first Englishman in Virginia.

"The whites in the Congo can go back home to Belgium or
France," an Afrikaner professor told us. "There'll always be
an England for the African-Englishman in Africa. Most of
them think of themselves only as displaced Englishmen anyhow. But we Afrikaners have been here for 300 years. We
can't go anywhere else except as aliens and we don't want
to go anywhere else."

In much the same way that the Southerner tells his ques-
tioner that the Yankees brought the black slaves to America,
the Afrikaners' first line of defense is that his white forebears
got to South Africa before the black man did. We heard at
least a hundred times that when Van Riebeck's Dutch
pioneers arrived at the Cape in 1652 they found only the
yellow, nomadic Hottentots and the tiny Stone Age Bush-
men, neither of whom were black Africans. These relatively

few unfortunates were all but wiped out by the white man's
muskets and diseases, the womanless white man's tendency
to miscegenate, and, in time, by the black invaders from the
North. Our Afrikaner friends insisted that the real racial conflict in South Africa did not begin until about 130 years
after the first Dutch settlement. Not until about 1780 did
the white pioneers, trekking ever northward into the then
nearly empty South African hinterland, collide, 600 miles
from the Cape, with the onrushing Bantu tribes pressing
down from Central Africa. We were reminded emphatically
that in the desperate years which followed, a hundred
blacks were slain in tribal wars by fellow Africans for every
tribesman who fell before the rifles of the Voortrekkers. A
Voortrekker, more than incidentally, is one who moves forward, a pioneer. The Afrikaners can match our Daniel
Boones and Jack Seviers with giants of their own, the Retiefs
and Maritzes and Potgieters who withstood the Zulus; the
Bothas and De Wets and Smuts and Reitzes who, outnumbered more than ten to one, held off the British for nearly
four years. Of that dismal war they will relate in yet white-
hot anger that the number of Boer women and children
who died in the British concentration camps—some 38,000
—was greater than the toll of Bantus taken by the Boer
commandos in the half century of decisive struggle.

Nor did we feel at home only because of the like-as-like
hero legends and the burning memories of a lost war. The
folk similarity between Afrikaner and Southerner is all but
complete. If they are not farmers themselves, most Afrikaners are the immediate descendants of yeoman farmers or
great landholders. They are a pietistic, homogeneous Protestant people, whose Dutch Reformed Church resembled
in many and basic respects the Presbyterian Church of those
Scots-Irish pioneers who so largely settled the South. The
community church is the first building that almost every
Afrikaner wants to take you to see. Many an Afrikaner bears
a good Scots name, the legacy of an ancestral Scots minister
who came out a century and a half ago to spread the gospel
in Boer town and village and across the rolling veld. They

share the Southern clansman's respect for patriarchal authority, which from the days of Abraham has come naturally to pastoral, closely knit people. And, as does many a Southerner, though in decreasing numbers, the Afrikaner cherishes the notion that his Dutch-descended kinsmen form a nation within a nation. Like ours, too many of his politicians willfully and wickedly use that notion to keep the South African citizenry divided and to keep themselves in power. Listening to some of the extreme Afrikaner Nationalists in Parliament, I almost came to believe that the bloody shirt which Ben Butler waved in Congress during Reconstruction debate was only a palely pink garment.

But South Africans, whatever their national heritage, do not spend most of their waking hours remembering old wrongs or brooding upon present crises any more than do we. Southerners take pride in the hospitality which we like to think meets stranger as well as friend so long as the stranger is not meddlesome. But never before had we met such hospitality as was extended to us by South Africans of every racial and national and political grouping. We learned from guitar-playing professors at Stellenbosch University, the seat of Afrikaner culture, the rollicking Malay chantey "Hier kom die Alabama," which has to do with the call made at Cape Town nearly a hundred years ago by the famed Confederate raider. We found that these academic hosts knew more verses to almost every Southern song than did we. We gorged upon fantastically diverse delicacies at the day-long feasting which precedes, accompanies, and follows a Malay wedding ceremony. We were present simply because we were friends of Afrikaner friends of the bride's parents. In merriment remindful of celebrations in the old South, we danced and feasted night-long at the wedding reception for the daughter of a Western Transvaal farmer whose acreage dwarfs almost any Mississippi Delta plantation. We had tea in the homes of angrily anti-government black African professors at Cape Town University and the University College at Fort Hare, institutions whose multi-racial status was doomed last spring by the Afrikaner Nationalist Parliamentary majority. We drank the inevitable tea also with Filipino and Colored fishermen of entrancing Kalk Bay beyond Cape Town and with embittered, morose Indians in Durban and Johannesburg and elsewhere, sometimes proceeding from such gatherings to exceedingly formal evenings at Government House, the official residence of the Governor-General.

Wherever we were—in farmhouse, hunting lodge, academic hall, native hut, urban slum, suburban estate, or dominee's study, and whatever the circumstances, we almost invariably encountered friendliness that could not be mistaken. But we also sensed or were made directly aware of the white man's spirit of resistance, expressed sometimes in frustration or despair and sometimes in confidence, to any suggestion of change. In foreboding contrast we found among most of the non-white leaders a determination upon change as quickly as possible, and little willingness to compromise.

We also soon discovered that most South Africans, whatever their race or attitude, shared, as do most Southerners, a strong self-identifying affection for their beset land. I know no better interpreter of that love than a long-time friend, Thomas Chalmers Robertson, who despite his Scots name is as much an Afrikaner as any who rode with Smuts. On one memorable weekend we roved together the farmlands of the eastern Transvaal, not far from Johannesburg. It is a countryside where, as Robbie has written of it, "the landscape flattens out and the veld was once a sea of rooiegras sailed by herds of game . . . and whose old families had more in common with the rugged frontiersmen of the South than with Virginia's cavaliers."

Robbie pointed out to us century-old and older farmhouses of mud brick, counterparts of the South's log cabins. He showed us also ancient Dutch mansions as stately as any to be found in Charleston or New Orleans or Natchez. He drew for us the lesson that we were late in learning in the cotton South, relating how, after the discovery of gold and the mushrooming of the Johannesburg area, the industrial giant's demand for food resulted in merciless farming of lands that should have been kept in pasturage, so that the veld was threatened with the fate of too much of the old South's cotton land. Robbie's kinsmen are discovering what we have discovered in the South, that the beloved land cannot be dealt with harshly or foolishly.

The Afrikaners' love for their homeland, and their accompanying resentment of its critics, is responsible for another and tragi-comic resemblance to Southerners. In self-defense they pretend that they are indifferent to foreign comment, which they dismiss as the product of ignorance, malice, or the insidious doings of Communists. In reality they are greatly sensitive to such criticism; and in the long run this sensitivity can be a blessing. During our stay much of the nation was outraged when a visiting Dutch professor unwisely described South Africa's university as "super high schools," peopled largely by "asthmatic thinkers." The Afrikaners reacted similarly when students in a number of American colleges dispatched a ten-foot-long petition in behalf of the four South African universities that were still unsegregated and described apartheid as "antithetical to Christian principles." Familiar to us also was the proud listing by the South African Information Service of favorable stories written by foreign journalists. And, if the only news I read about Mississippi in the South African newspapers while we were there concerned the lynching in Poplarville, I am sure that at the same time many a Southern paper was headlining stories of racial disorders and discrimination in New York or Chicago or wherever examples of man's ill will to man can be found north of our divisive line. Next to hunting, playing the game of "You're another" is the principal sport we have in common.

In happier similarity, white South Africans pointed out to us many examples of decent human relationships that eased or contradicted the rigid racial patterns. They are not often publicized outside South Africa any more than similar Southern examples are heralded in the United States outside of the South. But they occur with probably the same frequency: the white man coming to the rescue of the drowning African; the African laborer subduing his employer's assailant; the individual or organized assistance in time of disaster; the kindly, unpublicized adaptations or departures from racial taboos, especially in the smaller communities and on the better farms; the presence of a courageous judiciary; the genuine concern of many civil servants and not a few private employers, for the improvement in health, living standards, working conditions, and wages of the Africans.

In this last may lie the germ of what can save South Africa, or at least postpone a final showdown, just as it has helped save us in the South where no such dreadful showdown as threatens South Africa is possible. As do we Southerners, white South Africans of every political hue share an almost mystical belief that greater industrialization can bring about at least amelioration of the problems of a land whose agricultural acreage cannot adequately support its black majority or its white minority. Listening to hopeful predictions of industrial growth, we could have been in any community in Mississippi, or anywhere else in the South. During an evening with such a man as Harry Goldberg, a leading Johannesburg industrialist and a principal apostle of higher wages for the African worker, we could hear our own perceptive Southern employers echoing Booker T. Washington's comment that the white man cannot keep the Negro in the ditch without staying there with him.

Few white South African dissenters advocate an absolute end to segregation or unrestricted suffrage for the three-to-one black majority. Neither would I. But the South African critics of racial injustice are much more outspoken and militant than are most of their white Southern counterparts. As with us, the dissenters are to be found principally among the clergy, the university professors and students, and the newspapermen and writers.

The clerical opponents of the status quo appear far more frequently among the numerically subordinate Roman Catholic, Anglican, and Jewish churchmen and clergy than within the Dutch Reformed Church. It is no happenstance that South Africa's most publicized feud is that waged by the Dutch-born Anglican bishop of Cape Town, the Most Reverend Joost de Blank, and Prime Minister Hendrick F. Verwoerd, likewise a Hollander by birth, who is a member of the Dutch Reformed Church and the spiritual as well as political leader of the extreme racist wing of the Nationalist party. Even so, a relatively liberal leaven seems to be at work among younger Dutch Reformed clergymen, especially those whose ministry is among Colored and African congregations. So it is with us.

Likewise, as in the South, there is a stirring of dissatisfaction among university professors and university students with prevailing majority racial attitudes. Its expression is very limited in the predominantly Afrikans Nationalist-oriented universities of Pretoria, Stellenbosch, Potchefstroom, and Orange Free State, although a significant movement of South African intellectuals in behalf of moderate adjustments, known as Sabra—for South African Bureau of Racial Affairs—draws much of its inspiration and leadership from the faculties of these institutions. Criticism of the prevailing mores is pronounced in the universities attended principally by students of non-Afrikaner descent—Cape Town, Rhodes, Natal, and Witwatersrand—which for years have enrolled non-white students. The Nationalist majority in Parliament insured last spring that these universities cannot admit non-white students much longer.

We were startled by the vigor and the openness of the criticism in these and other government-supported schools, which means all the institutions of higher learning in South Africa; all of them receive their principal financial support from the state. We were impressed by the fact that despite its obvious authoritarian and censorial tendencies, the Nationalist government has not interfered with the universities to the extent of curbing unfriendly professors. The result is that there is more academic freedom in South Africa's state-supported institutions than in similar institutions in the South.

South Africa's white-owned newspapers are divided by language, by political loyalties, and by attitudes toward the racial problems into the Afrikaner and "English-speaking" camps; but, although the latter number only forty per cent of the white population, the principal English-language newspapers have better than a three-to-one readership lead over the Afrikaner dailies. It is no secret that many Afrikaners rely primarily on these newspapers for information if not editorial guidance. The Afrikans-language papers almost unanimously support the Nationalist party's stringent segregation policies. Some of them, like some of our all-out segregationist papers in the South, are brilliantly edited. The English-language papers are likewise partisan, much more so than are the so-called moderate or liberal Southern papers. None of our own newspapers would go this far in attacking white traditions as do some of theirs. Additionally there are a handful of weekly or monthly publications, without parallel in the South, which forthrightly champion the black man's quest for full and equal citizenship. Among them are the highly readable *Drum,* a picture and text magazine primarily for non-whites, and *Contact,* a belligerently crusading bimonthly review.

The South can match South Africa's roster of writers of protest literature of whom Alan Paton, Nadine Gordimer, and Harry Bloom are best known in our country. Like them, Southern authors have found far wider and friendlier acceptance beyond their borders than within them. But the South African writers have proportionately a larger and more sympathetic readership among their fellow white South Africans than, for instance, William Faulkner, Tennessee Williams, and Elizabeth Spencer find in their native Mississippi. There are probably more book stores in Johannesburg than in all Mississippi.

This singling out of the clergy, university professors and students, the newspapers and the creative writers is unfair to the sizable minority outside these ranks which does not go along with the excessive racism of the Nationalist party's program and political techniques. Many Afrikaners themselves can be found in the United party, the coalition formed by moderate Boer and English-descended leaders after union and from which a liberal wing has recently split to form a "Progressive" party. These and other groups and individuals provide, to a far greater degree than is the case in the South, persistent if frustrated opposition to one-party rule and immoderate racial policies.

Often it seemed to us as if time and place had gone awry in South Africa and that we were living simultaneously in the South of Reconstruction, the South of my childhood, and the South of only yesterday or today.

The South's answer to emancipation was a different kind of subjugation. We imposed, by state law, regional custom, threat, and indifference, a rigid segregation and an accompanying discrimination in education, civil rights, and employment. South Africa has written her discriminatory practices into the law of an entire nation, not just a policy in force in one fourth of the country against the national will, as with us. Under the laws of South Africa, black Africans cannot obtain, save in rare instances, an education comparable to that of a white student, although South Africa does afford a better opportunity for secondary education for its black people than does any other country or colony in Africa. South African law bars the black man from the best jobs. Not unexpectedly, the income of the white South African is seventeen times that of the black man. Nevertheless, there is an excess labor supply, much of it flowing in from outside South Africa's borders. Black men wait for jobs in the gold mines which pay in addition to food and compound lodging forty-two cents a day. South Africa's system of residential and occupational passes and other onerous restrictions upon the African's movements are little different from the Black Codes with which the fearful South of Reconstruction enmeshed the Negro freedman. Time and again Africans with whom I talked, the educated and the illiterate alike, placed the pass system, and the too frequent police brutality which accompanies it, above low wages as their principal complaint.

As among the Southern whites of Reconstruction, South Africa's whites are gravely concerned over the continuing threat and frequent incidence of African violence. Similarly, many appear relatively indifferent to the economic and social reasons for such violence. When it occurs, whether in infrequent mass outbreaks or frequent gang lawlessness and individual offenses, the police crackdowns are severe indeed. The average South African constable is as rough on the black man as is any Southern marshal; and in respect to police surveillance of the African, South Africa is certainly a police state. But, as in the South, public opinion, publicity, and the judiciary are increasingly a deterrent to police excesses.

Public opinion is becoming effective in another area of white-black relationships, reminiscent also of the South of a half century ago. While we were in South Africa, numerous newspaper exposés of peonage and the abuse of convict laborers on farms and other exploitations of the fantastically underpaid African farm workers shocked many English-speaking and Afrikaner whites alike. Under similar circumstances Mississippi was moved fifty years ago to outlaw the leasing of convict labor to cotton planters.

In most of the South until World War II and in parts of it today the Negro has been disfranchised through legal devices, economic pressures, and even the threat or the actuality of violence. But while the Southern Negro is entering the voting booth in ever-mounting numbers, the Nationalist government is taking away what few political rights non-white South Africans once enjoyed. Throughout my life I have heard other Southerners say, most of them believing it, that such political and economic subjugation was needful to save the white man from drowning in a black sea. This is precisely what the white man in South Africa says today. He defends and attacks in phrases identical to our own; white South Africans of moderate or liberal racial

views are derisively labeled "Kaffir boetjies," which simply
means "nigger lover." We were asked time and again as
at home the rhetorical question, "You wouldn't want your
daughter to marry a kaffir, would you?" As at home we
listened time and again also to fundamentalist interpretation of the Bible as evidence that the black man is forever
ordained to be a subservient, inferior being, a hewer of wood
and drawer of water in eternal atonement for his shortcom-
ings.

South Africa's political demagogues rival our own. They
have certain advantages. The Southern spellbinder has only
Yankees, nigger lovers, Reds, and federal interference to go
after. The Afrikaner Nationalist politicians can set up a far
greater number of targets: Great Britain and the English-
speaking South Africans, the Coloreds, black South Africans
and black Africans, the United Nations, Communists, Anglican church leaders, English-language newspapers, and
occasionally the United States. As with us, these rabble-
rousers find their most wholehearted disciples among the
lower-income whites; but in a curious and heartening parallel to the South, little anti-Semitism can be found among
them, even though a considerable number were pro-German
during the war. To the contrary, South Africa sent supplies
of various kinds to Israel during its war with the Arab world.

In and out of Parliament, political hucksters and men who
are not hucksters speak and talk of a solution which has
been advanced in the South for more than a century and a
half. Thomas Jefferson and Abraham Lincoln alike proposed
the resettlement of Negro freedmen far from the United
States. Today the Nationalist government of South Africa
is creating so-called Bantustans, political entities which will
have a modicum of self-government, designed to set the
black man apart in education, culture, political activity,
and in every other way save where his labor is required on
the farms and in the cities and mines.

Yet even while we felt so completely at home, we were
aware of the sadly, meaningful differences. As one of our

Afrikaner friends said perceptively, South Africa is made up of several nations with a common boundary, each mistrustful of the other. Neither the resisting white South nor the protesting Southern Negro feels alien in the United States. Even in the worst pockets of oppression in the South, the Negro remains an American with no thought of turning upon his country; the least advanced Negro is identifiable as a citizen of the United States. The South is an indissoluble and important section of the most powerful and predominantly white nation in the world. But in South Africa, 3,000,000 isolated whites seek to preserve nationhood and culture and racial identity on a continent that counts 200,000,000 militant Africans whose unity is based on color and not nationhood. The Southern Negro moves forward, however slowly. In South Africa he has been spun around, if ever in fact he once faced the sun.

If any of this should make us feel more virtuous than the whites of South Africa, we might ask ourselves one question. How would a majority of the 162,000,000 white Americans react if the 18,000,000 American Negroes became more than 500,000,000 multi-tribal, culturally disparate, and long-exploited people pressing suffocatingly upon the driver's seat. The whites of South Africa think that they know what our answer would be. When they told it to us, endlessly, we never felt more at home.

PART III

Hunting Is for Fun

17

WE HUNTED WITHOUT GUNS IN THE BUSHVELD
1960

I am not certain just where and when the story of our family's week of camera-hunting in South Africa's Kruger National Park should properly begin. In a literal sense it starts late on a South African winter afternoon in June—that's right—when we and South African friends drove through the gates at Malelane, the southwest entrance to the park, in two automobiles, and we Americans, being tenderfeet, yelled in near unison, "Zebras," as if the three striped, timorous grazers were indeed something to see.

If this is inappropriately sudden, I could go back five months to an evening in our home in Greenville, Mississippi. There our South African guests, Jan and Susan Moolman of Pretoria, easily persuaded us that our forthcoming trip to their vast and beautiful country on an exchange program would be incomplete without such a holiday, and promised to be our guides. Again, in a hauntingly real and personal sense, I could begin with the long-ago time when as a Southern youngster I read *Jock of the Bushveld,* Sir Percy Fitzpatrick's classic tale of hunters and game and a courageous mongrel named Jock in a never-never land of dangerous adventure. Or to give credit where it is due, I could tell first of Paul Kruger, the last President of the Boer Republic, who in 1884 first recommended to his lawmakers that the government protect the decimated wildlife of the Transvaal from mass, indiscriminate slaughter by white and African hunters. The reserve was finally proclaimed in 1898 —or the first 1800 square miles of it—just ahead of the Anglo-Boer War; and Paul Kruger, the doughty old Voortrekker, lived to see the British conqueror resume in 1902 the visionary undertaking that the one-sided conflict had interrupted.

Or I might begin with the lioness and the wildebeeste, but that might not be believed so early. . . .

We added up to quite a safari. There were Jan and Susan Moolman and Bernard and Jan Hendrik, their two sons, small, observant veterans of former excursions. There were two of our sons, Philip, nineteen, and Tommy, fourteen, who were sharing the experiences of four months in South Africa. And there was Hans Knopf, the versatile American photographer, whom the *Saturday Evening Post*—having much experience with amateur picture takers—had dispatched from France to backstop us.

Most definitely this was an expedition which had no intention of living off the land. The Boer pioneers, whose descendants call themselves Afrikaners, had a reputation for hearty eating, and Jan and Susan were their unmistakable heirs. In boxes and jars, in tins and vacuum containers and ice chests, we carried what seemed to be a ton of assorted Afrikaner delicacies which must have taken Susan and her servants a good week to prepare against our coming, and enough accompanying staples to have protracted the siege of Vicksburg another month: babootie, a conglomerate of minced lamb, onions, egg, milk, and curry powder, which Malay slaves and political prisoners concocted when first they came unwillingly to South Africa 200 years ago; yards of homemade boerwors, the spiced beef and pork sausage without which no Afrikaner breakfast is complete; a cracker tin full of rusks, turned out in the Moolman kitchen to a great-grandmother's recipe; several jars of insidious, honey-soaked shortcake called koeksisters; slabs of mutton for the making of sasarties, the South African equivalent of shish kebob; boxes and hampers of vegetables and fruit, and much else—food exotic and food familiar, food enough to last a month, I thought and wrongly. And cooking utensils, a minimum of personal luggage, and cameras, cameras, cameras, but not a weapon except a pocket knife did we carry to a homeland of lions and leopards and elephants and hippopotamuses.

It is a temptation to dwell overlong on the six-hour drive eastward from clean, bustling Pretoria, co-capital with Cape Town of South Africa, to the park, from the 5000-foot plateau of the Highveld to the escarpment of the Berg that descends into a lush valley between Highveld and Low. Here in the shadow of the mountains grow in abundance and in infinite variety much of South Africa's subtropical fruit and vegetables: oranges and bananas, pineapples, lemons, pawpaws and kumquats, tomatoes and avocados to be had, freshly picked, at innumerable highway stands in a wintertime which is like Mississippi's late spring. Bordering the fields and highways rise red and yellow and pink poinsettia trees, acacia and eucalyptus, lombardy poplar and cypress, green against the purple mountain backdrop; and walking or resting beneath them, sometimes against the incongruous background of a drive-in movie, Mapogga tribesmen who still prefer leg and neck bangles and clay-dyed blankets to our prosaic garb. . . .

But this is about a game reserve and not the approaches to it. The Bushveld country in which the park itself is mostly situated is not as appealing to the eye. Most of its trees appear stunted and, in wintertime, drab. Above the thorn trees and mimosa bushes, the tall buffalo grass and the green and gold reeds of the little rivers, protrude forbidding outcroppings of stone and desolate little hills called kopjes. Here and there the surface is deeply scarred with dongas, the handiwork of erosion. But it is oddly appealing and greatly suited to the requirements of the creatures who populate it; and if it is least attractive in wintertime, it is far more acceptable then to the visitor, for in the relatively denuded scrub it is easier to spot game.

We were late in reaching Malelane, one of the park's six entry points, thirty-eight miles from Skukuza Rest Camp, where we were to spend our first three days, for we had tarried too long on the way to picnic and take pictures. It is one of the few and sensible rules of Kruger Park that visitors be inside the gates, not only of the entrances but of the rest camps themselves, by nightfall—5:30 P.M. from April to August and 6:30 from September to March—and we avoided only by seconds the payment of fines. It is not that human beings will be in danger after dark that prompts this regulation as much as it is the threat that automobiles at night pose for the animals themselves.

We were familiar with all the rules before we reached Kruger. We could not alight from our automobiles anywhere else than in a rest camp nor drive elsewhere than on an authorized automobile trail and at a speed no greater than twenty-five miles an hour. We were not to feed or disturb any form of wildlife or deface any plant or tree, or scribble our names on any object in the park. We must not toss any matches or cigarette butts in any place that could be set afire. Pets were taboo.

The area for which these rules were laid down is so large that we could not cover more than half of it in our week; and there was much about the park and its inhabitants that we could not have learned in many weeks more. But we did find out enough about the region itself to make us properly awed before and during our expedition.

The reserve occupies the extreme northeastern corner of South Africa, with Portugal's Mozambique as its eastern limits and Southern Rhodesia to the north. Its 4,300,000 wilderness acres are contained within boundaries that are some 200 miles long with an average width of forty miles; and man has touched it skillfully but lightly in converting wilderness to the world's largest wildlife sanctuary. Fourteen immaculately maintained rest camps accommodate most of the 120,000 visitors who explore Kruger each year, the others setting up tents in prescribed areas. Some of the rest camps are primitive, some offer surprisingly civilized facilities; almost every cottage is a counterpart of the beehive-shaped rondavels, the traditional huts of the South African natives, and they range from family size "self-contained" rondavels—meaning interior plumbing—to huts for two campers. Each camp and tent campsite is provided with running water and outdoor, communal cook stoves, protected by grass-thatched roofs. Each has a multitude of native attendants to keep the fires going and the cottages tidy. Beyond their confines, civilization ends; all else is a tangle of thorn tree and bush and tall grass, haven for the widest variety of wildlife under protection anywhere on any continent.

Our family has camped and sailed and hunted together ever since my oldest boy was born. But never had any of us experienced nor were we prepared to experience what we found almost from the moment when, after the small preliminaries of registering and paying the modest camp fees at Malelane gate, we five American newcomers and our experienced South African companions drove through the bush to Skukuza. From then on we would change some of the occupants of our automobiles each half day, almost always managing to keep at least one quick-eyed Moolman among us outlanders.

It took less than a day for us to become selective hunters of big game, mentally and audibly discarding the prolific, high-jumping little impalas and the plentiful zebras and baboons and even the giraffes in favor of the hoped-for and evasive lion and elephant and sportive hippopotamus. But nothing later on—or almost nothing—could rival that first moment of goggle-eyed, unbelieving discovery just inside Malelane gate when a small, mixed company of zebras and blue-black wildebeeste, bearded and hump-backed, galloped away from us in near-military formation. At the gate, each of us had put up a shilling for a pool which would go to whoever saw the first animal. When Susan won, Jan said it was only because she was raised a farm girl; but I know that at least part of the reason she bested us Americans was that we were distracted by the huge ant hills and fallen trees, uprooted by elephants, and the topsy-turvy feeling which Tommy best expressed sometime later: "The people are in the cages and the animals are free."

It was dark when we reached our quarters at Skukuza Camp. Here was the red-carpet treatment indeed, two family-size rondavels connected by a breezeway, for the Moolmans and my wife and me, and a smaller rondavel not far away for Hans, Phil, and Tommy, together with a cook shack and outdoor fireplace where our special attendant, a generally silent, efficient man named Joel, had the fires going; and when we went to bed two hours later it was with the beams of the full, golden African moon in our eyes and in our ears the mournful protest of a nearby hyena.

Looking through my notebook I find that I kept an overly detailed and wondering account of everything we saw in the bush that first day, beginning at 5:30 when we waited with other early risers for the gate to open. The tame impala and the guinea fowl which skittered about us as we drank coffee and ate rusks, hunger stoppers until the midmorning breakfast when we would return from the first hunt. . . . That later breakfast itself, the biggest I had ever eaten: flaxed wheat with honey and milk, papayas and pineapples, mealie meal, almost the equivalent of our Southern grits, scrambled eggs, bacon, boerwors and fried potatoes. . . . The three baboons who greeted us surlily from a roadside ledge just beyond the camp gate and the little gray duiker drinking from the first little river we crossed. . . . Our first small herd of impala and sulking near them an outcast old buck, kept at a distance by the younger males. We must have asked Jan and Susan a thousand questions and we accepted their answers as coming from oracles. "It is like hunting," Jan warned as we started out. "There are good days and bad, so don't be disappointed if we don't get much today." But it wasn't *like* hunting, it *was* hunting, two automobile loads of hunters shooting with cameras at everything we saw. It would likely rain that day, Jan had added as we set out, and if only a little rain fell it would not be bad; but if it rained heavily, the game would scatter from the river banks and established water holes from which the animals did not wander very far in the dry period. And it did rain more than a little, though not greatly, that first drizzly morning. We were mildly disappointed, so quickly did we become all but indifferent to "only impala" and "just baboons" and "more zebra and wildebeeste" when movement in the bush turned out not to be some magnificent rarity. Even so, we shot everything we saw, and I marveled at how quickly our youngsters and even ourselves learned to detect motion and with the coaching of the Moolmans to identify quickly what we discovered.

At the day's end we felt better. In our afternoon bag we could count three tremendous kudus, corkscrew-horned and taller at the forehead than a six-foot man. Some jackals had slunk across our path, the only animals Jan expressed a wish to shoot, for they are cunning scourges of sheep farms. We saw, though at some distance, five giraffes, three and then two, the last engaged in a comical wrestling match, mostly with their necks, and whether in sport or in anger, we couldn't tell. An anteater had faced us from atop an ant hill. We had laughed at our first wart hogs, the ugliest creatures in all Africa, with mean tusks and fleshy projections like great warts jutting out below their eyes, and the side-splitting habit of holding their tuft-tipped, longish tails straight up like flagpoles when they run. For an hour we had stalked a marshy lion pan, a reed-lined, spring-fed catchment for water, after hearing from other hunters that a lion and a lioness had been seen there earlier in the day; but all we saw was a herd of wildebeeste coming down to drink, the bulls shielding and turning the cows on the way to the pan. And so home to another gargantuan meal of lamb chops and sasarties grilled out-of-doors over the open fire, the omnipresent boerwors, with baked potatoes and fresh green beans cooked with onions on the side, and fruit and koeksisters to top it all off. Afterward we shopped in the camp store's fine gift shop, where our boys acquired a three-foot, carved

giraffe, some native figures in ebony, a tribal mask, a circular rug of six springbok skins, a silver fox robe called
a kaross, a ceremonial drum, all seeming amazingly cheap
to us. But after they had finished, my wife and I settled on
a couple of dozen postcards.

We were in luck later that night. Warden and Mrs. Steyn
dropped in on us and we kept them for longer than they
must have planned to stay. Warden Steyn, his beard white
and trim, has served at Kruger for twenty-nine years and
his is the biggest job of its kind anywhere. Under him is
what we thought a very small force when he told us—
three regional wardens, twelve white rangers, and 150 native
rangers. His job, he said, is a matter of control—control
over white and native poachers and of careless visitors and
over nature which cannot always maintain a perfect balance
within artificial boundaries, however wide. He told us of a
warden who had stabbed a lion to death as it dragged
him by the shoulder through the bush, and of other wardens
not so fortunate; and of an incredible lack of casualties
among visitors, though some had been mauled or shaken
up. And we learned that of all the animals in Kruger we
should give the widest berth to the water buffalo and the
unpredictable elephant. Before the Steyns said goodnight,
Warden Steyn promised to assign to us the next day an
African ranger who would take us to an area temporarily
closed to visitors. He was sure that there we would find
some lions and elephants.

After they left, the boys went to bed and the grownups
added up the day's gains. Under the tutelage of Bernard
and Jan Hendrik, Tommy had improved his knowledge of
Afrikans, to the extent of five stanzas of "Jan Pieterwiet,"
an Afrikaner folk song with the same tune as that of our
"Pretty Foot." Bernard and Jan Hendrik had likewise improved their English or at least some Mississippi slang
variants thereof; Phil his photography under Hans' direction,
and the rest of us our bush lore and, we agreed, our dis-
positions. For two days we had read no newspapers, listened
to no radios, heard no phones jangle.

"That was a great supper and everything," Tommy said as he took to bed. "I feel all relaxed and no part of me is specially itchy," an observation which made us realize that not a chigger or mosquito or fly had bothered us all day. Nor would they.

Tomorrow we would find our lion. Surely the native warden would oblige.

He was waiting for us the next morning when we came out of our huts, a cheerful giant of a man, neat in khaki shorts, bush jacket, and bush hat. He said his name was Judas—later that morning Philip tagged our automobile Judas' Chariot—and he answered "yes" to every question. But despite Judas, Friday was not a good day. That may seem an overstatement when I add that we followed for fifteen minutes a herd of perhaps 500 wildebeeste who fled from a water hole as we approached; and saw literally thousands of frolicking impalas, zebras by the hundreds, and many wart hogs and giraffes. Elephants had been around not long before. Three times we had to skirt newly uprooted trees lying across the trail; and at a water hole formed by a dam across a small, nearly dry river, where under Judas' watchful eye we got out of our automobiles, he pointed out to us the spore of buffalo and leopard. The boys questioned him continuously.

"You ever kill lion, Judas?"

"Yes." (laugh)

"He scare you, Judas?"

"Yes." (laugh)

"Which animal is baas?"

"Buffalo. He too much strong. Take five lions kill buffalo."

"You know we American, Judas?"

"America? Must find lion." (laugh)

Once that day, rounding a bend in the trail, we came upon a startlingly solitary figure, a wiry African ranger, patrolling on foot with a Lee-Mitford .303 slung over his shoulder and an oversize hunting knife and club at his belt. He and Judas conversed in Shangaans and when they had finished Judas turned to us, shaking his head.

"Not much lion." (laugh)

All day we hunted along the western border of the reserve. Jan's car mired temporarily on the steep bankside of a shallow river and we all had to pile out and push, nervously wondering if we would find our lions when we didn't want to. But never a sign of big game. I don't know who felt the worst about it all, Jan and Susan or Judas, as if it were the fault of any of them.

But that night after supper we walked in the near dazzling moonlight on the banks above the Mutshidaka River where it forms the southern border of Skukuza, and there we came upon a spectacle which made us forget the disappointments of the day. Crowded along a small wire fence on the low bluff above the river were some fifty chattering, gesticulating Afrikaner schoolchildren, some of them directing flashlights upon the river almost directly below us and perhaps 200 feet away. In the light of the moon and incandescent torches we saw three shiny black hippopotamuses, their yawning mouths wide enough to swallow any two of us, wallowing, submerging, and rising again unconcernedly. The blond-haired children, the hippos, the dark river in the moonlight. . . . "It's just not true," Betty said.

Jan and Susan were less impressed. I think they felt their nation's honor was at stake. "Tomorrow we'll get our lion," Susan said.

And tomorrow we did.

Susan had suggested that we again try the lion pan, some eighteen miles from camp. Someone had told her that despite the showers it was very dry in that section. Animals would be coming there to drink, and where there were thirsty animals, lions shouldn't be far away. We should get there sometime between eleven and twelve.

But Susan didn't get to go. Jan Hendrik came down with a high but short-lasting fever, and she stayed in camp with him. And the rest of us almost didn't make it to the pan in time. A few miles away from it we came upon a pack of baboons congregated in the road, scowling fathers, nerv-

ous mothers, and their inquisitive, almost unafraid young,
all of them fascinating caricatures of human beings. They
were too irresistible to pass by. We parked on the side of
the road. The little fellows swarmed over our cars, the parents prowled warningly near, and Hans and Philip took
picture after picture. After fifteen minutes of exchanging
pleasantries with the baboons, we moved on, and lucky
for us that we did.

When we turned off the road and drove to the lion pan,
we found about twenty cars already there, parked closely
together and leaving little choice for us. We asked the
first carload we came to whether anything was going on.
"Daar ess n' leeu in die gras," somebody answered in
Afrikans. "A lion is in the grass." He pointed to the far
bank of the pan, 300 feet from us.

We became panicky then, for so crowded was the park-
ing area that we were afraid we would have to line up behind the front rankers. Hans, Philip, and Tommy were in
one car, Betty, Jan, young Bernard, and I in the other.
Jan, who was driving, spotted a narrow space and wedged
into it. Philip began jockeying for another.

I think I was the last person in either car to detect the
head that was raised now and then in the grass beyond
the rushes on the far bank, high enough to see but apparently
not to be seen by the thirsty assortment of animals who,
upwind of what turned out to be lioness instead of lion,
were moving cautiously and nervously toward the pan. There
seemed to be more than a hundred wildebeeste, as many
zebras, and perhaps a dozen giraffes; and among them there
may have been other and smaller creatures which I did not
notice, and all only vaguely aware, if at all, of what lay in
predatory wait. If they were aware, their thirst was about to
conquer their fear.

It took me an eternity to make out the lioness. I looked at
my watch. It was 11:20. Near us Philip was trying to enter
a satisfactory place. In the split second when my eyes lifted
from my watch to the far bank, the lioness came up out of
the grass and streaked toward the heterogeneous herd that

now milled at the water side; and at almost the same moment the wildebeeste and zebras and giraffes stampeded. In the dust raised by their frantic hoofs, hunter and hunted were briefly obscured; and then, as the dust began to settle, we could see that two luckless wildebeeste had veered away from the rest, or perhaps had been cut out by the lioness herself, and she was after them. It was all over almost before we could draw our breaths. The lioness leaped a good fifteen feet onto the back of the nearer of the two. Her head hid the neck of the wildebeeste and they went down in a thrashing tangle.

Almost in my line of vision Hans had jumped out of the other car and scrambled atop it and was shooting pictures madly, meanwhile shouting what may have been directions to the lioness and the wildebeeste. Phil was leaning out of their car and likewise taking pictures and Tommy was shouting, and though they were very near us I could hardly hear him above the excited cacophony, the rumbling all about us of voices that rose almost to a roar; and somehow out of it the voice of what must have been a cultivated and distracted Englishwoman giving pitying commentary on the unequal contest. "The poor thing is trying to fight . . . it may get away, it's trying . . . oh no, it can't." In the bright sunlight the survivors were disappearing into the dun of the bush. The dust settled and we could see in the grass beyond the green rushes a movement that was not the wind's doing, as the lioness dragged the dead wildebeeste out of sight. We saw nothing move for a while, not even a rustling of the grass.

I looked around. A young warden was telling Hans to get down, apologetically notifying him of the fine for leaving an automobile. Hans kept nodding and taking pictures. Two or three others were likewise caught. We luckier ones laughed. The spell was broken. In a few minutes the lioness rose to her full height. Then she sank to the ground and we did not see her again that day.

We waited for the next act. It wasn't long in coming. Ten minutes later the scattered herds began returning to

the pan, first the giraffes, next the zebras and the wildebeeste. They did not drink at once nor for long, nuzzling
the water only fleetingly instead, then breaking for cover
and returning hesitantly again. Finally they began drinking in earnest, undisturbed. On our side and downwind
from the hidden lioness across the water, a pair of kudus
picked their way toward the pan, sniffing at the scent that
could mean death, and then broke and leaped away in
beautiful unison. Soon thereafter the last of the drinkers
had vanished again into the bush. Again on our side another
file of wildebeeste approached from the north and lumbered
to within fifty feet of the pan. Then as if at a single command they turned and fled. Save for us humans and the
hidden lioness and the dead wildebeeste, the lion pan was
deserted. Once more I looked at my watch. It was 11:55.
The lioness had made her kill only thirty minutes before. In
another half hour we drove away. Our expedition was now
undoubtedly a success. I think we all felt a little sad.

But our hunting day was only half over. After lunch we
roamed the trails for another four hours, our minds and our
conversations so much on the noon-time drama that we
were unimpressed by the biggest herd of impala yet, by
the group of giraffes which at one point blocked the road
as if posing obligingly for a picture, or by our first and only
sable antelope, its scimitar-curved horns the finest of them
all. But near the close of day, returning to camp just ahead
of the long dusk, we saw what incredulous wardens and
campers were to tell us that night was just about the most
unusual sight, if not the most exciting, we could expect in
Kruger Park. As we drove over the crest of a slight rise not
six miles from camp, a leopardess and her cub confronted
us in the middle of the road. We stopped. They stopped.
We stared at each other for a few moments and then
mother and offspring seemed to fade into the gathering
haze. One warden told us that not in his seventeen years
in the reserve had he ever seen a cub in company of its
mother; for the leopard young are almost invariably hidden

in a cave or log or some other secure place before the parents set out in search of food.

At noon the next day, which was a Sunday, the Moolmans took leave of us. Jan had to return to his business. But we confident, four-day veterans still had nearly four more days to go. After our Saturday bag, these could not help but be anti-climactical, as full of surprises and fun and new game as they proved to be.

On Sunday afternoon we saw almost certainly the same lioness and were so assured by our young warden of the day before. She was drowsing in the grass, some three miles above the pan where she had brought down the wildebeeste and on the other side of the road. If she were not the same one, she was another whose belly had been filled. We waited two hours for her to move from where she stretched, as if in a stupor, Hans with his infinite patience seeking a perfect sequence. As we watched, a zebra came up behind and upwind from the lion and stood within ten feet of her. She only raised her head to look at him indifferently, having no urge to kill when she was full, and after a while the zebra strolled away. As we waited and watched, other automobiles began lining the road; and when the lioness finally rose and decided to cross, probably to return to the pan for water, a column of perhaps thirty automobiles, driving close together, kept pace with her as she loped lazily seeking a clear place in the road. Finally she began running in exasperation plain to see and crossed a mile farther down, just ahead of our automobile.

We were to visit four more camps before we left Kruger. At each of them, Olifants, Leteba, Orpen, and Satara, we were to add much to our bag, tenderfeet though we still were. We found our elephants the day before we left Kruger, a small herd, and they performed for us in fine style, uprooting several trees to get at the roots and the tender topmost branches, and ambling toward us afterward so fast that my wife was certain we would be overtaken and our car and ourselves battered to bits. But they were in good humor. At Olifants River, under guard of a native rifleman, we were permitted to go down to the hippopotamus pool. It was as if the gigantic bathers were waiting for us.

As the South Africans say, everything was laid on for us by nature and man, the full moon, the blanket-cool nights and the clear bright days, the food which still tasted good even after all the Moolmans' bounty had been eaten up, the friends we made in the camps, swapping hunting stories in which never an antelope bit the dust, and swapping recipes, too; and of the latter, nothing could have been more improbable than we Mississippians, whose Dutch was far scantier than our camp neighbors' English, swapping with a family of Hollanders a recipe for Seafood Gumbo for another for Scotch Cow, a hash of beef, sprouts, and potatoes, on a South African evening. Early on our last morning, when we halted by the Nwanetze River, the crocodiles obliged to our entire satisfaction, even though the native warden there said apologetically that if we would wait until nine o'clock there would be "too much crocodile." Also on our last day we saw our first waterbucks, their rumps ludicrously ringed with an outside white circle from which dangled an overly thin, tasseled tail. In those last days we began paying more attention to the birds of Kruger Park, so exotic to us in their own right that we wished they had a park of their own for us to visit. We saw many ostrich, though most of them at a distance, and a variety of guinea fowl and francolin and partridge which, more than the animals, made me wish Kruger did not have a ban on shooting. Always the little starlings and the turtle doves were holding conventions in the road. We sighted at least three different species of eagles and herons aplenty; but only occasionally were we really distracted by them for we had not come to hunt birds. And from the first day to the last we were spoiled by a succession of houseboys, though we never quite got used to their ministrations; Mister and Fernand and Petrus and others, all romper clad and as quiet and smilingly efficient as had been Joel of Skukuza, they swept not only our rondavels but the bare earth around them, and made our beds and built our fires and washed our pots and pans.

We left Kruger by the Malopena gate, 120 miles north of Malelane where we had entered. For another two days we relaxed near the mountain-girt, Sabie Bungalow resort in the magnificent lodge of Charles Engelhart, the American developer and investor in South Africa's future, a man of great hospitality who was away from South Africa at the time but who had offered his paradise to us through South African associates. But that is another story.

Tommy's sleepy evaluation of Kruger's inhabitants that first night at Sabie was brief and to the point. "I'd rather be a lion in Kruger Park than anything I know," he said. As for me, I'd rather be a member of a family which had gone camera hunting for lions and leopards and lesser prey in Kruger Park than any vacationer I know. I hope it doesn't sound fatuous to say that a good part of our fun came from our learning something—so many things—as we went along. Certainly we Americans learned from our South African friends and chance acquaintances, from guide books and from our own observations more about a greater variety of wild animals in eight days than in the sum total of our several lifetimes before our visit. And, perhaps most unexpectedly of all, my boys and I learned that it can be as much fun and perhaps even more to hunt without guns than with them.

18

MY SON SHOT HIMSELF WHILE HUNTING
1959

Ten years ago, when my son Philip was nine, I wrote, for an outdoor magazine the story of his first hunt, a proudly paternal bit of boasting about how he shot three mallards and acquitted himself in general like a veteran.

The story I am writing now might have been that of his last one. In it there is little to boast of save his and his older brother's stamina, the perseverance of the friend who was with us, and the skill of the doctors who saved his badly shattered right foot and possibly his life. What happened between the time a soft-nosed .30-.30 slug drove bone and flesh through his boot sole and our arrival with him at the General Hospital in Greenville, our home town, two and a half hours later is a nightmare of good luck and bad, and of things done well and done badly or not at all which will long haunt me.

This was to have been the hunt on which Phil would get his first buck. He, his older brother, a twenty-three-year old Marine lieutenant—which is important here—and I were the guests of my friend Jesse Brent at the Ashbrook Hunting Club as we had been every Christmas holiday for several years past. The year before, Phil had scored a near miss, and the penalty was the cutting off his red hunting shirttail, just below the neckband, the hitch being that the shirt happened to be one of my best.

The club takes its name from a vast, heavily wooded island in the Mississippi River, some twenty miles above Greenville, formed when the United States Engineers straightened out a number of tortuous bends in the river twenty-five years ago by creating new channels. Ashbrook lies between one such channel and the old river bed, beginning at their point of separation at the northern tip and extending south some eight miles to their joining.

Ashbrook is a hunter's paradise, abounding in deer and duck, squirrel and turkey and wild hogs, but it is difficult of access. Some of the members fly light planes which they land trickily on sand bars. The usual procedure is to drive north from Greenville to an abandoned landing on the east bank of the Mississippi, five or six miles below and across from the island and from there go by outboard to Ashbrook. During the deer hunting season the club keeps horses and several jeeps on the island, the only transportation that can cope with the forest and the old logging trails; and even these trails are all but impassable in wet weather.

On the morning of December 29th, my two sons, my friend Jesse, another hunting companion, Dr. Joe Walker, a Greenville dentist, and I set out from the clubhouse by jeep long before daylight to take our stands a half mile or so apart in an area about six trail miles from the club. Widely scattered elsewhere on the island would be some fifteen other hunters who, like ourselves, would wait, as immovable as possible after our manner of hunting, while riders and hounds harried the deer through the sodden wilderness.

As our party jolted and skidded along the trail we joked about Phil's failure to bring down his deer a year ago, and the shirttail penalty which I unwittingly paid in his behalf. Just before we let Phil off in the vicinity of his stand, Jesse suggested that he and Phil swap weapons. His rifle, a .30-.30 hammer-action repeating carbine, not only was equipped with a telescopic sight but had claimed a deer each season for the past six years. Philip was carrying a 12-gauge pump with rifled slugs, which is what most of us use in our dense woods.

So they exchanged. Phil had never handled a hammer-action before but he was familiar with almost every other kind of firearm. We thought nothing of it. After all, he had been hunting for ten years.

Forty-five minutes and four miles from camp we let Jesse

off. Fifteen minutes later Joe Walker, who was driving, let me off and he and Hod continued on. It had been agreed beforehand that they would leave the jeep another mile down the trail where we would rendezvous at noon. It was about six o'clock in the morning and still pitch dark though only a half hour until daylight. I didn't have a second thought about Phil and the unfamiliar carbine. I hoped only that it would bring him luck.

None of us had that kind of luck. Does and fawns I saw a-plenty; but this wasn't to be our day. None of us in our zone shot at all that morning—not until eleven o'clock. Two or three times a few hounds ambled by me, following what must have been old scents; and once a rider galloped past about fifty yards away. Throughout the morning I could hear the hallooing of riders, the fluting of their horns, and the yelping of the dogs; and now and then distant shots which indicated that others were having better luck than ourselves.

I knew the shot which I heard at eleven had been fired by Philip. It was unmistakably a rifle shot and from the direction where Philip would be, but there followed neither a second shot nor a shout for assistance. He's missed again, the unlucky kid, I thought; and that wouldn't help anyone but hunting-shirt dealers.

At about quarter of twelve Joe Walker came by my stand and we walked together to the rendezvous. Young Hod had beaten us there by a few minutes. Now it was noon and Phil would be along any minute. We lounged around, talking about the great numbers of does and fawns and the scarcity of buck in our neck of the woods.

We began shouting for Phil at 12:15 or so and by 12:30 I was beginning to get irritated with my second son. It was a camp rule to end the morning hunt by noon and for all hunters to be in camp by one. "Phil should have been back at the jeep on time like the rest of us," I fumed. Then Joe Walker and I recalled that Phil had said something offhand about walking back to camp before noon if he hadn't had any luck. That is probably what he had done, we told ourselves, specially since he'd undoubtedly missed his one shot.

"We might as well go on in," I said. "He's there and eating by now." But Hod dissuaded us. "Not Phil," he said. "I can't see him walking through these woods in the mud. He's probably asleep under a tree." We shouted some more.

Joe and Hod were facing in another direction, calling out at intervals, when I heard Phil. "Come help me! Come!" I thought I heard him call "I've shot a deer." He sounded a long way away. I told Hod and Joe that I'd thought I'd heard him call something like "Help me" again. Hod bellowed, "Yes, we know—we're coming."

The three of us began walking eastward, in the direction of Phil's voice, our progress slowed by the tangle of fallen trees and underbrush and the mud. We called out again from time to time and could hear Phil answering, "Here," his voice still sounding far away. But we suspected nothing. "The lazy rascal didn't even try to drag his deer out," Hod said. "He's waiting for us to help him." He was about fifty feet ahead of me. Joe was somewhere between us.

Hod reached Phil first. I saw him jump a fallen tree trunk and bend over. I couldn't see Phil. Joe caught up with Hod; as I approached he turned. "Your boy's shot himself," he said.

Not until then did I see Philip. He was lying on the far side of the log. His right leg was propped up on his left knee and pointing skyward. His right boot was off, and his heavy gray hunting sock was darkly wet with blood. A tourniquet was tied about his ankle and blood was dripping to the earth. I didn't see the rifle. But what I remember mostly about the next few minutes was that I began shaking uncontrollably and thinking that I was going to faint. Phil's face was almost a parchment yellow. I put my arms around him and I don't remember what I said. He kept answering, "I'm all right, Dad," but he wasn't. The jeep was about a half mile away. Hod had shifted the tourniquet to just above Phil's knee and he and Joe were already conferring on what should be done. In a few moments I was calm enough—which wasn't very calm—to join in. What we needed was a litter, we decided. It would be easy to make one quickly from saplings and our hunting jackets.

Not until then did we discover the unbelievable. None of us had taken along a hunting knife. It was the first time that any of us had ever gone into these woods without a knife or ax. We began looking for fallen trees small enough and still hale enough to be used.

In a few minutes we found two dead saplings which might do. We made a litter out of jackets. Oddly enough, it was Phil who told us not to forget Jesse's rifle. It lay some forty or so feet away, where he had left it after he tried to make his way out of the woods toward us before discovering how badly his foot was hurt.

We got him onto the litter. Hod and Joe lifted it while I held Phil's foot high and tried to manipulate the tourniquet. We started off, but we didn't get ten steps before one pole broke. Then Hod and Joe tried a hand-carry. The poor footing made it impossible for them to work together. We stopped and Joe said that he would go back to the jeep and try to bring it closer in.

It was then that I first thanked God for the physical fitness that the Marines had given my eldest son. He picked up Phil, all 175 pounds of him, slung him over his shoulder, and we set out in Joe's wake, with me still trying to keep the right foot as high as possible. For nearly a half mile Hod carried his brother through the mud and fallen trees until we reached Joe and the jeep.

There is no need to recount here in detail the dreadful hour and a half that it took us to reach the hospital. The jeep made it through a mudhole which had almost snared us earlier that morning; but it fetched up against a cotton-wood tree on the far side, bending the axle and fouling up the radius rod and spring so that we couldn't go on. We fiddled with the damaged radius rod a few minutes, desperately. Phil was getting weaker and, though he didn't complain, it was obvious that he was suffering great pain. Joe had wrapped the foot tightly in bandages made from the jeep seat covers, but, even so, blood was still seeping through. By now Hod was as distraught as I. He said he would run to the camp for help. And he took off his slip-on, jodhpur-type shortboots, which wouldn't have stayed on his feet two minutes in the mud, and loped off.

But before he and the search party returned to where Hod had left us, Joe had wedged a jack handle between the spring and the axle and somehow we started off again. Instead of heading for camp, however, we decided to make for the island landing where he had left his own speedboat the day before, tied to a concrete revetment which was the club's "dock." It was two miles closer to where we were and Joe reasoned correctly that the time which could be saved and the condition of the jeep made this change necessary even though the hunters might wonder what had happened when they arrived at the break-down site.

The jeep made it to the levee. A group of Negro timber workers and their employer helped us down the steep side, carrying Philip and getting him into the speedboat with relatively little discomfort to him. The logger himself—Bentley —accompanied us across the river for he had his truck parked on the east bank. Phil became very cold on the trip down and across the river and we piled everything available, including life jackets, on top of him. Some forty-five minutes later after a seventy-mile-an-hour truck ride we reached the General Hospital. Less than an hour later, Dr. Thomas Barnes told us that Phil might lose his foot, that he had lost a great deal of blood—he required six pints—and was dangerously injured, and that if the foot itself was saved, a long time would elapse before it would be restored to any usefulness.

Tommy Barnes, who had much wartime experience with gunshot wounds, performed surgical wonders in two operations, spurred on, perhaps, by Phil's written admonition, affixed to his bandaged foot before the decisive operation. It read in part: "This, my right foot and I have been closely connected for 19 years and do not wish our connection severed. . . . Remember, what God has joined together, let no man rend asunder."

Less than three months later, long before any of us had
expected, Phil had discarded the walking cast. A month
later the crutches went and then the cane, in favor of a
built-in arch support to replace the destroyed metatarsal
bones of his foot. Today his limp has all but gone. So the
ending to my son's hunting mishap has been in a very real
sense a happy one.

But, looking back, I am still concerned over how nearly
the ending came to being a tragic one and why. And, because our experience was neither unique nor inevitable, I
am putting down now for the possible benefit of others who
hunt in remote areas the mistakes we made and the things
we did properly when Phil's life was at stake.

The right things first. . . .

To begin with, Phil himself. He apparently did not give
way to the shock and pain of his wound or to the real fear
that we might not get to him in time. He did make a tourniquet from his bootlace. After he realized he couldn't make
his way to the jeep, and after he had no answer to his
shouts, he did lie down and elevate his foot and begin to
shout for help. It was not his fault that his voice was weaker
than it otherwise might have been.

On our part, we made him as warm as possible as soon as
we found him, readjusted the tourniquet, and tried to make
a litter to get him out. Hod and Joe were calm, or relatively
so, throughout. The best that I can say for myself was that
I didn't faint or have the heart attack that my boys feared.
We kept Phil's foot elevated throughout and, for most of the
time, the tourniquet was adequately compressed. Joe's decision to head the crippled jeep for the landing was wise,
even though we might have had difficulty in finding transportation quickly on the east bank of the river had not
Bentley been providentially on the island and his truck
ready on the eastern bank. We did think to drop Joe off
at the first house we reached in Bentley's truck to telephone
the hospital to be ready for our arrival. And the members of
the Ashbrook Hunting Club had acted with promptness

after we failed to turn up, although there had never been a serious accident on an Ashbrook deer hunt before. The search party had set out about an hour after the twelve o'clock rendezvous time and soon after Hod had begun running from the stalled jeep to camp. Even so he had covered about four miles when he met them. They must have reached the mudhole only a few minutes after Joe and I arrived at the landing, so that, as it happened, we would not have lost more than another half hour had we waited— which may or may not have affected Phil's chances.

But I shudder at the mistakes which could have made the difference between life and death.

First among them, I think, was Phil's decision to use a rifle with which he was completely unfamiliar. A hammer-action rifle can be treacherous to a novice user as Phil found out the hard way. The carbine's muzzle must have been point-blank above his foot when the buck came within range and he cocked the hammer and unconsciously squeezed the trigger.

Two other mistakes, which could have been fatal had we not heard Phil's shouts, were his failure to fire the three-shot signal for help which we may, or may not, have recognized as such; and his misapplication of the bootlace tourniquet below instead of above the knee. Today he says that he didn't fire the signal for two reasons: he wanted to use, and did use, the rifle as a cane, butt down, when he tried to make his way to the trail and so had ejected the shells; and, in his state of shock and revulsion, he had the fixed notion that the carbine was jammed and might explode if he tried to fire it. As for the tourniquet, he says he simply forgot his Boy Scout tests, an explanation which will have to do and which underscores the need of hunters to know more about the treatment of injuries than most of us do.

The memory of my own bone-headedness put me into a cold sweat. It was I who suggested that Hod, Joe, and I head for camp when Phil didn't show up. It is imperative for hunters to have a firm commitment as to the time and place of rendezvous and to start looking when a companion doesn't appear. Instead we—and especially I—were casual to the point of not even being sure in what general area each of us had taken our stands once we had separated early that morning. Moreover, like many a hunter over—and even under—fifty, while I was in good enough shape for ordinary hunting, or wandering through the woods, I certainly was not fit to meet physically an emergency which demanded considerable fitness; and this handicap was emotionally aggravated by the fact that my son was the victim—an aggravation so pronounced that Hod, Joe, and Phil were more concerned about my condition than his.

No single one of us can be blamed for our other mistakes. It is incredible that with a combined hunting experience of at least seventy years, each of us forgot to strap on a hunting knife that morning though all of us had brought knives with us to the camp. With those knives we could have quickly cut down small trees for litter poles and so saved precious time and avoided the rough handling that caused Phil to lose more blood.

Finally, none of us carried even a rudimentary first-aid kit nor was there a kit in the jeep. A few aspirins and a bottle of water were all Phil had to help him along. And neither Joe nor I could be sure that we would find an automobile or truck on the far side of the river ready for use after we had crossed. As it happened, Bentley was on hand and even had he not been we would have discovered once we got across that Jesse had left his key in the locker of his station wagon—and always did—in the very event that someone might need transportation in a hurry.

Phil isn't so sure that he will go deer hunting again. He says he's found out how the deer feels. The rest of us probably will, and so will thousands of others this winter, and the next, and the next and for as long as man is a hunter, which is a long time ahead. And some will be maimed as was my son, and some will die through mistakes that might have been avoided and through others which might have been unavoidable; and many will suffer, as did I, the mental agony of a kinsman or a friend who finds himself helpless or nearly so, and self-reproachful for his ignorance, his unfitness, his forgetfulness, and his mistakes when the penalty can be death.

19

THE MYSTERIOUS ULOK

One Christmas Eve I arrived in Manila from Singapore on the last leg of a round-the-world trip, and wishing I was home after being away nearly three months. I was met by an old friend, Colonel Egbert White, whom I'd known first in North Africa when he directed *Stars and Stripes*. Bert was heading our government's regional printing organization in Manila, which was then publishing and distributing through Southeast Asia a great variety of publications designed to combat communism in a wide area.

After we'd had dinner we went to a tree-decorating party, with frequent and pleasant interruptions from Filipino and American carolers, all of which added to my dejection.

Just before I was about to jump into Manila Bay, I fell into conversation with Tom Britt, who has published his own paper in Ohio and who, at the time, was serving as Bert's chief assistant. We started swapping lies about hunting, and after I had duly impressed him with the duck, deer, dove, and squirrel hunting in our Yazoo-Mississippi Delta, he said he'd arranged a new kind of hunting trip for the day after Christmas, and would I care to come along?

The invitation didn't give me much time to get properly dressed for hunting, and there was no one my size in sight. But Tom said not to worry, just wear something light, and he'd find a gun. I hadn't even asked what we would hunt. I didn't care.

The only thing I could find to wear were a dark blue nylon shirt, a pair of white trousers, which will never be useful again, and leather bedroom slippers. Tom said we wouldn't need khaki or boots or similar gear. "Our game doesn't mind colors," he said, "and it's too hot for anything heavy."

So I met him at 4:30 the morning after Christmas, feeling even sillier than I was sleepy. I was reassured when I found out in the light of Tom's living room that he was dressed pretty much the same as I except he wore tennis shoes. He also had a gun, a sack of shells, a few assorted cans of spaghetti, meat, and pineapple—any fresh food spoils, he said—a jug of water, and a loaf of bread.

We drove in darkness about eight miles north of town to a barrio. That's a new word I picked up, and it means village. There we met Roque Santos, the Filipino foreman of Tom's printing department, and a friend of Roque's named Beneveniente. Their equipment was as light as ours. In pitch darkness we stumbled down to the banks of the Pasig River, which runs from a big lake, Laguna de Bay, some twelve miles southeast of Manila, then through the city, and empties into Manila Bay.

On the bank we piled into a craft about twenty-two feet long and two feet wide which had bamboo outriggers, a ragged, temporary canvas draped over it like a tent, and was powered by a wheezy outboard motor. It was sort of a river taxi and was filled with Filipinos, mostly villagers and fishermen.

Just before we took off, a chill rain began to fall, a decided error on the part of the weatherman who had predicted it would be warm and dry. We reached the tiny barrio at daylight, and there we were to meet our combined guides-and-paddlers, who would take us upriver in search of game which hadn't yet been identified.

The barrio was a conglomerate of elevated palm-thatched huts woven on bamboo frames, and even that early was swarming with partly naked children, pigs, chickens, ducks, and nursing mothers. Most of the menfolk, apparently, were still taking their rest.

Our three guides appeared in shorts and clean, ragged singlets. They brought along for my use a rusted but serviceable Winchester 12-gauge pump gun. I found out later that it was rusty because its owner had buried it, smeared with grease and wrapped in sacking, when the Japs came, for the Japs cut off the head of anyone found with firearms. Later, when the area's men turned guerrilla, the gun had helped him and the village get even with the invaders. My guide said the Winchester had two Japs to its credit.

It was raining hard by this time, so I decided to leave my slippers behind and hunt barefooted, since they told me our shooting would be done from small boats or in soft mud.

When I saw the skiffs in which we were to embark, I decided at once they were far too small for me. They resembled the pirogues of southern Louisiana, though higher in the prow and narrower. They were hollowed from single mahogany logs, and their bottoms tapered into very shallow V's. All in all, those skiffs were the tippiest, trickiest small craft I've ever got into—or fallen out of. I barely squeezed into a sitting position in an inch of water.

We set out upriver in a strong current, sticking close to the bank, which made me feel easier. On each side was the low-lying jungle. After about an hour and a half, the river began to flatten and spread over the countryside. Roque called to us and said that we were in flooded rice paddies, and that in other seasons the place would be green with rice. Now it stood from two to four feet deep in water. Out of the water rose the thickest, highest masses of water hyacinths I've ever seen. Almost identical in appearance to Louisiana's pestiferous hyacinths, they stood in great clusters as much as four feet above the water. And among and between them shot up all manner of reeds and ribbon grasses, what seemed to be dead palmetto fronds, and much more.

The varied growth made the paddy fields appear to be solid ground, but our guides, shifting from paddles to long bamboo poles, began maneuvering the skiffs into the tangle of water and weeds, sometimes atop the growth, sometimes through it, and I saw no land anywhere. All this time the rain continued and I had a hard time seeing ahead since there was no point in trying to wear my eyeglasses.

I realized about this time that I still didn't know what we were hunting or how we'd go about it. I called to Tom and asked. "Beats me, too," he said. Then we asked Roque and his friend, who were sharing a slightly longer skiff with one guide.

Roque yelled something that sounded like "You look," and repeated it over and over until we finally got the idea that we were hunting for some kind of waterfowl with a name that resembled his shouted phrase. By this time Roque was standing erect, without shimmying, in the bow of his skiff, though I'm ready to swear right now it can't be done. That was the only way to see the birds rising and to get in any shots except just ahead and on each quarter. But Tom and I never managed to stand up long even without a gun.

And then the "You looks," which are variously spelled uloks and ulucs, began rising. Our three small craft had separated, and I couldn't see the others. My guide began shouting guttural warnings, which turned out to be addressed to the uloks, and now and then he'd smack the water or the hyacinths with his bamboo pole.

He could speak almost no English, but when he yelled, "One, one," and I heard a shot, I steadied for my first sight of the mysterious ulok. In a couple of seconds I saw it, dimly and wetly, skimming the reeds ahead. I blazed away. On the second shot the ulok fell into the water, and so did I and my guide. With no effort at all I'd turned the skiff over.

We came up and stood in about three feet of muck, water, and greenery, laughing at each other, and the guide said, "You got." We tilted the skiff until it was empty, and after some false starts I got back in it while the guide found my first ulok.

I can hear my hunting friends in Greenville, Mississippi, saying that what follows is just a big lie and can't be possible. But the ulok has a head shaped like a dove's, with a red tuft and bill, the body of a teal which it resembles in flight, bright-green legs, and green feet which are not webbed and are something like a chicken's except they have no spur. Believe it or not, despite the absence of webs, the bird swims. It also is good eating, particularly if soaked overnight in water to which three jiggers of whiskey have been added. That's supposed to take away any gamy taste. Later I found that the ulok is a variety of marsh hen common in the Philippine Islands.

The rain kept falling and we kept hunting, and I fell out of the skiff once more before the day was over. Tom went overboard twice. I knocked down seven uloks, including one we couldn't find, and, by mistake, a tiny yellow marsh bird that looks like our snipe except for its color. That shot sent all the Filipinos into stitches.

On toward noon the weather turned unseasonably cold, and the Filipinos were freezing. We'd already made camp in a bamboo-stilt shed, without sides, rising out of the submerged fields, where the rice farmers stay during the season. It wasn't high enough at the ridge pole for me to stand upright, but we sought shelter in it and had a go at our food.

Beneveniente went into a hard chill just after we finished eating an amazing mess of cold canned spaghetti, cold, weak, and very sweet Filipino coffee, canned meat, wet brownies, canned pineapple, damp bread, and—one try at it—a gob of cold Filipino rice, unsalted and pressed gooily together, topped with a sliver of fish.

My nylon shirt dried in a few minutes, and since I wasn't cold then, we persuaded Beneveniente to take off his wet clothes and drape himself in the shirt. It went around him about three times.

Then Tom and I built a preposterous fire inside half an empty can. We started it with toilet paper and some strips from a paper sack in Roque's providential cracker tin, and fed it with bits of wood sliced from a dry and rotting stick we found on an upper berth in the shed. All this time our feet were in water, but it was warmer than the air. As an experiment, I sprinkled the fuel with a bottle of insect repellent I'd tucked in my pocket and set a match to the pile. It worked. When the fire began blazing, we propped up the cracker tin's top for a reflector.

All of us took a clinical interest in thawing out Beneveniente. Thanks to my surplus padding of flesh, I didn't feel too cold. The rest did, but none so much as our patient. We kneaded him, maneuvered his back scorchingly close to our can of heat, promised him a slug of whiskey when we got home, and tried psychology by telling him how cold it gets in Minnesota, where Tom lives, and Maine, where I've hunted.

It was amazing how much heat bounced out of that can and off the reflector, and how warm and dry the nylon shirt felt to Benny. But as the rain and wind continued to beat down, I found it difficult to keep pretending I was warm in a sopping undershirt and pants and minus shoes and socks.

An hour and a half later we were ready to go out again, all but our patient. The rain had slowed to a drizzle, so we decided to hunt until four o'clock in the afternoon. Those hours were not among my most productive. I don't know whether I was too stiff from cold or too homesick to concentrate on the uloks, but out of twelve shots I brought down one bird—embarrassing for a Mississippian who that morning had used only thirteen shells for seven uloks and one unmentionable, without glasses and in a heavy rain.

But it was a good hunt all the same, and one calculated to chase away the absent-for-Christmas blues. I won't forget those little uloks rising out of a watery, jungle-thick undergrowth, and skimming the hyacinths three feet above my head while I tried to shoot from a seagoing tightrope.

Nor will I forget, if it's all right to bring in a small sermon, some of the stories Roque and Beneveniente told me, with interjections from the guides, about the days of the Japanese occupation.

In the very area in which we'd been hunting, the men from the barrio where we'd paused had rescued two American fliers and spirited them off to the mountains. The Japs executed more than ten villagers for that feat.

They executed others after a Jap pilot had gone down within half a mile from our paddy shed and hadn't been rescued. He sank like a stone, one guide explained—after some Filipino fishermen had clubbed him.

What I'm saying is that in the Philippines we have a warm backlog of friends, the legacy of a generally sensible, fair, and humane policy which had its culmination in the gift of freedom. I say, too, that if men can hunt together, wear each other's shirts when they're cold, and eat each other's food, they should stick together against the icy, evil wind that sweeps down, as it did that day after Christmas, straight from Siberia.

20

THE EXTRA CORPSE

1954

This is a secret I can no longer keep; one that haunts me by day and makes me leap in nightmarish terror from my bed. I see all of us cornered by every game warden in Arkansas and shunned by decent turkey hunters everywhere. My only hope lies in telling all. Or nearly all.

I am weak enough to plead that I wasn't the party of either the first or the second part, but I know the excuse won't hold up. All of us were guilty: Jim Robertshaw, who got the extra turkey, and who, being a lawyer, is especially culpable; Ferd Moyse, who parachuted into Normandy the night before D-Day but says that White River mosquitoes are deadlier than SS troopers; Johnny Gibson, who is my partner and business manager of our *Delta Democrat-Times* in Greenville, Mississippi, and who planned the fatal turkey hunt for a whole year; grizzled Conyers Sosbee, who guided us; and myself, who am herewith atoning for our sins. I guess Leonard Jones, our cook, was guilty, too, though all he did that fateful April week was prove he wasn't bragging when he said that offenders often came back voluntarily for meals at the Greenville city jail, where he worked and whence we borrowed him.

It all started innocently enough. The woods along the White River, which empties into the Arkansas side of the Mississippi about seventy miles north of Greenville, were full of the fattest, most cooperative turkeys in all history —or so everybody said. Especially Johnny Gibson, who said it all winter and who had been making elaborate preparations for a week of turkey hunting long before the Arkansas season opened on April 1. Even today we won't tell our wives about the provisions that were called for in the six-day menu that Jim Robertshaw drew up: the roasts and steaks and hams and chops and fish, the fruit and fresh vegetables, the snacks and the case of snakebite remedy—all adding up to a far richer table than any of us enjoyed at home.

Johnny attended to just about everything else. He got it on the best authority that Montgomery towhead, an island not far above the mouth of the White, was the original turkey paradise. He drove up to Rosedale, that flower-and-tree-hidden little Mississippi town across the river from the mouth of the White, to find a proper turkey caller in the person of Conyers Sosbee, a highway-department worker by vocation but a hunter by preference and long habit. From Mr. Sosbee, whom the rest of us were not to see until the day the hunt began, Johnny learned about box calls and the relative merits of hand and mouth in fooling a tom turkey into cracking a chunk. And from the day he invei-gled Mr. Sosbee into coming along, our newspaper office was a banshee's haunt, with profit-and-loss statements hid-den beneath strips of rubber, and with the *squank-squank-squank* of the box call drowning out the voices of the pro-testing staff. Johnny even rounded up Leonard, the cook, and talked Jimmy into drawing up the week's menu. All Ferd and I did was save our strength for the big hunt.

And so, on the drizzling daybreak of April 2, our cabin cruiser, *Mistuh Charley,* headed up the Mississippi for Rose-dale and Mr. Sosbee, sixty miles or so north. With what we had aboard in arms and foodstuffs we could have stormed Gibraltar and lived there a month without foraging.

We reached Rosedale's landing a little after noon, and there was Mr. Sosbee, a lean, weathery man in his late fifties, looking just as I thought a turkey hunter should. He car-ried a rucksack and was dressed in worn khakis, and under his left shoulder—surprisingly to anyone who doesn't know Rosedale—nestled a shoulder holster.

Without ado he recommended that we first cross the river to Arkansas and bear a little north to where some of the boys had found some pretty good turkey hunting on opening day. With that, Johnny began making noises on his caller which so distracted Mr. Sosbee that he gave us no more instructions. Instead, in self-defense, he devoted himself to the impossible assignment of showing Johnny how.

When we reached the opposite bank it was late afternoon. We hadn't figured on hunting that day anyhow, so when Mr. Sosbee suggested that we go ashore and look for turkey sign all of us went clambering up the bank and, sticking close to our guide, entered the woods. We took Mr. Sosbee's word that what we saw in the dusk was real sign, including a dust bath, and we were back aboard by dark, for poker, rummy, and no end of boastful predictions as to who would get his turkey first.

But nobody got anything the next day except the thrill that is found in the river-valley woodland on a cool, sunshiny day, with the leaves damply green and the wind—too much of it for good turkey spotting—rustling the unusually heavy foliage of a wet, early spring. I saw my first wild turkey that morning, but he was too far away, or rather I was too unready to do anything about him. The gobbler was perched in a lightning-seared tree, and when he heard us he parachuted to earth. I first caught sight of him just as he hit the ground, and I could have sworn that the fat, black object was a hog. I didn't shoot, nor did Mr. Sosbee or Ferd, who was closest to him, but it set us up mightily, and we knew that Turkey No. 1 was waiting out in those woods for somebody.

Maybe he was, but we didn't get him. We scattered, after sighting the gobbler, and settled ourselves, according to Mr. Sosbee's advice, in a way calculated to make the smartest tom think he had the woods all to himself, our backs against tree trunks or fallen logs, immobile, straining to outlisten, outwait, and outsee the big birds. All morning we heard turkeys stalking, and sometimes they seemed quite near, the hens yelping once in a great while and the toms, wings drumming, calling to them; and all around, too, the orchestration of the whippoorwill and mockingbird, and the patter of surprised deer.

John and I, the first in at noon, decided that the original hunting grounds we had earlier chosen, an island a few miles up the White, was the proper place. Our unprofessional surmise was strengthened by the recommendation of two rivermen who pulled alongside in their twenty-foot fishing skiff powered by an old auto engine. Friendly souls, they came aboard at our invitation for a drink and settled down to an hour of yarn spinning after their innards had been warmed by two or three slugs. Turkey, said one of them, was all right, but he preferred cold coon and collards himself. They complained that most of the good hunting land was all clubbed up—they meant that private clubs had bought it—and while such usurpation didn't bother them much, it was hard on the fainter of heart.

Our interest perked up when they said they had a cabin a good deal farther up the White than we were going; for, as even the tenderfoot on the Lower Mississippi knows, the islands, swamp land, and backwoods along the White are home not only to honest fishermen and whiskey makers and shanty-boaters but also to a shadowy collection of outlaws—hideaway folk who walked away from civilization or escaped just ahead of the sheriff, and who collectively could fill a city jail. White River outlaws rarely bother anyone except themselves and are seldom bothered, though sometimes a careless fugitive may forget his past and pick a fight in a river town on a drunken Saturday night, and that can lead to trouble.

We plied our visitors with questions about these derelicts, and they seemed to enjoy telling us stories of their neighbors, though how true they were I don't know. But I do believe the tale that one of them, low-voiced and a little thick-tongued, told about his companion, who had gone forward. Our tale teller jerked a thumb in his partner's direction and said that he had once owned a prosperous business and considerable commercial property in a sizable Southern city.

"Found another fellow dating his wife," our confidant said. "He killed him and come clear, but he didn't have

the heart to stay around. Been here about fifteen years."
His considered opinion was that women, one way or
another, had caused most of the sudden withdrawals from
society, but he volunteered nothing about himself.

The two rivermen took friendly leave of us half an hour
or so before Ferd, Jimmy, and Mr. Sosbee came aboard.

We got under way then, before three in the afternoon,
for everybody agreed that we'd better head up the White.
Before dark we had tied up, bow and stern, to a couple
of willows against a heavily wooded island whose banks
rose some fifteen feet above the falling river. Mr. Sosbee
laid the plan of battle. We would leave the boat by 3:30
in the morning and he'd place each of us in ambush.
Jimmy could use a turkey call reasonably well, and Johnny
thought he could, so Ferd and I elected to stay in the
general neighborhood of Mr. Sosbee.

It was something less than a picnic next morning to
work our way up that bank and through the dense woods,
in darkness broken only by an occasional flashlight beam.
But we all made it, though my 200-odd pounds were protesting severally and together, and much hard breathing
warned the wild things of White River that we were on
our way. It was worth it, I thought, when just before daybreak I lay hunched against a fallen log, with my presence
hidden—so I thought—from the most observant turkey.

The predawn silence was uncanny. I couldn't relax the
slightest. Luckily I had smeared my face and hands with
mosquito dope, or I'd have been eaten alive; for unlike the
relative freedom from the pests which we had enjoyed on
the Mississippi bank, with a steady down river wind, we
were plagued by millions of mosquitoes.

Mr. Sosbee's calling that day should have summoned
every turkey on the island; but again, though Ferd and
I heard them in plenty, we saw none. We only hoped that
the sounds of shooting we heard now and then meant that
Jimmy and John were in luck. We switched stations several times, and saw much sign; and finally, after more than
eight hours in the woods, Ferd and I decided in disgust

to return to the boat. We had a good enough excuse at that time, for we were both allergic to poison ivy, of which there was a bounteous crop around, and we wanted to follow up the poison-ivy shots we had already taken by scrubbing with lye soap. So we left Mr. Sosbee and somehow found the *Mistuh Charley*. We washed up and then settled down to gin rummy.

A little later Jimmy hailed us from shore, and we went on deck to greet him. He was carrying over his shoulder, with great nonchalance, a turkey—a tremendous tom. There is no greater envy than a hunter feels when another comes in with a kill that seems forever beyond the viewer's hope, and we sure felt it that day. Jimmy's damn modesty, his "Nothing to it," added to our sense of personal wrong. It was a beautiful bird, all of thirty pounds.

As Leonard handled him, preparatory to drawing, he said, "Must of killed him mighty early, Mr. Jim," and Jim gave him a quizzical look. But we thought nothing of it. Jimmy basked in our admiration until almost suppertime. Then, after Johnny and Mr. Sosbee had come aboard and likewise marveled, he confessed.

"Believe it or not," he said, "I found that turkey. Stumbled right on it in a clearing about noon. It must have been dead two or three hours then. I shouted and shouted"— this was the only thing that was hard to believe—"but I couldn't raise anybody. So here he is."

All of us felt better. Here was proof that turkeys could be killed. And by Jim's own admission, he was not a better hunter than we. We slapped him on the back, complimented him for his truthfulness, and loudly praised the turkey.

And then the horrible thought came to all of us.

Game wardens were thick as river fog all over the White River's bird grounds. Somebody would have to take credit for that turkey by the time the warden came around, and the hunter who did wouldn't be able to hunt any more. One turkey to one hunter was the limit.

Immediately the non-turkey finders declared that Jim

would have to take credit for the kill. Jim's legal mind got busy. The turkey shouldn't count against a limit, he said, because none of us had killed it. But right then, as so often happens, the spirit of the law ran afoul of practicalities. What warden would believe such a story if he found an unclaimed turkey aboard and five hunters in the woods? Or if, as we were sure would inevitably happen, five hunters ended up with six turkeys? But now the turkey was on ice in the big fish box on the stern of *Mistuh Charley*.

It was then that Ferd Moyse, who is a spiritual blood brother to all White River outlaws, had his idea. "Hide it in the woods each day," he said. "Bring it back at night. When we've got five more turkeys, let's eat this one."

That seemed eminently fair. Jim said that we could put the turkey in a gunny sack the next morning—soaking the bag awhile in the river first to cool it—and then tie it in a tree on the bank where no warden could see it. And so we did, in inky blackness, and set out with clear consciences to find five legitimate turkeys. But rain and a driving wind kept the turkeys out of sight that day, and all we got was a thorough wetting.

Crestfallen, we came in that afternoon to a friendly waiting warden. He commiserated with us, said there'd been some turkeys killed on the far side of the island, and wished us luck. After he left, Jim hauled down the turkey and put it back in the ice chest, and we made plans for hunting the far side on what would be our last day. And so, next morning, we went through the established ritual: in the woods long before daybreak and hidden by ones and twos in the area which the warden had described. This would be the day.

And, in a way, it was. At the crack of dawn the shooting began. Johnny was somewhere to my left, and I think it was he who first blazed away at a very real turkey. Mr. Sosbee shot, too, and that waked up Ferd, who had developed a technique of slumbering on the ground until (he said) a seventh sense told him turkeys were nigh. It told him too late this time, and, as he said afterward, when he shot at a turkey the turkey simply took aim and shot back. Maybe he was dreaming.

And then, out of a tree to my left, plummeted a tom. It flew in a split second across a cleared space, and I shot twice, yelling, "I got him." That was premature, because if I did hit that turkey the load made no impression. Violating all the rules of the chase—except for Jim, who didn't turn up—we yelled to one another and finally joined up, each sure that the others had got their turkeys.

No one had. No one could understand why. Mr. Sosbee said then that we'd better scatter out by pairs, the four of us, and take new stands. By that time Ferd and I had earned somehow the reputation of being rather casual turkey hunters, so we were left together. When Johnny and Mr. Sosbee departed, we consulted. If we were turkeys, we finally concluded, we'd come right back to this spot later in the morning. Besides, each of us had a comfortable bivouac, and the mosquitoes in the vicinity seemed fairly discouraged by the dope. So we elected to stay more or less where we were. Ferd went off to sleep and I began thinking the long thoughts of an unsuccessful turkey hunter.

I assume that Ferd was still asleep, a few hundred feet away, when I heard the sound, an hour or so later. "Don't move your head, not even your eyes." Mr. Sosbee had said: "Just wait for old tom to come into view." So I sat, cramped and rigid, waiting for my victim. Perhaps a minute later it appeared, black and slow-moving, and almost hidden by low bushes. I waited until I was sure that it wasn't Ferd, and then I fired. There came a mighty squalling and off into the thick stuff dashed a woods hog.

Let it be said that I thought fast. Even before Ferd came stumbling to his feet I had stretched out peacefully on the ground, my gun leaning an arm's length away against a tree. When he burst into view, scaring any chance turkey within five miles, and yelling, "Did you get it?" I was stretching and looking around with the blank stare of the newly awakened.

"Sounded like some fool shooting a hog," I said. "Might

have been the same fellow that killed the turkey for Jim."
As a cautious afterthought I added, "Let's get somewhere
else. Isn't safe around here with that kind of carelessness."
I had read of hogs who got awfully mad when they were
so positively mistaken for a turkey.

Ferd was low in spirit anyway. He had mosquito welts
wherever he didn't have poison ivy. He was also too heavily
dressed, and the weather had turned warm. Like me, he
was almost willing to wait until next year to try again.
We trudged away, found another likely-looking place, and
brooded until such time as we could decently return to the
boat. There the only solace to be had was the discovery
that Johnny and Mr. Sosbee were already aboard when
we arrived, and as turkeyless and discomfited as we. Mr.
Sosbee insisted that we cut off his shirttail for missing his
turkey.

Then it was that Jim appeared, almost like a replay of the
first time he came in with a turkey on his back. If anything,
the turkey he carried now was bigger than the first, and
from his grin and strut we knew he hadn't stumbled over
this one. And this time we were glad. At least we were
bringing back two turkeys, and one of them legitimate. We
hefted Jim's newest victim, admired its beard and plumage,
and listened to how he had called it in and in until it
had practically spat in his eyes before he saw and shot it.
Just as easy as that.

And we came to an amicable solution of what to do
with the dead bird up the tree. Mr. Sosbee didn't want
it and Jim didn't need it, so the three that were left would
play gin rummy for it. While we planned this compromise,
Jim went ashore again to get the original, and even before
we had played one hand we heard him yell. Everything
he said won't do to repeat, because he's running for the
legislature, but he came crashing through the bushes, and
without the sack or the turkey.

"Goddlemighty," he yelled. "It's just about melted."
And Jim smelled of dead, ripe, and melted turkey for the
rest of the day and night and all the way back to Greenville

the next day. Served him right, too. Any man who tries to beat the law that way deserves to have his companions blackmail him into putting on a turkey dinner with all the fixings that very Sunday night.

But just wait until next April. We know the very place——

PART IV

Something Different Every Day

21

A SEPTEMBER TO REMEMBER

1957

At a certain or uncertain age, anniversaries take on meanings that escape younger folk. So it was that September of 1954 had for me an importance which I did not try to explain to my oldest son who was nineteen and who intended to become a newspaperman, and did.

In September 1929 I got my first newspaper job on the New Orleans *Item,* to which, after five years of college and one year of college teaching, I was worth $12.50 for a fifty- to sixty-hour work week. In September 1936 my wife and I came to Greenville to establish a then competitive and now monopolistic afternoon daily after selling the tiny tabloid daily which we had established four years before in Louisiana and had somehow kept alive. In September 1954 my son returned to college from his own first newspaper job, also on the *Item,* where his starting pay was roughly four times as much as his father's had been.

That superior earning power pleased him almost as much as the first byline, which he had won far sooner than I had been given my first. He had been proud, too, of the stories that the four or five oldtimers on the *Item* had told him about my own cub days, tales which I modestly almost disclaimed while making a mental note to set 'em up for those friendly survivors when next I journeyed to New Orleans. They should have left out one or two, however, for young Hod interrupted some parental warnings about the French Quarter with an inquiry as to why I had chosen in my bachelor days to live there myself.

But beneath this give-and-take ran an undercurrent of serious examination of our respective times. For me this was the best legacy of the summer. We found ourselves agreeing on far more matters than usual. (Two summers before, he was the family's lone Stevenson man.) He carried a Guild card, as once I also had, and we decided that the Guild was principally responsible for higher wages, together with inflation, more prosperous times, more enlightened publishers, and the emergence of better-trained and more career-minded young newspapermen.

We agreed also that it was too bad that there were fewer daily newspapers and more newspaper monopolies than when I started out, although we were both in favor of the present newspaper monopoly in Greenville. We concluded, however, that despite the nostalgic reminiscences of older reporters and editors, most newspapers today are better than they were twenty-five years ago.

I really think they are. A principal reason, and not altogether a pleasant difference, is that young and old reporters, like almost all Americans, were living in a fool's paradise a quarter of a century ago. I doubt that in September 1929 I had ever used the word depression or ever thought of one except during history or economics exams. Wars were over for the foreseeable future, no person or idea could ever successfully challenge American democracy and the capitalistic system, and about the only things that troubled my waking hours were the recent refusal of the American electorate to make a President out of an energetic enemy of Prohibition named Al Smith and the popularity of a brash Louisianian named Huey Long. Good old normalcy would endure forever, along with the same headlines; and don't bore the readers with dispatches from Europe.

I find it hard to make young Hod believe that we were not quite as naïve and trusting as our Page Ones would indicate. His generation is neither naïve nor insular nor trusting, and this makes better newspapermen out of those who become such. But they, along with their elders, have paid a high price to see more clearly.

Now what I have said about the meaning of our talk has had to do mainly with a father's prideful reactions to a son's first venture into journalism. As for the personal anniversaries, they remind me that today's threats to press freedom may differ in degree from the perils that were present earlier, but they do not differ in kind.

Three weeks after I started reporting I was manhandled and tossed bodily out of a strike meeting. In the years of Long's domination, Louisiana's press was confronted with punitive taxation, its representatives were slugged, its existence jeopardized by organized boycott, its principal critics of Longism threatened and libeled. It was almost as hard to get into meetings of so-called public bodies, when they wanted to act in secret, as it is now.

We're still having the same troubles and some others. In my own little city, our reporters and myself have a tough time finding out what the school board or the city council or the county board of supervisors don't want us to know. We have a harder time at the state level because we can't maintain a full-time correspondent in Jackson, the state capital. How infinitely more difficult it is to penetrate the Washington maze, as any Washington correspondent, struggling with the handout technique, the loose invoking of the national security issue, and the conflicting claims of partisan politics, can tell you. It all adds up to an expanded version of what newspapermen have always been subjected to, but in our infinitely more complex world the difficulties are far greater.

And this brings me to a final reason why September 1954 was personally memorable. All newspapermen are aware of how so much of the public can be aroused to a high and dangerously emotional pitch by demagogues and the causes demagogues espouse. In my younger days Long was the most effective but not the only such demagogue, just as his Share Our Wealth program was the most appealing but not the only political confidence game. Newspaper critics of the Longs and the Gerald Smiths, the Townsends and Father Coughlins came in for rough handling. We felt the temper of the mob.

That temper flourished in 1954, as any critic of McCarthy

knows. But in September 1954, its evil vigor became known to me in a way I had never experienced before, and I pass the experience on as a reminder that we cannot take our freedoms for granted.

In the wake of the Supreme Court's decision on the public schools, there have been organized in Mississippi widespread and still loosely bound groups which are called Citizens' Councils. Their avowed purpose is to fight integration of the races in Mississippi's public schools by non-violent means, including economic pressure. By and large, the Councils have been led by well-known and law-abiding men, though their operations have been quasi-secret.

But the organization of these Councils has emboldened bigoted and violent men, within and outside the Councils. So it is that in September 1954 there were circulated in our county and elsewhere three anonymous circulars. One threatened a boycott of Greenville because the directors of our baseball association had leased the ball park to a Memphis promoter who proposed to put on an exhibition ball game between Negro and white barnstorming clubs. Two of the directors are Jewish. The second circular was violently anti-Semitic. We had said editorially that we saw nothing wrong in such a game. The third circular was a crudely versified attack on me personally, in which racial fears and personal innuendoes slimily competed.

I am not so sure that the Citizen's Councils can keep their members within the announced bounds.

Which makes me feel that this is where I came in. We thought back in 1929 that the Klan had just been laid to rest. Newspapers and newspapermen must remember that the enemies we fight are never stilled.

22

1955

It happened on April Fools' Day. But it wasn't a joke to me or to the majority of the Mississippi House of Representatives who, by formal resolution, voted on April 1, 1955, that I had lied, slandered my state, and betrayed the South in a *Look* magazine article (March 22 issue) about the Citizens' Councils—the militant Southern white groups which have been organized to discourage school integration and Negro suffrage.

Perhaps in the history of state legislatures, often citizens have been made liars by legislation. But I doubt that any of them received the accolade under the same conditions as I did.

April 1 was the final day of a special legislative session at which our Mississippi lawmakers had been seeking feverishly, and finally with success, to find new money to equalize the dual school systems, as a means of avoiding racial integration. April 1 was as usual the opening day of the turkey hunting season. With four friends, a cook, and a guide, I was turkey hunting forty miles from my home town, Greenville, Mississippi. Our headquarters was the *Mistuh Charley*, my newspaper's cabin cruiser, and we were playing cards aboard her that afternoon after an unsuccessful opening day.

The game was interrupted by a low-flying plane that dropped a bundle near the wooded shoreline. I kept on playing cards, but John Gibson, the *Delta Democrat-Times* business manager and my publishing associate, went out and found the bundle. He returned and handed me some sheets of paper. "You'd better read this," he said.

I did, and for the time being I lost interest in cards and

turkeys. Joe Call, a cotton-duster pilot and friend, had dropped a press association report of what the House of Representatives had done, together with a note from my wife. I read the note first:

"We've played the story on page one as second lead. Everybody's calling for your answer. When can we get it and what else shall we do? Love, Betty."

Then I read the wire service report. It was like being kicked in the stomach by eighty-nine angry jackasses. That number of state legislators, with nineteen opposed and thirty-two others not voting, had officially branded me a liar. During two hours of angry debate preceding the vote, I had been described in terms not often used by lawmakers. I was a Negro lover and a scalawag, a lying newspaperman, a person who "as far as the white people of Mississippi are concerned, should have no rights." I had sold out the South for 50,000 pieces of silver. (Note to *Look*: You owe me money.)

The elderly Speaker of the House, a perpetual seceder and a backer of the Citizens' Councils, cast a vote for the resolution, gratuitously, although ordinarily he would not vote on any measure except to break a tie. I was defended by a few, notably the two young lawyer-legislators from Greenville and another young representative, Joel Blass of Stone County. Blass told how he also had felt the Councils' lash because he had opposed a Council-backed constitutional amendment making it possible to abandon the state's public school system. The fact that these men are young is important to this story and to the future of Mississippi.

My hunting companions thought the whole thing was funny. I didn't, even though they assured me—and I agreed—that a Mississippi legislative majority was mentally and morally incapable of insulting anybody. I ducked below and started writing. I'm glad, I guess, that my fellow turkey stalkers talked me into watering down the original editorial. [The watered-down version is reproduced here. *Ed.*]

LIAR BY LEGISLATION

BY A VOTE OF 89 TO 19, THE MISSISSIPPI HOUSE OF REP-
RESENTATIVES HAS RESOLUTED THE EDITOR OF THIS NEWSPA-
PER INTO A LIAR BECAUSE OF AN ARTICLE I WROTE ABOUT
THE CITIZENS' COUNCILS FOR LOOK MAGAZINE. IF THIS CHARGE
WERE TRUE IT WOULD MAKE ME WELL QUALIFIED TO SERVE
WITH THAT BODY. IT IS NOT TRUE. SO, TO EVEN THINGS UP,
I HEREWITH RESOLVE BY A VOTE OF 1 TO 0 THAT THERE
ARE 89 LIARS IN THE STATE LEGISLATURE BEGINNING WITH
SPEAKER SILLERS AND WORKING WAY ON DOWN TO REP. ECK
WINDHAM OF PRENTISS, A POLITICAL LOON WHOSE NAME IS
FITTINGLY MADE UP OF THE WORDS "WIND" AND "HAM."

AS FOR THE ARTICLE, I STAND BY IT. THIS ACTION BY A MA-
JORITY OF THE HOUSE OF REPRESENTATIVES ONLY SERVES TO
ADD NEW PROOF TO WHAT I WROTE. THERE IS ONE EDITOR
OF THIS NEWSPAPER. I VOTE ONLY IN WASHINGTON COUNTY.
THE CITIZENS' COUNCILS CLAIM 30,000 MEMBERS WHO VOTE
ALL OVER THE STATE. THAT IS EXPLANATION ENOUGH FOR
THE RESOLUTION.

I AM GRATEFUL TO THE 19 LEGISLATORS, AND ESPECIALLY
TO GREENVILLE'S TWO REPRESENTATIVES, WHO VOTED
AGAINST THE RESOLUTION. I AM ALSO APPRECIATIVE OF THE
SANE COMMENTS OF REP. JOEL BLASS OF STONE COUNTY WHO
LIKEWISE HAS BEEN A TARGET OF THE DISHONEST AND CON-
TEMPTIBLE TACTICS USED BY THE CITIZENS' COUNCILS
AGAINST ANYONE WHO DIFFERS WITH THEM OR THEIR METH-
ODS.

I AM HOPEFUL THAT THIS FEVER, LIKE THE KU KLUXISM
WHICH ROSE FROM THE SAME KIND OF INFECTION WILL RUN
ITS COURSE BEFORE TOO LONG A TIME. MEANWHILE, THOSE
89 CHARACTER MOBBERS CAN GO TO HELL, COLLECTIVELY
OR SINGLY, AND WAIT THERE UNTIL I BACK DOWN. THEY
NEEDN'T PLAN ON RETURNING.

HODDING CARTER

I decided to wait until the next morning to telephone in the reply I had written. We turned on the radio and heard how I had been done in, and then went on playing cards.

But in the woods on the rest of the hunt I couldn't forget what had happened. I did a lot of thinking about my twenty-three years as editor and publisher of small newspapers, four years in Louisiana and the last nineteen in Mississippi. I had never looked on myself as a starry-eyed crusader or an unfriendly critic of my homeland. No book or editorial or article I had ever written, including the *Look* article, would so identify me. I do like to believe that we've tried on our paper to take seriously the idea of man's equality. But we've been generally orthodox newspaper people, my wife and I.

I have noted, however, that an editor is remembered longest for his unpleasant comments—and for comments made about him. Long ago in Louisiana that odious anti-Semite, Gerald L. K. Smith, said that I had been run out of Mississippi as a young newspaperman and would be run out of Louisiana. Every now and then, some politician will repeat that preposterous fantasy as gospel. When I won a Pulitzer Prize for editorial writing in 1946, the late Theodore G. Bilbo, then running for re-election to the United States Senate, told his listeners that "no self-respecting Southern white man would accept a prize given by a bunch of nigger-loving, Yankeefied Communists for editorials advocating the mongrelization of the race."

When, ten years earlier, in 1936, ours had been the first Mississippi paper to print a picture showing a Negro in a favorable light—it was of Jesse Owens, the Olympic triple winner—some of the readers who canceled their subscriptions said that our action was part of a Communist plot to end segregation.

When (and this again was unique in Mississippi) we began using the courtesy title "Mrs." before the names of Negro women in news stories, the tale spread that we would soon demand "social equality" for Negroes. And every time we have come out for anything that some of our special pleaders or Stone Agers haven't liked—from the Blue Cross nearly twenty years ago to a good word for the United Nations—we have known we could expect the same emotional cacophony, and that the cumulative roaring would echo loudest during political campaigns. But never had we been ganged up on by a state legislature. Most of all, I wanted to know what this thing portended.

I've been trying to figure it out ever since. I think I've come up with some answers, and I'd like to say first that I'm not as worried as I was about Mississippi or our newspaper or anything except our politicians. Perhaps the reaction of so many of my home town and Southern fellow citizens, and my fellow newspapermen, particularly in Mississippi, is what keeps me from being worried.

When I got home, I asked our two Greenville legislators what they thought about the resolution. Both had strongly defended me on the floor. Young Joe Wroten, a lawyer and a minister's son, didn't mince words. "Some of our people who pay lip service to constitutional government pay homage in practice to a government of men," he said. "The resolution was abortive thought control by legislation against facts, and I don't like it. But maybe those venomous attacks on freedom of the press may wake people to the danger of a clandestine government of men." And Joe punned: "—a Klandestine klavern of men. . . ."

Jimmy Robertshaw, likewise a lawyer, was more amused than disturbed. "It's partly because they were scared, partly because they're sore at the Supreme Court, and partly because they were on edge after twelve weeks of looking for money," he said. "And some of them, don't forget, are Council members. But I would like to think that they're ashamed, too, and don't want people outside to know that the Councils really exist."

Joe and Jimmy are two of the legislative minority that wouldn't go along. Numerically, they aren't important. But numerically and otherwise, the letters that continue to pile up as an aftermath of the *Look* article and its legislative sequel do seem to me to be important. I have received more than 2000 letters about the Council piece. They've run about three to two in my favor in the South, and better than that elsewhere. Heartening is the preponderance of letters from young people, especially servicemen; clergymen of all faiths; educators and fellow newspapermen, and the accent of so many of them has been upon the Christian challenge. The several hundred that quickly followed the resolution favored our side at least nineteen to one. I think this shows that Americans dislike seeing people ganged up on.

It is significant, too, that the critical letters were overwhelmingly emotional, often anti-Semitic, and, when unsigned as many were, contained filthy personal attacks and threats. Some, of course, came from people honestly disturbed over the Supreme Court ruling and wondering whether the Council's program of economic terrorism is not the South's only anti-integration weapon.

A man in Alaska sent $100 to be used as I saw fit to oppose the Councils. Three priests, each from different communities and one of them 300 miles away, came to Greenville within a few days of each other to offer aid and comfort to this battered Episcopalian. But an unidentified telephone caller told me to get out of town before I was carried out.

Less trivial than threats or insults have been the efforts at boycott, only spasmodic before the *Look* article appeared, but now accelerated. We've lost circulation in some areas, but we've managed to hold to our 12,500 average. We've been hurt a little in our commercial printing and office-supply sidelines. So far, none of our advertisers has knuckled under to the arrogant demands of Council spokesmen that they join the Councils, or take away their advertising from us on penalty of losing the trade of Council members. This economic weapon was announced last summer as being planned for use only against Negroes who tried to vote or enter their children in white schools, but it has been turned against anyone who doesn't go along with the Councils.

It seems to me that the general reaction to the legislature's blast, and the failure so far of any boycott, points up something that our non-Southern friends possibly don't know. The thinking people of Mississippi and the South are a long way ahead of their politicians; and those of us who seem to be in a completely rebuffed minority aren't as alone or as out of step as legislators and Councils might lead the outsider to believe.

I don't mean that many white Southerners are willing to have public schools integrated now, especially in the Deep South where numerical pressures are greatest. But they know that inflammatory political behavior and the formation of vigilante groups aren't the answer any more than would be a Supreme Court edict ordering complete integration next fall. There must be a middle ground.

That brings up something personal. I've been pretty much a middle-of-the-roader all my life. Some of my fellow Southerners think otherwise. They've been conditioned largely by political demagogues to believe that anybody who challenges extremism in the South is in league with the Supreme Court, the N.A.A.C.P., the Communist party, the mass-circulation magazines, and everybody north of the Mason-Dixon Line to destroy the Southern way of life. There's a lot of it I do want destroyed. There's a lot I want to keep.

And some of my non-Southern correspondents have been wrong also, though in a kindlier way. They envision a dangerous life for the Southern dissenter, or, at the best, a social and economic martyrdom. That, I am glad to say, just isn't so, though it could have been twenty years ago.

We live normal small-town lives in Greenville. That means we're busy with all kinds of matters besides racial problems. According to my calendar for the general period between the *Look* article and the legislature's resolution, I was chairman, so help me, of the Rotary Club's Ladies' Night; planned a spring boating weekend with the skipper of the Sea Scouts whose unofficial flagship is the *Mistuh Charley*, and gave a wiener roast for the Cub Scouts, including my youngest, whose den father I am; met three times with my fellow directors of the Chamber of Commerce; awarded the annual *Democrat-Times* plaques to the outstanding man and woman citizen; served as ringmaster for our neighborhood teen-agers' Cypress Saddle Club show; met with our monthly discussion group, a dozen business and professional men, in my home; judged a college and high school newspaper contest; went to two square dances; attended the Tulane University annual Board of Visitors meeting; began work on a talk for the convention of the Mississippi Bankers Association; helped my wife entertain for two engaged daughters of friends, and for each of our two older sons home from college and school for Easter holidays; planned a board meeting of the Mississippi Historical Society, of which I'm president; and worked with my wife on the 150-year history of the Episcopal Diocese of Louisiana. This accounting is only partial, but it doesn't leave much time for scalawagging.

A great many of my friends, and uncounted thousands of other Southerners, are too busy to spend time on boycotts and threats even were they so inclined. A good many other thousands, however, do seem to have the time and inclination, too. The Southern struggle, it seems to me, is not so much between two races as between these groups. In four or five Deep Southern states, the Supreme Court and the Negro stand on the sidelines. In these states, integration is distant. In their public schools, it will be no more than token for as far ahead as I can see. The gradual adjustment will be aided by accompanying improvement in the Negro's economic status; by Negro migration which will reduce the pressure of numbers; by the tolerance of those who today are our young; and by the persistent growth of the idea that democracy and Christianity and man's responsibility for his brother are all facets of the same bright dream.

I know that, against these forces, the South's braying demagogues, its Klans and Councils and Southern Gentlemen, Inc., cannot forever stand. As our eldest son, who is twenty, disdainfully told our ten-year-old, who has been delighted with all the excitement:

"If you think this is something, you should have been around when I was in the fifth grade. . . ."

Or when I was.

23

WOMAN EDITOR'S WAR ON BIGOTS

The fetchingly helpless and beautiful Southern belle and the gallant Southern gentleman are two of the principal stage props for those who write or dream or prate of the South that never really was.

Hazel Brannon Smith, editor and publisher of four small weekly newspapers in Mississippi, is fortunate in that, except for her good looks, she does not fit the first stereotype. She is unfortunate in that the dominant male citizens of Holmes County, in whose county seat she publishes the Lexington *Advertiser,* her largest weekly, have about as much of the chivalry ascribed to the old South as does a cottonmouth moccasin.

That the attractive Mrs. Smith is still in business after twenty-five latterly stormy years in Holmes County is a tribute to her resolute and resourceful spirit. That she is having an increasingly hard time keeping going is also a tribute of sorts to the persistence of a small but powerful group of Holmes Countians who are trying to put her out of business.

These gentry, I am hopeful, are not typical of most Southern men. But it so happens that Holmes County is made up partly of hill and partly of flat delta land; and too many of its citizens combine the worse rather than the better qualities of each region: the arrogant feudalism and reactionary outlook of the old-time, life-and-death masters of vast acres; and the provincial suspicion, the racial and religious bigotry and the predilection for violence which have traditionally been part of the character of hillmen everywhere.

In some similar areas the good and the bad qualities

of the homefolks are mixed; sometimes the favorable qualities dominate. But not with Hazel Brannon Smith's somewhat less than courageous foemen in Holmes County.

Until a few years ago Hazel Smith's career made an enviable success story. She came breezing into Holmes County, Mississippi, in 1936, a high-spirited, energetic, and joyful girl with a journalism degree from the University of Alabama, and a loan of $3000 to go toward the purchase of a broken-down weekly, the Durant *News*.

My wife and I had come to Mississippi to found our own daily in Greenville at about the same time. We remember meeting Hazel at our first press-association meeting and hearing her tell her dream of making something out of what was then almost nothing. We worried a little because we doubted that the execution could ever match the vision.

We were wrong. In less than ten years Hazel had transformed the Durant *News* and bought the larger Lexington *Advertiser*. Later she was to acquire a third and much smaller one; and in the recent past acquire in Jackson a suburban weekly.

Working day and night, learning the art of printing as well as of publishing, tirelessly striving to make Lexington, Durant, and all of Holmes County better and more profitable places in which to live, Hazel wrought miracles in the old shop in Lexington in which the papers were printed.

Today, one of the most modern and complete weekly printing plants in the state is housed in a pleasant building; Hazel and Walter Dyer Smith, the talented and friendly Yankee husband from Philadelphia whom she acquired when on a round-the-world trip after her pioneering trials were over, live in a more than comfortable home on a tract of some twenty rolling, tree-shaded acres within the city limits of Lexington. Despite the economic setbacks caused by the implacable hostility of the Holmes County bosses, they have hung onto a small cattle ranch where she and "Smitty," as everyone calls her husband, have for seven years been trying to improve the quality of their beef cattle.

But all that is only the material side of it.

Twenty or so years ago, people began reading each week's issues of the Durant paper with eagerness rather than with the long-accustomed boredom; for Hazel was making good her promise to let the citizens know what was going on, to crusade for law and order, which to a considerable degree were strangers to Holmes County, and to bespeak the rights of all citizens—the last-named purpose probably being the most dangerous notion that had ever been publicly voiced in the county.

With the purchase of the Lexington *Advertiser* in 1943, Hazel stepped up her fight against the slot-machine operators, liquor racketeers, gamblers, and conniving officials who were finding easy pickings and little opposition in the clique-ridden rural county. In 1946, thanks principally to her persistence, a grand jury voted sixty-four indictments, after investigating organized crime in Holmes County.

But Hazel became one of the objects of court action herself when the trial judge found her guilty of contempt of court for interviewing a witness, the widow of a Negro for whose death by whipping five white men were indicted but not convicted.

The judge fined her fifty dollars and sentenced her to fifteen days in jail, but suspended sentence and put her "under good behavior" for two years. Hazel refused the gag and appealed to the State Supreme Court (which later ruled in her favor). Hazel won the cheers of her fellow editors in and outside of the state. But she had made dangerous enemies.

In 1948, a World War II veteran was killed in an automobile collision with a man who had just been acquitted, bewilderingly, on bootlegging charges in still wide-open Holmes County. Hazel's editorial denouncing the jury won her the year's top award from the National Association of Press Women. It also won her some new opponents. In the same year she received the certificate of merit for outstanding service to Mississippi in the field of human relations from the Mississippi Association of Teachers in Colored Schools.

Holmes County, in a state whose people vote dry and drink wetter than most any sister Southern state, was still honeycombed with bootleggers and other law violators whom the apparently complacent city and county officers couldn't detect. Again and again, from 1951 to 1954, Hazel Smith kept up the fight against the sheriff and his general disinterest in cleaning up the county.

Then, in 1954, Hazel really got in bad with the other whites. On the July 4 weekend, incumbent Sheriff Richard F. Byrd, accompanied by three other peace officers, drove his car up to a group of Negroes who had gathered at a roadside café, probably for a few illegal drinks.

He asked one of them, a twenty-seven-year-old man, why he was "whooping" so loudly. When the Negro denied that he was guilty of this serious violation of the peace, the sheriff shouted to him to get going. As the Negro ran, the sheriff shot him in the thigh.

In her first news story reporting the affair, Editor Smith recounted that she had not been able to get a statement from the sheriff. In the next issue of the Lexington *Advertiser*, Hazel told the story of how the man was shot by the sheriff when he hadn't violated any law and how the sheriff had not even threatened him with arrest before the shooting. In a front page signed editorial she followed up the newspaper report with a denunciation of the sheriff for brutality in this and other cases involving Negroes. Wrote the angry young woman:

"The laws in America are for everyone—rich and poor, strong and weak, black and white. The vast majority of Holmes County people are not rednecks who look with favor on the abuse of people because their skins are black. Byrd has violated every concept of justice, decency and right. He is not fit to occupy office."

The sheriff filed a libel suit for actual and punitive damages in the amount of $57,500. At the October term of court a trial jury awarded Sheriff Byrd $10,000, after each juror allegedly dropped into a hat for drawing slips of paper upon which he had written down the amount he thought the sheriff deserved. The Holmes County grand jury adjourned without indicting anyone in the shooting of the young Negro.

The year 1954 was a tense one in Holmes County for another and more significant reason. In the wake of the United States Supreme Court's decision on school desegregation, the citizens of little Indianola, less than fifty miles from Lexington, organized the first White Citizens' Council, the white-supremacy group which, while abjuring violence or masking, pledged itself to hold down Negro voting, fight "moderates," and prevent school integration by economic and social pressures. A second unit was almost immediately organized in Holmes County. Among its leading members were men actively aligned with the sheriff in his feud with the editor and suspicious of her advocacy of equal justice.

That summer a respectable Negro woman, a teacher for twenty years, was shot in her own home by a leading Lexington white man after she had remonstrated with him for driving his automobile into her yard and damaging it while turning around.

White Citizens' Council members and others tried to persuade Hazel Smith to kill the story. She printed it. Telling the story did no good, for no arrest was made. The wounded teacher was dismissed from the school and her husband was fired by the filling station operator for whom he worked. The pair then moved to Chicago.

The White Citizens' Council gathered momentum. County and state and Southern politicians began to cash in on the fear and unrest of the white people over the Supreme Court's frontal assault. Tensions in Holmes County increased.

A mass meeting was called by the White Citizens' Council in the little village of Tchula so that citizens could hear a tape recording of a so-called investigation, conducted by the sheriff and members of the Council, of a Negro teen-age boy who had been charged with insulting a white schoolgirl. The boy was found blameless, but the meeting turned into a mass denunciation of idealistic Dr. David Minter, a physician, and his friend and associate, A. E. Cox, who directed a biracial, cooperative farm in Holmes County.

Both men were present at the meeting when speakers demanded that they leave the county because they assertedly advocated and practiced racial integration. Dr. Minter and Cox were booed when they tried to answer, and soon were repeatedly threatened by letters and anonymous calls.

The Reverend Marsh M. Callaway, a white Presbyterian minister of Durant, who had protested at the meeting "the un-Christian and un-American treatment of the pair by a kangaroo court," was dismissed by his church before the end of the year, and left the state.

So did the two men whom the genteel Holmes mobsters had threatened, though in their own good time. Hazel Smith meanwhile had kept fighting for the rights of all three.

The embattled editor won a round in November 1955, when the Mississippi Supreme Court unanimously and caustically reversed the libel judgment and dismissed the sheriff's suit. Said the court in part:

"Under the facts in this record there was no justification whatever for hitting this Negro with a blackjack or shooting him. . . . It follows that the Negro was unjustly assaulted in both instances.

"The right to publish the truth with good motive and to justifiable ends, is inherent in Section 13, Article III, Constitution of 1890 . . . 'the freedom of speech and of the press shall be held sacred. . . .' Out of the testimony of the officers themselves, the news items and other pertinent comment in question are believed to be substantially true and the plaintiff was, therefore, not entitled to recover anything."

And for the second time Hazel won the National Federation of Press Women's principal award for the libel-case editorial. But the victory was relatively a hollow one; for in January 1956 a set of Council-dominated trustees in the Holmes County Hospital fired her husband as administrator of the hospital, despite the medical staff's unanimous resolution asking that he be retained. One trustee in a newspaper statement said: "There is nothing against him or his record, but his wife has become a controversial person."

Hazel went on winning more and more awards while losing more and more dollars. In 1956 the National Editorial Association in convention in Louisville, Kentucky, awarded the Herrick Award to Hazel Smith "for editorial writing, embracing the highest type of American principles and ideals." In the next year the Fund for the Republic presented her a citation for "an American whose actions have made an unusual contribution to advancing the principles of freedom and justice and the Bill of Rights."

Since every Citizens' Council member knew that the Fund for the Republic was a dangerous organization, Hazel also received another black eye. But in her own state, in the same year, the Mississippi Press Association in convention adopted by unanimous vote a resolution "commending Mrs. Hazel Smith, editor of the Lexington *Advertiser* and the Durant *News* for her epochal fight in the interest of freedom of the press."

Clearly she was becoming far too much a problem of the atavists to be dealt with lightly. The White Citizens' Council leaders began organizing a concerted advertising boycott. Her local advertising volume shortly fell off some fifty per cent, a loss which she has never recovered. She kept and even gained readership; but without the necessary advertising and commercial-printing volume, her papers began to suffer.

And in 1958 her enemies organized a new weekly paper at a meeting at which an officer of the local Citizens' Council presided and asked for stock subscriptions from those present—mostly Council members. The new weekly, the Holmes County *Herald,* has been subsidized from the beginning by well-to-do Council leaders. It couldn't have lasted three months without pressure in its behalf from county politicians and White Citizens' Council leaders, generally the same persons and all of the same readily recognizable stripe.

Hazel Smith, lacking subsidy, began to show the strain. Once again the same pattern was repeated—professional recognition at the cost of financial setbacks. Marquette University in Milwaukee honored her at the twenty-seventh annual Matrix Table sponsored by Theta Sigma Psi. But some of her gallant foes got even in 1960 with an act that shocked the better citizens. A cross was burned on her lawn by a group of teen-agers, including the son of a man prominent in Council circles. Hazel herself descended upon them as the cross burned and, after they had fled, removed the license tag from their car so that proof of ownership and occupancy could be made.

The year before she had received the Elijah Lovejoy Award from the University of Southern Illinois: "for demonstrating the ability to perform under great stress . . . her role as editor of the community's newspapers so effectively as to win the approval and support, in growing numbers, of the right thinking people of her town and county. . . ."

So what will happen next? There is no real wealth in Holmes County. It is unlikely that the other newspaper will survive if Hazel's friends begin to speak out, as some already are doing. Men get tired of indulging their prejudices at the expense of their pocketbooks. And this is exactly what is happening in the case of the Holmes County *Herald,* a travesty of a newspaper which is only an instrument devised to destroy a brave woman, who twenty-five years ago came to Mississippi with eyes shining and dreaming a dream that had to do with the rights of all men and the freedom of newspapers to speak their pieces.

Maybe the brave bigots will stop putting up. Maybe the now silent, decent people will begin speaking up. Maybe next year the Lexington *Advertiser,* which is celebrating its 125th anniversary this year, will still be Hazel Brannon Smith's editorial voice. If not, another light will have gone out in a shadowed state.

And perhaps the supreme irony is that nowhere outside the Deep South would Hazel Brannon Smith be labeled even a liberal in her racial views. If she must be categorized, then call her a moderate; a churchgoing, humanity-loving newspaper woman who takes seriously her responsibilities toward her fellow men. But that doesn't fit well in Holmes County where the most benighted are today also the most powerful.

24

1962

Like millions of other Americans, I have often been exasperated by that obstructive tactic known as the filibuster, used by United States senators from time to time in efforts to talk to death measures which they dislike.

When a filibuster is successful, as was the one conducted by Southern senators against the Administration's voter-literacy bill in May of 1962, editorial writers frequently demand that this parliamentary tactic be outlawed. They denounce it as a tool of the devil (disguised as a Southern demagogue) to prevent passage of civil rights measures, and as an undemocratic, un-American means of thwarting the will of a legislative and popular majority.

Even though I am against the devil and demagogues, I must dissent. The filibuster is not undemocratic; to the contrary, it is as democratic as any other procedure in our system. It has not been employed very often in racial issues. Only rarely has it thwarted the will of the majority.

Filibusters were common in the assemblies of the thirteen colonies and our infant republic. As early as 1790, senators sought to talk to extinction a bill to fix the permanent seat of the federal government, "the gentlemen from Virginia and South Carolina" being especially criticized for being long-winded. Unlimited and angry debate persisted in the Senate throughout the Civil War and both world wars. Senators have filibustered against such diverse measures as the readmission of Louisiana after the Civil War; the Versailles Peace Treaty in 1919; a migratory-bird bill in 1926; and the Prohibition Reorganization Bill of 1927.

The filibuster's defenders have been an oddly assorted

lot. After the late Charles G. Dawes was sworn in as Republican Vice-President in 1925, he denounced the filibuster. The American Federation of Labor was among the first to lash back at Mr. Dawes, asserting that the filibuster was the laboring man's best defense. Among the Presidents who have defended the tactic are Thomas Jefferson, Abraham Lincoln, and Woodrow Wilson. The great Midwestern liberals, Senators George Norris and Robert LaFollette, were outspoken in its defense. LaFollette said in 1917: "Sir, the moment that the majority imposes the [filibuster] restriction . . . you will have broken down one of the greatest weapons against wrong and oppression that the members of this body possess."

In a remarkable letter written when he was seeking the Republican nomination for President, Senator Arthur Vandenberg wrote the Negro religious cultist, Father Divine, in part: "I am definitely and specifically in favor of the pending Federal antilynch legislation. . . . You also ask me whether I will endorse a bill making it a crime to filibuster against any bill that has been carried by a majority vote. The answer is I will not. . . . This [the antilynch] bill protects minorities . . . [the filibuster] also protects minorities."

What do opponents of the filibuster want? They desire restrictions upon debate—including cloture by a simple majority vote—far more stringent than those set down in Senate Rule 22 of the Standing Rules of the Senate, adopted in 1917 and twice amended. Rule Number 22 initially provided that, upon the motion of any sixteen senators, the presiding officer must submit to the Senate the question of closing debate on a pending measure. If two thirds of the entire Senate membership were to vote for such cloture, debate was thereafter to be limited to one hour for each senator. The rule was amended in 1949 to permit cloture by a constitutional majority on any "measure, motion or other matter," not just the pending measure. The second amendment came in January 1959, under the prodding of then Senator Lyndon B. Johnson. It required a two-thirds vote only of the senators "present and voting."

Filibuster participants, generally playing to an inattentive, sleepy handful, have provided drama and comedy as well as boredom as they go through such routine paces as demanding a full reading of the journal of the previous day and moving endless corrections; obtaining repeated quorum calls; offering unacceptable riders and amendments to the pending measure; raising of parliamentary objections and points of order; asking interminable questions; and, above all, making long and often irrelevant speeches.

Drama, comedy, boredom.

Here is President Wilson in 1917, white-lipped with fury, denouncing the eleven senators who held up his Armed Neutrality Bill as that "little group of willful men . . . [who] have rendered the great Government of the United States helpless and contemptible."

Here is Senator Smoot of Utah, speaking in 1915 completely without relief and sticking to his subject to set an all-time record for a completely uninterrupted speech (on a ship purchase bill) of eleven hours and thirty-five minutes.

Here are the runners-up: Wisconsin's LaFollette, going on for more than eighteen hours, with the aid of quorum calls and friendly interruptions in his fight against a national banking bill; Wayne Morse, the maverick from Oregon, speaking for twenty-two hours and twenty-six minutes without a breather from quorum calls but with some respite through yielding for questions; Strom Thurmond of South Carolina orating against civil rights proposals for twenty-four hours and eighteen minutes in August 1957, but with about an hour and a half of rest-giving questions and quorum calls. During the 1960 civil rights filibuster, Allen J. Ellender of Louisiana amused even his opponents by hiding from the Senate sergeant at arms in a secret Capitol cranny which he had stocked with oysters, shrimp, ham, eggs, bacon, vegetables, and an electric hot plate.

Since measures can be filibustered in committees as well

as on the floor of the Senate, the perhaps apocryphal tale of a closed session in August 1959 of the Senate Judiciary Committee, presided over by Mississippi's James Eastland, might not be out of place. Among the topics allegedly discussed were Noah's Ark, the laws of the Medes and the Persians, the habits of the Scribes and the Pharisees, Einstein's theory of relativity, the spelling of aurora borealis, the Ten Commandments, Mormonism and, especially, the provocative English novel *Lady Chatterley's Lover*. New York's Kenneth Keating, a civil rights advocate, was quoted as saying, "We talked more about her husband than her lover. We decided the lover was getting all the publicity while the husband was more interesting and was being slighted. This led to a discussion of husband slighting."

Race-related debates over civil rights legislation have created the political drama and tensions of latter-day filibusters. Three months of debate in 1957 won for Southern senators a compromise on the first civil rights bill passed since Reconstruction. They succeeded in limiting to forty-five days and fines of no more than $300 the sentences which federal judges could hand out, without trial by jury, in criminal contempt cases arising from the denial of the right to vote. During the civil rights filibuster by eighteen Southern senators in March 1960, the Senate chalked up nearly six days and five nights of continuous oratory—125 hours and thirty-one minutes, broken only by one fifteen-minute recess. The ages of not a few of the senators present make this record all the more amazing; Senator Ernest Gruening of Alaska, who presided, was seventy-three. Senator Theodore Green of Rhode Island, ninety-two, missed only a few of the forty-two quorum calls demanded by the Southerners. Wisconsin's Alexander Wiley was seventy-five, Harry Byrd and Willis Robertson of Virginia were both seventy-two, and Hawaii's Oren Long, seventy-one. And the pajamas, bedroom slippers, and snacks brought by pro-civil rights senators, so as to catch naps between quorum calls, made the Senate and its antechambers resemble a flophouse.

As for the political morality of the filibuster, I am convinced that a rational defense can be made on four counts.

(1) If adjournment of the Senate is a considerable way off and if a substantial majority of the Senate is determined to take action, a handful of senators can rarely conduct a successful filibuster. If they are in an extremely small minority, not only can cloture be invoked but they must fall by the wayside through fatigue. Moreover, the worst aspects of filibustering could be done away with through strict enforcement of present parliamentary rules, especially the rule of relevancy.

(2) The most shallow concept of a democracy is that which sees it as government by majority rule, without adequate legislative protection for the minority. In many important aspects of American self-government, majority rule does not figure. Through the presidential veto, one more than one third of either house of Congress can prevent a majority-approved measure from becoming law. One more than one third can nullify ratification of a treaty, and one more than two fifths of the House can prevent the submission to the Senate of a constitutional amendment.

(3) With my fellow Mississippian, John Stennis, I believe that open debate is man's greatest political invention. The United States Senate is the last great legislative body in the world where unlimited debate is possible. The privilege is a legacy from Greece and Rome. The Senate was conceived by the founding Fathers as a counterbalance to the House of Representatives. It was not envisaged as being susceptible to the will of a national majority; were it otherwise, Nevada and Alaska would not have the same number of senators as New York and California. Whether a minority be racial, religious, regional, or numerical, it deserves, I believe, the marginal protection that a handful of senators can sometimes gain by their stubbornness.

(4) In a speech on the Senate floor in September 1961, Senator Eastland of Mississippi said a considerable mouthful, to wit, that the power in the executive and judicial branches historically has been "loaded in the interest of the

large states." The five most populous states have consistently produced an extraordinarily disproportionate number of Presidents, Cabinet members, and Supreme Court justices. Only one President, Franklin Pierce of New Hampshire, has ever been elected as a citizen of a small state.

"In the 1960 census the five largest states were New York, Pennsylvania, California, Illinois, and Ohio, with thirty per cent of the population," Eastland said. "The forty-three other states contain seventy per cent. Yet fifty-five per cent of the top offices in the government were held by individuals from the five largest states."

The statistics are not reassuring to those of us who live in the less populous states. Nine of the small states have never been represented in either the Supreme Court or the Cabinet. Sixteen states have had no Cabinet appointments since 1900. It is hardly coincidental that the principal sponsors of proposals to permit closing of debate by a mere majority of votes are from the big states.

The Senate is the only remaining body where the small states can raise their voices as equals. If a state's senators are gagged by majority-vote cloture, the state is being denied its right of equal representation.

And as a clincher I quote Senator William Fulbright of Arkansas, a man who has never been accused of being a professional Southerner or a conformist: "To those who argue that the Senate simply cannot function as a legislative body without such a [gag] rule, it should be pointed out that, during the years since the present rule has been operative, we have passed through two wars, a major depression, and serious inflation without being handicapped to any appreciable extent. . . . We have taken billions in taxes. We have legislated to the extent of drafting men into service, fixing prices, rents. . . . We have somehow managed to exercise most of our powers and sometimes in excess of our powers."

Will the gentlemen yield?

25

I'LL NEVER LEAVE MY TOWN

1961

For nearly twenty-five years I have been the editor and publisher of the *Delta Democrat-Times*, a daily newspaper in Greenville, Mississippi, a community of some 50,000 in the flat, fertile Yazoo-Mississippi Delta.

This fact is more satisfying than surprising to me. But many friends and well-wishing strangers elsewhere in our country tell me, with an admixture of sympathy and indignation, that they can't understand the how or why of it. They are especially commiserative when a Mississippi legislature resolves that I am anti-Southern and a liar; when a state legislative investigating committee proclaims that I am Red-tainted; or when our most powerful figure in state politics, the elderly speaker of the House of Representatives, intones publicly that I am unfit to mingle in decent Southern society.

My reassuring answers vary. Sometimes I point out that politicians and newspapermen are not natural allies. But mostly I tell them that whatever the spiritual, mental or democratic climate elsewhere in my state or the South or the nation, it is my happy lot to live in an oasis. Greenville was already an oasis when I came here from my native Louisiana. It is even more an oasis now.

So this is an unabashed account of why one man loves his town and why he knows it to be all but unique in a sad, arid time of regional travail. I would like to begin with four lines of a poem written about Greenville by the late William Alexander Percy, a gentle, courageous aristocrat and gifted poet. He also was one of the eight Greenvillians who in 1935 invited me to establish a competing newspaper in their own town and backed up their invitation with cash to match my own. This is what Will Percy wrote:

> The river town that water oaks
> And myrtles hide and bless,
> Has broken every law except
> The law of kindliness.

So, first I will tell of the kindliness and a rare toleration, a respect for the dissenter and the dissimilar, which are the spiritual hallmarks of my town. These are the qualities which have made it possible for us to go our own way in Greenville—happily, hopefully, and profitably.

Eight out of ten of Greenville's citizens are Protestants. In the past thirty years we have had only two city judges, each serving by appointment of our city council. One is Emmet Harty, an Irish-American Catholic who voluntarily resigned ten years ago. The second is Earl Solomon, a Jew. They epitomize a religious harmony concerning which I can cite many an example—such as the dinner meeting a few years back at which some thirty Protestant and Jewish citizens raised more than $20,000 to help our Catholic fellow citizens complete their new parochial high school; the ten consecutive years when Catholics and Protestants united to contribute an average of $5000 a year to the United Jewish Appeal; the year the Methodists worshiped in the Greenville Synagogue while their own new church was abuilding.

I have personal verification. Through all our years in Greenville the *Delta Democrat-Times* has been a controversial newspaper. No matter what else the morning mail may bring, there will be some letters giving me unshirted hell. An unending spate of political candidates have found it useful to make our newspaper and me their favorite whipping boys—I am "a nigger-loving, Yankeefied Communist" who advocates "the mongrelization of the race"; the *Democrat-Times* is "owned by a millionaire Northern Negro" who uses me as his mouthpiece; my office is the "secret headquarters of the N.A.A.C.P." It has even been said—oh, slander of slanders—that I am Yankee born, and conversely that I was "run out of Louisiana." It has also been said that my home is a haven for visiting subversives from Europe, Africa, Asia, and New York City, that our editorial support of any candidate is proof positive that he is a radical, a liberal, or, currently in Mississippi the dirtiest word of all, a moderate.

Some of my fellow Greenvillians believe some of these accusations. A few may believe all of them. But it doesn't seem to matter as far as most Greenvillians are concerned.

Over the years, I have served on our library board, our school board, the Delta Area Council of the Boy Scouts, and the board of directors of the Chamber of Commerce. The week that the state legislature resolved me into a liar, Greenville High School's journalism fraternity gave my name to its newly organized chapter. The very day last winter when the legislative investigating committee encouraged a professional witness to link me with Communist-front organizations, I addressed high school students on flora and fauna of darkest Africa.

The next day, twenty-five citizens of Greenville—including our four incoming members of the legislature, Greenville's only lieutenant general, our rabbi, and the chancery-court judge—joined in a public statement of confidence in my patriotism and, more meaningfully, denounced the smear tactics. The board of directors of the Rotary Club reacted similarly. Three weeks later I was re-elected senior warden of St. James Episcopal Church. My wife is, or has been, president of just about every woman's organization in Greenville —garden clubs, P.T.A.s, church auxiliary, study clubs, music associations, and the like—despite the repeated calls from clarion voices elsewhere in the state calling for our "ostracism."

Ostracism—during our prolonged Christmas season we even yearn to be ostracized a little, for the Delta celebrates Christmastime in a fantastically thorough manner which leaves us weak from an almost endless succession of cotil-

lions, debutante balls, eggnog gatherings, duck-hunt break-
fasts, and rounds of visiting.

I am certain that Greenville's non-white population,
nearly one half of the total, is not as contented to live in
Greenville as I am. As the black man in the South draws
nearer abreast of the white, the two move farther apart. Yet
I believe that the Negroes of Greenville would rather live
here than in any other place I know of in Mississippi or,
indeed, in the South—or, for that matter, in many another
area of our country.

Why? I think I know some reasons. Nearly 1,000,000
Negroes live in Mississippi's eighty-two counties. Fewer
than 15,000 of them vote, but approximately one seventh
of these voters are registered in Washington County, of
which Greenville is the county seat. If Ed Cocke, registrar
of voters for some sixteen years, makes a habit of turning
down any prospective voter who can meet an unrigged
examination, regardless of race, it has escaped the attention of the *Democrat-Times* news staff.

Negroes were included on jury lists in Greenville well
before a Supreme Court decision made such inclusion necessary if conviction of a Negro is to be upheld on appeal.
Greenville is one of but four towns in the entire state of
Mississippi employing Negro policemen.

What is more important to our Negro citizens is the
evenhanded, color-blind quality of the justice that is
traditional in our city court. Nor are we plagued by police brutality or discrimination against Negroes under
arrest. My reporters can vouch for this. Not for twenty-five
years have we experienced a disturbance that could be
ascribed primarily to racial tensions. Individual incidents,
usually among drunks, have occurred, but never a threat
of mob action or one-sided victimization. Red Taggart, who
was police chief when we came here and who retired fifteen
years ago, was proud that during twenty-five years of police work he had seen "men shot over and under him and
beside him, but had never killed a man." Al Hollingsworth,
the assistant chief who succeeded him, resigned last sum-

mer to enter and win the race for county sheriff. And Bill
Burnley, the present chief, came up from the ranks and
is an FBI-trained career officer, as were his predecessors.

I am not concerned here with segregation. It is a fact
in Greenville and largely will remain a fact for a long,
long time. But, within the pattern, Greenville has been
extraordinarily fair. Ours was the first Mississippi community to provide a public swimming pool for Negroes, a
counterpart of the one constructed for whites. Our new General Hospital houses Negro and white patients in identically
equipped wings. The operating rooms are common to both
races; qualified Negro doctors can operate there—a privilege
that is rare in more places than Mississippi.

I cannot say that our separate school systems are truly
equal. But, since the war, we have built a new Negro high
school and two new Negro grammar schools and have re-
modeled two others. Most of this was done before the South
was prodded by the courts into trying to live up to the
separate but equal principle, if only as a deterrent to integration. Also, we had moved a long way toward equal pay
for equally qualified teachers, regardless of race, before our
state recognized that principle.

Too many of Greenville's Negroes live in substandard
houses—so do too many of our white citizens. We are now
trying to do something about our slums with a proposed
building code and clearance projects. Yet more than half of
our Negro families own their own homes, and some of these
are as good as or better than most of the white dwellings.

We have discrimination in labor. But 1100 Negroes are
employed in skilled and semiskilled categories in our industries. Almost as many Negroes as whites work as carpen-
ters, masons, electricians, plumbers, and mechanics. A
Negro is one of our principal masonry contractors. Another
is a house mover whose equipment is worth more
than $75,000. And if this is still a long way from perfec-
tion, it is an even longer way from the imperfection that
challenges the national conscience.

"Civic teamwork" and "cultural values" are overused and

often undeserved phrases. But were my town the very epitome of tolerance, I still might not find it so green an oasis if its community life lacked these qualities.

Our teamwork is responsible for the fact that in twenty-five years, in depression and war and prosperity, not a single community-wide campaign—Chamber of Commerce, Community Fund, Red Cross—has failed to reach its goals. Teamwork put across the financing which brought us four major industries and a dozen small ones since World War II. Community teamwork impelled citizens of no great wealth to finance jointly one of the South's largest poultry-processing plants, an experimental rice-growing plantation, an insurance company with Greenville as its headquarters, and a $1,000,000 hotel-motel in the making.

We've pushed many another project in which economic gain has not been the consideration. A handful of boatmen bought an aged United States Engineers quarterboat and converted it into our fine floating yacht club, which has probably the lowest family membership dues to be found anywhere.

Our old people's home is one of the most attractive in the country because Dr. Charles Berry and Jake Stein and Hubert Crosby and Mrs. Edmund Taylor saw in the closed, four-story student nurses' home a place of dignified refuge for the old. They persuaded their fellow citizens to contribute $100,000 for its remodeling.

Greenville has a Junior Auxiliary, a small-town Junior League, because Louise Crump decided twenty years ago that, if the privileged could help the underprivileged in larger cities, we could do it here. Our ten garden clubs are largely responsible for Greenville's winning second place two years ago, first place last year, and second again this year in Mississippi's new hometown development campaign.

As our community mushroomed, our original country club became the site of three new churches, Mississippi's second-largest high school, a public swimming pool and a community-and-youth center—all enjoying the loveliest prospect in town. This was made possible because every member of

the club agreed—not all of them without some persuasion—
to turn his shares back at par so that the school board, the
city government, and interested churches could buy portions
of the land for less than one tenth of what real estate de-
velopers would have paid.

Because of the shift to missiles, the Greenville Air Force
Base, where jet pilots have been trained ever since the war,
is scheduled to be closed down. It will be converted to a
center for training Air Force enlisted, administrative, and
fire-fighting personnel. Air base personnel have coached our
Little League. For ten years each squadron has assumed
responsibility for supplying food, clothing, and toys to
needy Greenville families at Christmastime. Officers and
their wives play with the Greenville Little Symphony, assume leading roles in the Theater Guild productions, and
engage in almost every other community activity. Some citizens, of whom we are not proud, may have gouged air base
families who live in our town, but Colonel Jasper Bell, base
commander, still tells all comers that nowhere else has he
found as fine a relationship between civilians and airmen as
that existing here.

Once, after I had extolled Greenville's culture to a New
England Philistine, he commented witheringly that my
town must be the Athens of Northwest Mississippi. That's
all right with me. Don't ask me why, for example, Greenvillians have turned out about as many books in the past
twenty years—textbooks excepted—as have the authors of
all the rest of Mississippi. David Cohn, who described
Greenville so lovingly that my wife and I were persuaded
to come here even before we had seen his home town, has
published ten books and scores of magazine articles.
Louise Crump is working on her third novel. Shelby Foote,
who cubbed on the *Democrat-Times*, has six books to his
credit, including *Shiloh*, a notable novel. Shortly before his
death, Will Percy, our poet, produced his classic auto-
biography, *Lanterns on the Levee*. Ben Wasson wrote one
novel before turning critic and publishing-house editor.
Lucile Finlay's historical novel, *The Coat I Wore*, went

through several English editions. Charles Bell, one of our
two recent Rhodes scholars, has published two volumes of
verse which rank him with the country's better younger
poets. My twenty-five-year-old oldest son, Hodding III, now
on the *Democrat-Times*, got into the act last fall with *The
South Strikes Back*, a book on the Citizens' Council movement. My wife, Betty, and I collaborated on two books, and
I've written a number of others myself. All together, over
the past twenty years, we Northwest Mississippi Athenians
have turned out some thirty-five books. Pericles would have
been proud.

Our writers don't have a corner on things cultural. During the past six months the Twin City Theater Guild performed to packed houses for five three-night stands. The
last two productions were presented in our new Theater
Guild building, midway between Greenville and near-by
Leland, a gay structure that is the sum of a variety of
donated parts—including the colonnade, hallway, and par-
lor of a lovely old home, a few hundred vintage theater
seats, two gilt mirrors, and some discarded marble toilet
fixtures, structural steel girders, and the use of Hal Bur-
dine's earth movers. Many a Greenvillian and Lelander
had a hand in this creation, but we all agree that the late
Matsy Wynn Taylor was the spark plug. Even in her mid-
seventies, Matsy refused to take seriously her retirement as
one of New York's topflight photographers. She came back
to her home town to bring life to the Theater Guild.

Other Greenvillians put spare time into music. Our concert series has 1100 members; and among the artists we have
heard in recent years are the late Leonard Warren, Blanche
Thebom, Robert Merrill, and Gina Bachauer. Young Kenneth Haxton, a creative musician disguised as a department-
store-co-owner, decided that those four concerts a season
weren't enough, so he moved on to the organization of the
Greenville Little Symphony, with fifty-three members.

But, some of our friends protest, culture isn't altogether
a matter of books and music and theater—there are also the
weddings, barbecues, dinners, suppers, and cocktail parties

which, for good or ill, make so much of small city life so
like its magnified counterparts everywhere. What I am trying to say is that we escape boredom in a variety of ways.

The South's earliest culture was an earthy product of
the plantation outdoors. Greenville is traditionally and
nostalgically still a plantation town. At the foot of Main
Street runs the levee, and on the other side of the levee
lies Lake Ferguson, a fourteen-mile hairpin body of quiet,
river-replenished water that was part of the river's bed
until the United States Engineers changed the Mississippi's
twisting course. Lake Ferguson is an at-home resort where
water skiers and bass fishermen, swimmers and yachtsmen
and outboard racers can disport themselves five minutes
from home. And within a half hour of Greenville and the
lake are a dozen duck and deer camps for the man who
is hunt-minded; and if he is lucky, he can get his limit
before he goes to work of a winter morning.

Foremost among the ingredients which make our town
an oasis is the unity forged by the long sharing of tribula-
tion. For more than 125 years Greenville underwent, survived, and triumphed over most of the ordeals of an American frontier and some extra ones to boot. The land grantees,
the speculators, the younger sons of the seaboard cotton gentry, and the landless squatters, surging southward and westward, had to meet more trials than they had reckoned on.
So did their heirs. The old burial ground which we still call
Yellow Fever Cemetery is a testimonial in toppled marble
and granite headstones to the tenacious, puzzled, unprepared
folk who did not know for almost 100 years why so many
died with the coming of the mosquito season. The victims
perished unaware. The survivors stayed on.

The scourge of malaria was more embracing and lasted
longer, but it was less vengeful. Our grandparents and their
parents before them braced themselves with quinine and
whiskey and a host of home remedies. The hardiest lasted.

Intermittently the river flooded the land in springtime. A
man who was rich in January could be penniless in June.
Not until the superflood of 1927, a year more memorable

and meaningful than 1861 to my fellow citizens who lived
in Greenville in 1927, did the Congress of the United
States reach the overdue conclusion that flood control on
the Mississippi was a national job, that no community,
county, or state could or should be left alone to ward off
the drainage of almost half of the nation.

Since then, Greenville, whose men and women kept homes
and community intact through three months of six feet of
water in 1927, hasn't had to worry about floods. The myriad
of spillways, dams, cutoffs, and higher and wider levees has
seen to that. Yet our older citizens still divide the community
between those who were here before 1927 and those who
came afterward—something like separating the men from
the boys. I wish I had been here when the last flood swept
across our town.

Not all our tribulations were nature's doing. During the
Civil War, Greenville was put to the torch because a
handful of old men and boys persisted in taking potshots
at federal gunboats on the Mississippi. So effective was the
fire cure that Greenville eventually rebuilt herself eight
miles north of her funeral pyre.

Our people had to learn to unite in the common ordeal
of poverty. Lean years of cotton came often and bore most
heavily upon our dark perpetual poor; but their landlords
and employers also knew the bond of economic despair and
the art of making do. This I did not learn secondhand.
When we came to the Delta in 1936, cotton sold at a
measly nine cents a pound, and our cotton planters had
patches on the seats of their pants.

But there are happier, if more intangible, reasons for
Greenville's being what it is. Perhaps what I shall say first
is simply boasting; but it does seem to me that we who
dwell in port towns, be they on rivers or ocean or lakes,
are especially aware of far horizons; we realize that mores
other than our own not only exist but might even be
acceptable. Ours is a river town. On our flood plain the
Mississippi has deposited the rich soil of a continent for a
million years. It is a truism that good land produces good

people. If this is so—and I believe it is—we have been blessed even in our lean years in the Yazoo-Mississippi Delta.

Because our soil historically has been farmed by men who counted their acres in the thousands, we were shaped by a tradition of individual leadership and a ruling group which liked to think that it was completely motivated by a sense of "noblesse oblige"—though not all its members were. Yet, delving into the history of our town, I am certain that we were greatly blessed; for many of our landholders did take the obligation of their positions and holdings seriously and honorably.

The sense of obligation to community and fellow citizen was strong and deep when I first came to Greenville—and long before. It has not significantly lessened.

That leadership fortuitously resolved in Greenville an issue which was of lasting consequence not only to our community but even to the nation. The back of Mississippi's Ku Klux Klan of the 1920s was broken in our town; that noisome white-garbed snake was scotched because our braver leaders were men who would not brook organized, face-hidden evil. Older men still talk proudly of the fight, if they were on the side of decency; other older men, who were not on that side, do not speak so loudly today in behalf of wrong.

There is yet another reason for Greenville—not a unique one, but vastly helpful. However remote from the cities, our town is not a provincial one. The cotton planter was and has generally remained a cosmopolite. When crops were good, he and his family usually went traveling. When crops were bad, he often borrowed to travel anyhow. I dare say that the percentage of Greenvillians who have visited New York or Boston or Washington or Chicago or Los Angeles is higher than that of equally situated citizens of those cities who have journeyed to New Orleans or Atlanta or Houston or Nashville or Birmingham.

Because we symbolize some of the challenges and accomplishments in the Deep South—flood control, agricultural mechanization and diversification, racial adjustments—

Greenville and the Delta are jointly a mecca for many a visiting foreigner; and many of us have the pleasurable opportunity of meeting, entertaining, and debating with these questioning visitors.

Each industry we gain enriches our community with newcomers who are not in our tradition and who are willing to argue points of view which we thought secure. The federal-state agricultural experimental station a few miles from our town is a place where ideas of a different sort and of lasting worth can also be discovered. The air base has been a healthy leaven, too; the airmen who marry Greenville girls and settle down among us, and the brides from distant lands who have married Greenville's own veterans, alike help to mellow us.

I believe that a publisher should quit a community he does not embrace. I love my town. If I should ever feel otherwise, and if my three sons should decide in turn that our newspaper is not something they want to hold, I would sell the *Delta Democrat-Times*. And however bright a picture I have honestly tried to paint, I know that Greenville is far from perfect. In our newspaper we continually make known our awareness that we have our cheats and chiselers and free-loaders, our bigots and Scrooges, our slums and slum profiteers, our juvenile delinquents and pettifoggers and our shirkers and haters and just plain inert citizens. But I also believe that such civic aberrations haven't shaped the direction of Greenville. Nor am I alone in this belief. A few months before his separation from the Marine Corps, I asked young Hod whether he really wanted to begin newspaper work in Mississippi. His answer cinched it for me, too.

"It's not exactly coming back to Mississippi," Hod said. "That could be all right, too. But I'm coming back to Greenville."

26

THE EDITOR AS CITIZEN

1961

A clear division exists among newspapermen as to the editor's role as citizen. The cleavage is most apparent between metropolitan and small city daily editors. But it also cuts across each of these principal sectors of the American press. In opposition to my thoughts on the matter stand many newspapermen, on small as well as large newspapers, who are convinced that the editor should stay clear of what might be described as local entanglements, of which there can be many.

The argument for such detachment is reasonable. If the editor becomes actively identified with any organization or group which is likely to indulge in or be a subject of civic controversy or civic pressures, he cannot approach the issues thus created with the requisite Olympian detachment. Therefore, he should stand to one side, holding a mirror before his community, reporting what he sees in it, and, if he thinks editorial comment is required, make it from the vantage point of non-involvement.

We have pursued, especially during the last fifteen years, precisely the opposite course. As a result, our news columns may have reflected the civic, economic, political, social, and perhaps spiritual biases I have acquired through being a participant in a variety of community activities. It may be that our editorials have been similarly affected. I suspect they have. I also suspect that every newspaper reflects, in one way or another, the biases of the editor or the publisher, whether or not the said editor or publisher is a joiner. And it should be remembered that *bias* is not necessarily a dirty word.

Perhaps what I'm trying to say is that the editor can contribute more to the community's well-being if he thinks of himself first as a citizen of his town, who by good fortune happens to be a newspaper editor in that town, rather than as a newspaper editor who happens to be a citizen, permanently or in passing, of some particular town. Fortunate— though not yet rare—is the newspaperman who, in a day of newspaper monopolies, absentee and chain ownership and the dramatic, inevitable reduction in the number of daily and weekly newpapers, can make the choice of his own free will. I am thankful to be one of the lucky ones who can freely make a choice.

It may be argued that a man cannot serve two masters and that, accordingly, the danger of conflict of interest is too great; that the editor's chair is likely to be vacant too often if he is overly active in civic affairs; and that the concept of such participation is in itself provincial. Each of these criticisms may have validity. But I do not think them valid enough.

As for the threat of conflicting interests, it seems to me that the opportunity for good outweighs the likelihood that the editor might be improperly influenced by his participation in the diverse affairs of his town; and that if a newspaperman seriously doubts that he can be any less impartial or factual when dealing, as a newspaperman, with affairs with which he is closely identified as a citizen, he shouldn't be in the profession in the first place.

Concerning absences from the job, it must be admitted that were the newspaper under discussion much smaller, the editor could not have the freedom of movement which he now enjoys. But there are relatively few daily newspapers which are much smaller than this one. Besides, except for trips out of town on industrial missions, most of the time devoted to civic affairs is off-duty time.

I would like to discuss the matter of provincialism at greater length. Provincial is a word too loosely and too derisively applied to behavior and folkways associated with the American hinterlands which that brilliant old debunker,

the late H. L. Mencken, once populated exclusively with
his Booboisie. Provincialism should not be so glibly categorized. You can find hicks in New York City—a great many
hicks—in terms of their awareness of the nation and the
world in which they live. You can find world citizens in
Lawrence, or Emporia, or Greenville. In numbers, if not in
total combined circulation, a majority of America's dailies
and almost all its weeklies are provincial in purpose, outlook,
and achievement. There is nothing wrong about that. Provincialism is a healthy counterweight to concentrated ur-
banism. Politically, the small city newspapers have only
limited influence. Their editorials may contribute to the election of a mayor, a councilman, a state representative, even a
congressman, but beyond that they cannot aspire. They cannot help a federal administration reach a decision or influence social change save to the extent that they report or reflect the thinking of the areas that they serve. Most certainly,
they contribute nothing to the formulation of foreign policies.
But their usefulness is great. Their local news columns give a
sense of individual existence and individual worth to
millions of Americans. In this century of faceless man, their
editorial comments concern mainly, and give identification and sometimes direction to, the communities in which
these millions live. Their editors, whatever their personal
preferences, cannot live in ivory towers or in anonymity.

The small dailies have other similarities which combine
to make it proper and sensible for the editor to be first
of all a citizen. Here are the principal ones:

(1) Most of them are monopolies.

(2) Many of them have editorial policies which may
seem too vigorous or advanced for the essentially conserva-
tive character of the American small city.

(3) All of them compete for circulation with the metropolitan newspapers nearest to them and with other mass
media.

(4) The communities they serve are in unending competition with established metropolitan industrial and trade
centers and with each other.

The *Delta Democrat-Times* embodies each of these likenesses. Our circulation is small and our range of influence is
narrow. Our political and other comments are effective only
within a limited area. Our editorials are almost always
parochial. We emphasize local and regional events and
achievements at the expense of global or even national reporting. We now enjoy a monopoly. I hope we always will.
Our town is in active competition with our sister communities throughout the South which, like Greenville, must
adjust to a society in which agriculture now plays second
fiddle to industry. Our newspaper must compete for readership with two large city dailies. We are considered by many
of those who read our paper, and by almost everyone in
Mississippi who doesn't, to be out of step with most of
our fellow citizens. Incidentally, this suspicion apparently
exists because we take the Constitution and all of its amendments seriously; because we believe our public schools
should be kept open under any circumstances; and because
we do not believe that the justices of the United States Supreme Court are Reds in black robes.

Under these far from unique circumstances, I do not see
why I should refuse or how I could refuse to identify myself actively with those who seek to meet those challenges.
I have no right to be the town scold without taking part
in the town's life. I could have no better defense against
our critics than to prove that I am as much a citizen of
Greenville as is any other person who dwells there. If only
as a practical matter, I could take out no surer insurance
against competition than to make our newspaper the community's spokesman and its editor an active practitioner
of the civic effort that the newspaper preaches. Again, if
only from selfish motives, I should make whatever personal
contribution of time and money I can to the material welfare of Greenville. Every new citizen means a potential new
subscriber. Every new job he fills means new business.
New business means more advertising for our newspaper.
More advertising makes possible a better newspaper, a
larger and more competent staff. The larger and more com-

petent the staff, the more time the editor has to join in the extracurricular activities that build his town. Which brings us around full circle.

But practical, material, or selfish motives do not suffice. At the core of my interpretation of the editor's role lies what may be a too sentimental concept of the relationship of a man to his town. Some of us live where we live because it is a place where we can make a living. Some of us are citizens of our towns by inheritance; some because we cannot get away; some for other and assorted reasons; health, status achieved, living costs, scenery, climate, and so on. All of these reasons are understandable. None of this is bad. Not a few of them contribute to our liking where we live.

But there is another reason why we prefer Greenville above all places we know, and why, so preferring, are impelled to make its every cause our own. Nearly twenty-five years ago, Greenville accepted two young strangers from Louisana who came in the depths of the Depression to establish a competitive daily newspaper. Its citizens largely have stood beside us, whether in agreement or not, in these all but hysterical days of Southern trial.

This is not a happenstance. Our town's personality, its spiritual expression, is an amalgam of ordeals—of trials by flood, and yellow fever, by the destruction of a long-ago war, by a later struggle, waged against the Ku Klux Klan, in which the good in men triumphed over the evil. Out of it all has been forged a rare community tolerance for the dissimilar and the dissenter. Out of it has also come a community compulsion to close ranks when the chips are down. This spirit may not be as strong as it was when our town was smaller, and counted fewer citizens who, like ourselves twenty-five years ago, were newcomers. But the spirit is strong still and it must wax stronger. Our job on the *Democrat-Times* is to respond to every challenge which bigotry, social and economic evolution, and the shrill demand for conformity make to that spirit.

Most of what I have said here I have said before, though not at one time. Harry Ashmore, that all but Faubused newspaperman-turned-Encyclopaedia Britannica-intellectual, once introduced me to the members of the Arkansas Press Association thusly: "Our speaker gets more mileage out of one subject than any newspaperman in history." But Harry was wrong. I have another theme which can be stated briefly:

I would rather be a small city newspaper editor and publisher than anything I know.